THE BRITISH MUSEUM AND ITS COLLECTIONS

Published for the Trustees of the British Museum by British Museum Publications Limited

Upper levels

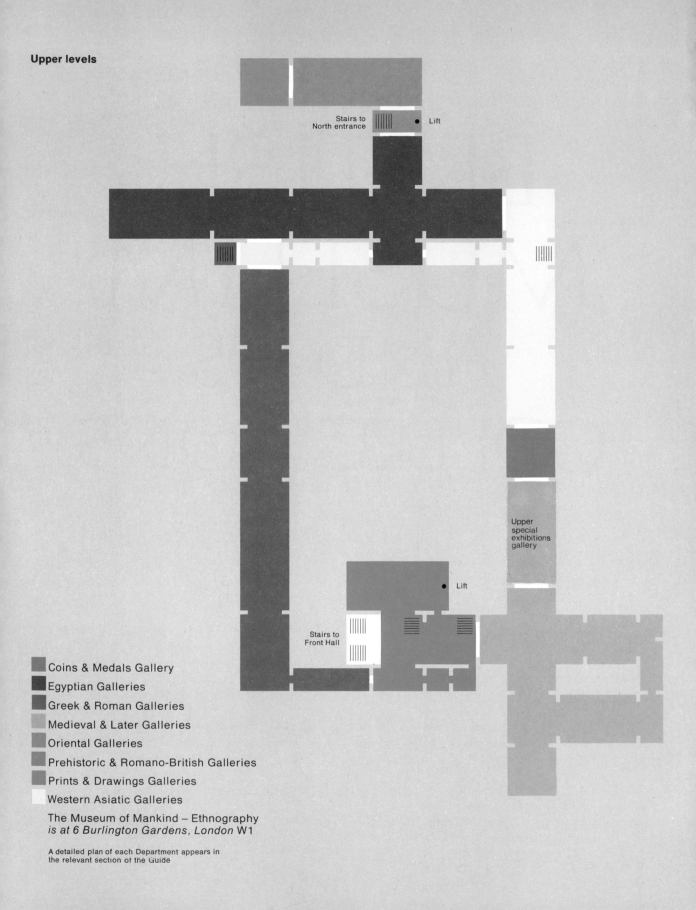

Stairs to
North entrance

Lift

Upper
special
exhibitions
gallery

Lift

Stairs to
Front Hall

Coins & Medals Gallery

Egyptian Galleries

Greek & Roman Galleries

Medieval & Later Galleries

Oriental Galleries

Prehistoric & Romano-British Galleries

Prints & Drawings Galleries

Western Asiatic Galleries

The Museum of Mankind – Ethnography
is at 6 Burlington Gardens, London W1

A detailed plan of each Department appears in
the relevant section of the Guide

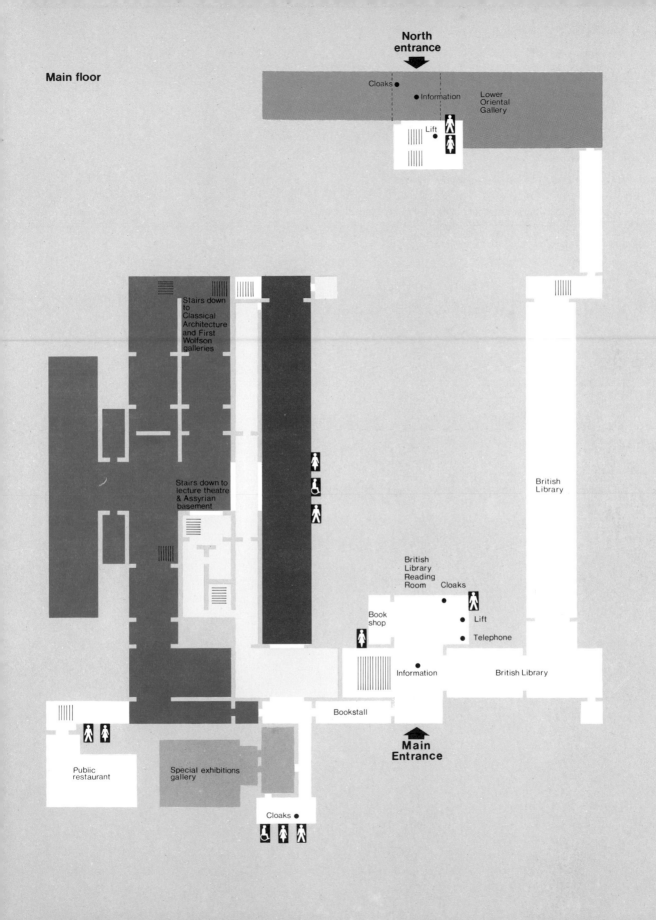

Main floor

North
entrance

Cloaks ●

● Information

Lower
Oriental
Gallery

Lift ●

Stairs down
to
Classical
Architecture
and First
Wolfson
galleries

Stairs down to
lecture theatre
& Assyrian
basement

British
Library

British
Library
Reading
Room

Cloaks

Book
shop

● Lift

● Telephone

● Information

British Library

Bookstall

**Main
Entrance**

Public
restaurant

Special exhibitions
gallery

Cloaks ●

© 1976, The Trustees of the British Museum

Twelfth impression 1988

ISBN 0 7141 2017 0 paper

Published by British Museum Publications Limited
46 Bloomsbury Street, London WC1B 3QQ

Cover design by Roger Davies
Book design by Alan Kitching

Maps drawn by Michael Robinson

Photography by British Museum Photographic Services
except Greek & Roman antiquities nos. 2, 3, 8, 12, 13, 26 by John Webb FRPS

Set in monophoto Sabon by Tradespools Limited, Frome, Somerset and
Filmtype Services Limited, Scarborough, North Yorkshire.
Litho reproduction by City Engraving Co. (Hull) Limited and Keene Engraving Ltd.
Printed in Great Britain by Ashdown Press Ltd.

Contents

The Trustees of the British Museum
acknowledge with gratitude the generosity of

BRITISH PETROLEUM
THE WOLFSON FOUNDATION
AN ANONYMOUS DONOR

for the grants made towards the
cost of producing this Guide

by the Director, Dr D. M. Wilson

THE BRITISH MUSEUM is unique. Behind its grand neo-classical façade lies one of the greatest storehouses of the world's treasures. It has more visitors than practically any other museum in the world – up to four million a year. It is a world within a world, it has its own publishing house, restaurants, security force, social workers, scientists, cleaners, teachers, engineers, and accountants. At base, however, it is a great collecting institution and the assembling, conservation and study of material is its central function.

Its founder was one of the greatest collectors of all time, Sir Hans Sloane, a fashionable physician in Queen Anne's London. Sloane assembled an immense private collection of plants, fossils, minerals, zoological, anatomical and pathological specimens, antiquities and artificial curiosities, prints, drawings, coins, books and manuscripts. When he died in 1753 at the age of ninety-two this collection, comprising some 80,000 objects, was by the terms of his will offered to the nation in return for the provision of a suitable repository and the payment of £20,000 to his heirs. An Act of Parliament was passed authorising the holding of a public lottery to raise the necessary money. Trustees, headed by the Archbishop of Canterbury, the Speaker of the House of Commons and the Lord Chancellor were appointed to oversee the new Museum. (The British Museum was, with relatively minor amendments, governed by this Act until the passing of the new British Museum Act in 1963.) To the Sloane collection were added the great Cotton and Harley libraries and the institution was opened on 15 January 1759 in a decaying seventeenth-century mansion, Montagu House, which stood on the present site of the Museum. It was, and remains, a universal museum which covers the whole of human knowledge, by collecting both natural and artificial products. Although today the paintings, the library and the natural history collections have been removed elsewhere, its collections still span the globe.

The collections increased rapidly through the generosity of private benefactors and a sometimes reluctant government. In 1756 George II presented the old royal library of England and with it the privilege of copyright deposit, now transferred to the British Library. In 1802 the Rosetta Stone and other Egyptian antiquities were acquired from George III. Two great collections of classical sculptures – the so-called Townley and Elgin marbles, which largely conditioned English Classical taste of the early nineteenth century – also came to Bloomsbury.

Montagu House was soon bursting at the seams and the Trustees, with the assistance of a young architect Robert (later Sir Robert) Smirke, began to plan for expansion. Impetus was given to this when in 1823 George IV presented his father's magnificent library and Parliament voted funds to house it fittingly. The East Wing, including the great King's Library, was completed in 1827 and the building as it is today gradually arose over the next thirty years. In 1846 Robert Smirke retired and was succeeded by his younger brother Sydney. The domed Reading Room in the quadrangle, not part of the original design, was opened in 1857 and is Sydney Smirke's work.

The original division of the collections had been tripartite – Printed Books (including prints), Manuscripts (including coins and drawings) and Natural and Artificial Productions (everything else). The growing importance of the antiquities collections was recognised in 1807 by the establishment of a separate department. The Department of Prints and Drawings was set up in 1836 and in 1860, on the retirement of the eighty-year-old Keeper, Edward Hawkins, the antiquities department was split three ways – into Coins and Medals, Greek and Roman and Oriental. The latter included ethnography and medieval antiquities and is the ancestor of six present departments.

In the late nineteenth century and during the first decades of the twentieth century the collections increased prodigiously, often as a result of excavation and expeditions by scholars and explorers all over the world. Early emphasis had been on Classical and Biblical material and in 1834 there were practically no British antiquities in the Museum. By mid-century, however, this part of the collections was growing rapidly as a result of the new developments in European archaeology triggered off by Danish, French and English research. The overcrowding was relieved by moving the Natural History collections to South Kensington in the early 1880s. Further space was provided by the completion in 1884 of a wing to the east of the main block, and the King Edward VII galleries to the north were opened in 1914. The Duveen Gallery which houses the Elgin marbles was completed in 1938; its opening was, however, delayed for more than twenty years because of war damage. An administrative wing containing a special exhibition gallery and a public restaurant was opened in 1980.

In 1970 the ethnography collection moved to a temporary home at the Museum of Mankind in Burlington Gardens, off Piccadilly. In 1973 the three library departments were divorced from the Museum and, with other library organisations, formed a new body, the British Library; ultimately they will be gathered together in a new purpose-built building.

Although its collections are largely of the past, the British Museum has, at times unwillingly, always looked to the future. As the collections develop, visitors increase and display techniques change so that the 'old curiosity shop in Great Russell Street' changes too. In 1981 a remodelled Egyptian Sculpture Gallery was opened, much of the cost of which had been met by private donations. The Wolfson Galleries (also made possible through the generosity of a private donor) will enable the public to see again the great Townley collection. Other major changes in galleries are being planned before the end of the century.

The British Museum, while acknowledging its debt to successive governments, has throughout its long history owed a particular debt to private individuals and institutions whose benefactions have ranged from gifts and bequests of money to the great Sutton Hoo treasure, to fragments of pottery and to single coins. The Museum trusts that this beneficial partnership will continue into the twenty-first century.

Coins & Medals

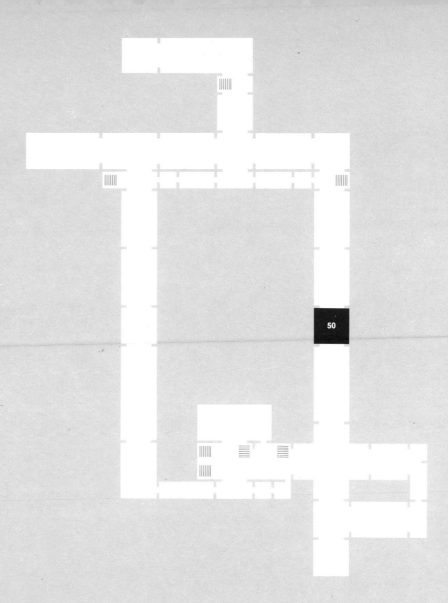

50 Coins & medals

The collection of the Department of Coins and Medals covers a number of different cultures and representative selections of material are placed in different galleries in the context of the relevant civilizations. They will be found described under the Departments of Greek and Roman Antiquities, Medieval and Later Antiquities, Oriental Antiquities and Western Asiatic Antiquities. In the Coins and Medals Gallery is displayed a selection of coins of the British Isles from pre-Roman times onwards. The bulk of the collection of Coins and European medals is available to the public by appointment. The illustrated coins throughout this Guide are shown actual size.

TWO THOUSAND YEARS OF COINS AND MEDALS
IN GREAT BRITAIN

The British series began as a direct result of major movements of people from Belgic Gaul, who brought the custom of striking coins with them. The type of coin first used in Britain was based on the gold stater of Philip of Macedon issued in 348 BC, which had become a universally accepted currency and was widely imitated. The generally barbaric appearance of these first British coins is changed with the appearance of the gold staters of Cunobeline (Shakespeare's Cymbeline). Their design is more representational, their technique more accomplished. On the obverse is an ear of corn dividing the mint name Camulodunum (Colchester, the centre of Cunobeline's sphere of influence) and on the reverse a horse prancing to the right with Cunobeline's name. This greater regularity has been attributed to the increasing influence of the Romans at this period, just before the Claudian invasion of AD 43.

During the occupation of Britain by the Romans the coinage was mostly imported from the Roman mints on the Continent, but numismatic evidence of the occupation is highlighted by the 'Britannia' type for the reverse on coins of the Emperor Hadrian. In AD 286 Carausius created for himself an independent empire in Britain which he maintained until AD 293 and he commemorated his success with coins struck at (?) Colchester and London and on a bronze medallion. The obverse portrait of Carausius in the dress and with the attributes of a consul provides a rare piece of evidence that he maintained this ancient Roman office in the establishment of his new regime in Britain. The reverse is a straightforward statement of his initial victory, but the mysterious formula I.N.P.C.D.A. in the exergue, below, still defies interpretation. After the departure of the Romans about a century later no further coins appear to have been issued and what gold and silver there was still in circulation was soon hoarded as bullion.

In the seventh century there was an increased absorption of Merovingian coins into southern and eastern England; examples of these types of coin produced in gold by the Merovingian Franks who lived in the area made up of modern France, Belgium,

1 CUNOBELINE. GOLD STATER

2 CARAUSIUS. MEDALLION

3 OFFA'S DINAR

4a HAROLD II. PENNY

4b WILLIAM I. PENNY

the Rhineland and Switzerland, can be seen in the Medieval Galleries among the Sutton Hoo treasure. This close contact with the Continent is further stressed by the marriage of Bertha, the daughter of King Charibert I of Paris, to Ethelbert king of Kent after AD 561. With her is associated the mounted gold coin attributed to her chaplain, Bishop Liudhardus, which formed part of the Saint Martin's hoard found at Canterbury and deposited towards the end of the sixth century. These coins still referred to Roman prototypes, but as the Merovingian coins became more commonly used the English coinage came more closely to resemble them. It was not long before this currency of gold was supplemented by, and in the end replaced by a silver coinage. By the end of the seventh century England can be seen to have adopted the northern European silver standard which was to survive without regular issues of gold for the next seven hundred years. With the regular coinage of these small Anglo-Saxon *sceattas* England achieved something like metallic and denominational parity with the coinage of continental Europe.

The link with Europe again provided the impetus for the change from the small, chunky *sceat* to the wider and thinner 'penny', which, apart from occasional exceptions, was the only English coin until the introduction of other denominations in the reign of Edward I. This new form of money, based on the Carolingian *denier* introduced into France by Pepin the Short in his great recoinage of 755, is first seen in a coin of Heaberht, king of Kent; but its general acceptance and availability was established by Offa, king of Mercia from 757 and virtual ruler of all England south of the Humber by 794. The high sense of artistic composition, the skill of the die-engraving and the variety of Offa's coinage are remarkable, but perhaps most 3 extraordinary is the copy of a gold *dinar* which bears his name. This is a copy of an Abassid coin of 744 issued by the Caliph Al-Mansur which has on the reverse 'Offa Rex' inserted upside down into the Arabic inscription. The legend was worked in the die and not counterstruck on the coin; this and the mistakes in the Arabic inscription prove that the dies were not made by Arab workmen and that the coin was copied in this country, providing a most interesting example of the extent of contact in the late eighth century. It also shows the preference for gold currency in southern and south-western Europe over the silver favoured in the north. The end of Offa's reign saw the standardizing of the new penny into a coin with a still broader flan and a higher weight; the penny, which was the standard currency until the fourteenth century. The history of Anglo-Saxon England can be adequately traced in the coinage through the kingdoms of Mercia, Kent, Northumbria and East Anglia until the final supremacy of Wessex ending in the primacy of Eadgar as King of all England in 959. Of particular note are the episcopal issues, the earliest of which is that of Jaenberht issued under Offa at Canterbury; the large offering penny of Alfred the Great produced for the payment of alms (*elimosina*) which he sent to Rome and Jerusalem; and the series of Viking pennies which document the Danish and Norse invasions. A

fine example of these is that of Anlaf Guthfrisson with his 'raven' type which reproduces the Viking standard. Some others can be seen in the Medieval Galleries as part of the Cuerdale hoard which also included Abassid coins. From Eadgar onwards the name of the monarch and the title '*Rex Anglorum*' surrounds the portrait of the king, and from late in his reign the name of the mint appears invariably with that of the moneyer on the reverse of the coins. The portraits are in profile and, apart from the issue of Edward the Confessor shown with a beard, make little attempt at realism. Variants from the usual type are shown in the heads of Cnut and Edward the Confessor with pointed helmets similar to those shown on the Bayeux tapestry, and in the seated full-length figure of the Confessor which recalls the Roman prototype of Theodosius I.

4 It is interesting to compare a penny of Harold II with one of William the Conqueror. The penny of the Saxon king shows a conventionalized bust to left with a sceptre, and on the reverse the inscription '*Pax*' (Peace) across the coin, presumably in an attempt to reassure those parts of the kingdom which were unnerved by the double threat of invasion by Harold Hardrada in the North and William of Normandy in the South. As William omitted the *Pax* inscription, his coin is in the direct line of English coinage since Eadgar, and illustrates William's political expedient of adopting native institutions by continuing the denomination, value and, initially at least, the design of the Anglo-Saxon coinage. The practice of changing the type of the coinage at regular intervals to supplement the king's income, which had been custom in the later Anglo-Saxon period, was also continued. It was in his second issue that the Conqueror introduced the facing bust on the obverse which in the end was to supersede the profile portrait until it was reintroduced by Henry VII. In Henry I's reign the periodic changes in type were continued but the quality and standard of the coins were not maintained, although they were restored at the end of his reign. During the reign of Stephen the chaos caused by the civil wars is amply shown by the variety of irregular coinage of lower weight and the generally miserable appearance of the coins. Particularly interesting are the pennies issued by Queen Matilda when Stephen was imprisoned, showing the full length figures of the Queen and her husband; these coins should not be confused with those of the Empress Matilda, Henry I's daughter, which have a bust to the right like the usual coins of the period.

Soon after Henry II came to the throne in 1154 he abandoned the old custom of regular changes of type. The first coins he issued, known as the Tealby type because of the large number discovered in a hoard at Tealby in Lincolnshire, continued to be struck until 1180. The appearance of the money was then deplorable because of the incompetence of the moneyers and the King decided to issue a new type under the supervision of Philip Aymery of Tours. When the new coins appeared, they were better rounded and more evenly struck than the Tealby type. The design – the king's head facing with his right hand holding a sceptre surrounded by the legend '*Henricus Rex*' and on the reverse the mint name and a moneyer's name enclosing a short cross voided with a four-pellet quatrefoil in each angle – was not much more distinguished than its predecessor. Nevertheless these 'short-cross' pennies proved most successful and the type was issued virtually unchanged from 1180–1247; even the name Henricus remaining on the coin during the reigns of Richard I and John. In 1247 Henry III, allegedly in the hope of putting an end to the clipping of coins, made another change in type, extending the arms of the cross on the reverse until they reached the outer edge. This new type is known as the 'long-cross' penny.

Following other European states Henry III decided to issue a gold penny which should be current for 5 twenty silver pennies. The gold penny was first struck in 1257 by William of Gloucester, the King's goldsmith; it shows Henry's full-length figure seated facing on a throne with orb and sceptre, with, on the reverse, an elaborated version of the long-cross design with rosettes accompanying the pellets in the angles. This fine example of English Gothic design failed because the gold was undervalued (indeed by 1265 it was worth 25 silver pennies) and it soon ceased to be struck; the experiment with bimetallism was put on one side until 1344.

In 1279, under Edward I, there was a great re-coinage and the style of the long-cross penny was changed; a penny bearing the name of Edward with a plain unvoided long-cross being substituted for it. This type of penny continued with only slight varieties in style until the end of the reign of Edward III in 1377, and remained basically unaltered until Henry VII in 1485. With this new coinage the practice of putting the moneyer's name on the coin disappears and the introduction of the groat, halfpenny and farthing set the pattern of English silver money for the next two centuries. Edward I's groat was short-lived, but the design was a brilliant example of the way late Gothic art forms could be applied to coins of a size larger than a penny. After the groat ceased to be struck the other denominations brought into currency under Edward I continued under Edward II and Edward III.

The occasion for the issue of gold coins was the increased importance of trade with Europe and particularly Flanders. There was a need to produce an internal currency which would be acceptable abroad in a society increasingly using gold and, not least, it was important at this particular time for Edward III to enhance his prestige abroad and to pay the mercenaries he wanted for his wars with France. The first gold currency which appeared in 1344 was the famous 'florin' issue, consisting of a florin or two leopard piece, a leopard or half florin and a helm or quarter florin. These coins were not well received despite the beauty of their design and its careful execution, as the gold was too highly valued in proportion to silver. Soon the series was withdrawn and the subsequent gold of Edward III was more individual in appearance; the international flavour of design was only maintained in the Anglo-Gallic series (coins produced in France in the name of the English

monarch as Duke of Aquitaine) most notably shown on the coins produced by Edward's son, Edward, the Black Prince. The noble with its half and quarter was proclaimed in 1344 at the value of 80 pennies, and after an intermediate step in 1346 the ratio between standard gold and silver was fixed in 1351. The name of the 'noble' is said to refer to its metal signifying the standard coin of gold, much as the name 'sterling' 6 signified first quality silver. Its design, the armed king standing with a drawn sword and a shield of arms which included the lilies of France displayed very prominently in a ship, was thought by some to refer amongst other things to the recent English naval victory at Sluys in 1340; but its purpose was in any event that of propaganda. In 1351 Edward was also able to carry through the reform which Edward I had tried and failed, namely to introduce the groat, a coin of the value of four pence. The great success of Edward III's monetary innovations can be seen by the fact that apart from the reduction of weight in 1412 the coinage remained unchanged in value, quality and design until Edward IV revised the coinage in 1464. Examples of the continuing types of noble can be seen in the Medieval Galleries as part of the Fishpool hoard which also included Burgundian nobles, riders and lions.

The monetary crisis which necessitated the revision of the comparative weights of gold and silver in 1464 was caused by the disappearance abroad of gold coins where they commanded a higher bullion value. Consequently the weight of the silver coins was reduced and the gold coins were increased proportionately in value; the noble was now worth 100 pennies instead of 80. In the following year a new gold coin, the ryal or rose noble worth ten shillings and another, the angel, which had the value of the old noble (80 pence) were introduced. The rose noble was distinguished from the old noble by the rose which it bore on the side of the ship, and a banner bearing the King's initial at the vessel's stern. The 7 angel derived its name from the obverse which showed the Archangel Michael transfixing the dragon; on the reverse was a ship with a cross set in front of the mast with a shield of arms below it. The King's initial and a rose, symbol of the house of York, were at either side. The propagandist element in this use of a rose was not lost on Henry VII when he won the throne in 1485 and the Tudor rose was a dominant feature on the reverse of the first coins of his reign, notably the revised ryal and more spectacularly with the sovereign of 1489.

8 The sovereign, with a current value of 20 shillings or two ryals, was produced in direct emulation of the great *real d'or* struck in the Netherlands for Maximilian, King of the Romans, in 1487. It was the heaviest coin so far produced for any king of England and its magnificence and the obvious display of royal power which it shows are paralleled in its name. The obverse shows the King enthroned with all the panoply of the regalia but it is well balanced by the elaborate double rose bearing the arms of England and France on the reverse – both splendid examples of the decorative elaboration so typical of the final phase of Gothic art in England. If the sovereign is an example of the

5 HENRY III. GOLD PENNY

6 EDWARD III. NOBLE

7 EDWARD IV. ANGEL

8 HENRY VII. SOVEREIGN

9 HENRY VII. GROAT

10*a* HENRY VIII. MEDAL

10*b* MARY. MEDAL

11 ELIZABETH I. ARMADA MEDAL

9 final brilliance of the late Gothic style, the groat of 1503–04 heralds the introduction of Renaissance portraiture. The abandonment of the old style of the full-face portrait of the king with a conventionalized appearance, regardless of age or individual characteristics, which had been in use for the last 300 years, in favour of a profile portrait of remarkable sensitivity and accuracy of portraiture really marks the beginning of the modern coinage. The testoon or shilling, groat and half groat with the authentic portrait of the king had considerable impact; and even though Henry VIII reverted to a full-face portrait at the end of his reign this still had a remarkable realism and the precedent had been set.

The influence on this new style of portraiture came from the Continent and continental influences can be 10 seen further in the medallic portraits of Henry VIII and Mary produced by Hans Schwartz and Jacopo da Trezzo respectively. These are superb examples of High Renaissance portraiture which show clearly a difference of approach between the German and Italian schools. It is instructive to compare them with 11 the Armada medal of Queen Elizabeth which, close in style to the design for the Great Seal by Nicholas Hilliard (now in the Department of Prints and Drawings), shows the Queen as a hieratic image, an icon glittering with the majesty of power, in sharp contrast to the genial realism of Schwartz or the withdrawn dignity of da Trezzo.

Henry VIII's coinage is notable for the introduction of the crown or five-shilling piece and the half-crown, both struck in gold; for the final cessation of the archiepiscopal mints of Canterbury and York – represented by the groat of Thomas Wolsey – and the episcopal mint of Durham, which was a result of the break with Rome; and for the truly remarkable debasement of the coinage. This was so widely disliked that the young Edward VI continued striking base groats in his father's name until three years after his accession when, in 1550 the quality and standard of the coinage was raised. An interesting variety of new types was introduced including the silver crown and half-crown showing the King on horse-back, and the introduction of Roman numerals beside the portrait of the King on the shillings, sixpences and threepences to show the denomination. Mary returned to the profile portraiture which has been in use ever since and her coinage falls into two sections; the issues before and after her marriage with Philip II of Spain in 1554. After this, his name and title appears with hers on the coinage and his bust is placed opposite hers on the shilling and sixpence. Elizabeth finally resolved the monetary confusion caused by her father's debasement of the coinage and by the end of her reign the coinage was remarkable for its intrinsic quality and the wide range of denominations from the gold sovereign to the silver half-penny. The designs of the later sixteenth century were clear and well executed, as pleasing to look at as they were simple. Another influence of the Renaissance was that Roman letters now replaced Lombardic lettering.

From the very beginnings of coinage in Britain there had been no change in the way in which coins were struck. The traditional method was for a moneyer to imprint the design upon the blank by hammering it between a pair of dies. Between 1561 and 1572 the first experiments took place in England in coinage by machinery. These were initiated by the arrival from the Paris mint of Eloye Mestrell who had fled to England. The series of coins he produced are more clearly and more elegantly struck than any of their precursors, and his sixpence shows great economy of 12 design and simplicity of lettering. The experiment was, however, expensive and unpopular with the moneyers, so Mestrell was dismissed.

James I produced a wide range of denominations and styles of coin in both his English and his Scottish series. His sovereigns and rose nobles were the last examples of these types of coin. The final survivor of the Gothic coinage, the angel, was continued as a ceremonial coin for the 'King's touch' (a traditional way of attempting to cure scrofula). Stylistically James's most interesting coin was produced in his third coinage of 1619. The laurel or unite of a value of 20 shillings showed the King laureate and draped like a Roman emperor. The reverse bore the legend *Faciam Eos In Gentem Unam*, referring to the unity of the Scottish and English crowns. The classicizing influence is reminiscent of the revived interest in classicism which focused on the work of Inigo Jones. An important innovation was the first use of a copper token farthing. These were issued under licence from the crown by Lord Harrington and not by the Royal Mint. The confusion caused by the semi-official nature of these coins made them unpopular; but the initial step to provide the need of an officially recognized token coinage had been taken.

The reign of Charles I, like that of Stephen, was dominated by Civil War and is similarly distinguished by the variety and complexity of its coinage. Hammered coins continued in the majority but further experimentation with machinery was undertaken by Nicholas Briot between 1632 and 1638. Briot's coins are neatly executed and skilfully engraved, and he continued to control the artistic side of the coinage until his death in 1646. In 1637 a mint had been established at Aberystwyth to strike money from the Welsh silver which until then had been sent up to the Tower mint; the money struck at Aberystwyth was distinguished by having a plume on both sides, the Prince of Wales's feathers. This experiment in decentralization in the interests of economy and efficiency was a great success and proved of singular importance to Charles after the outbreak of the Civil War in 1642 because the Welsh remained initially loyal and so the expertise and equipment from Aberystwyth enabled him to set up emergency mints elsewhere. War coinages were thus produced at various times at Shrewsbury, Oxford, Bristol, Truro and Exeter. A mint at York was set up by Briot and there were also mints at Weymouth and Worcester and perhaps elsewhere. An unrepresentative but fine example of these war coinages is the Oxford crown produced by Thomas Rawlins in 1644, which shows the King on horseback over a view of the city of Oxford. Less skilled but equally interesting pieces were struck at Carlisle, Chester, Colchester,

Newark, Pontefract and Scarborough while these were under siege. Mostly made from local plate they are very crude; some are stamped with no more than the royal cypher, place of origin, date and value. An intriguing example is the half-crown of Scarborough made from an oblong of silver upon which has been stamped a castle of ghost-like insubstantiality. Of the many medals of this period that of Prince Rupert has something of the bravura and glamour attached to his legend, and the memorial badge designed by Thomas Rawlins with the portrait of the King on the obverse and Queen Henrietta Maria on the reverse portrays them both with sympathy and great dignity.

Under the Commonwealth the monetary system remained unchanged and the coins are very simple and of universal type. On the obverse is the shield of St George within a garland of palm and laurel enclosed by the inscription 'The Commonwealth of England' and on the reverse 'God With Us' around the conjoined shields of St George and Ireland. Thomas Simon, who had been at the Mint since 1645, designed a series of superb coins for Cromwell as Lord Protector, showing him laureate and draped like a Roman emperor. The classical inspiration appears to be more direct here than that which inspired the laurel of James I. Simon's crown is altogether bolder and clearer: for pure distinction of style it remains unequalled in the English series. These coins were produced by machinery but never formally issued, and at the Restoration in 1660 Charles II continued the hammered coinage and type of coin of his father. Thomas Rawlins and Thomas Simon were both employed on the recoinage but in 1661 Charles decided that the demonetization of the Commonwealth issues would be much faster if he caused all coins to be milled, with the edges either lettered or grained. This new coinage was designed by a Fleming, Jan Roettier, whom Charles preferred to Simon despite the real accomplishment of the latter's Petition Crown made in protest at Roettier's appointment. Two coins were to have lasting importance: the first is yet another gold coin worth 20 shillings. Because some of these coins were struck from gold supplied by the Guinea Company they became popularly known as guineas. Coins actually made from this gold were distinguished by the mark of an elephant, sometimes with a castle. The second innovation was the copper halfpenny and farthing with the reverse of Britannia. The figure for this reverse was said to have been modelled on one of the beauties of Charles's court, Frances Stewart, Duchess of Richmond, of whom there is also a fine medal by Roettier.

The hammered silver coins were finally removed from circulation in 1696 and there was a complete recoinage which resulted in the guinea which had stood at 30 shillings in 1694 being revalued at 21s 6d by 1698, at which value it remained until 1717 when it was reduced once and for all to 21 shillings. Queen Anne's reign saw an influx of bullion taken from the galleons captured from the Spanish at Vigo Bay in 1702, and coins made from this have the word 'Vigo' under the bust. This practice of marking the coinage to show where the metal came from continued in George II's reign, the rose for England and plume for Wales being augmented by 'SSC' for the South Sea Company, and 'Lima' for the treasure brought back to England by Commodore Anson after sailing round the world in 1744. An interesting group in Anne's coinage is the series of copper halfpennies and farthings designed by John Croker and made at the end of her reign. One example shows Britannia in a chariot imitating the Roman *Biga* type, issued in honour of the Act of Union. The obverse shows Anne as Anna Augusta. When her cousin George, Elector of Hanover, came to the throne in 1714 the coinage continued unchanged except for the introduction of the Brunswick horse into his arms and his German titles into the legend.

In George III's reign the scarcity of silver which had been noticeable in William III's time became extreme and even gold was hard to come by. The result of this shortage was an increase in token copper coinage produced by the men in business who could not get enough small change from the Mint. The government eventually took steps to remedy this scarcity and in 1797 Matthew Boulton struck the first copper penny alongside a piece worth twopence at the Soho mint in Birmingham. These had a portrait of the King on the obverse and a figure of Britannia on the reverse, designed by C. H. Kückler. After this introduction, the copper coinage became increasingly important, although the twopence did not long survive as its weight and size made it too cumbersome. The lack of silver was so chronic by 1797 that the Treasury tried to make up the deficiency by issuing Spanish dollars countermarked with a stamped head of the king. In 1804, the Bank of England obtained permission to issue a dollar worth five shillings and in 1813 token pieces worth three shillings and one and sixpence. There were three issues of the guinea, the second designed by Lewis Pingo with a spade-shaped shield which caused the coin to be called a 'spade' guinea. The third issue was the most interesting; not only was it the last guinea to be issued, in 1813, but it also omitted the French arms and the French title which had been officially dropped in 1800, and showed a neoclassical inspiration in the laureate head of the King.

In 1816 an entirely new coinage was ordered, consisting in gold of the sovereign and half-sovereign, and in silver of the crown, half-crown, shilling and sixpence. The English coinage was based on this denominational structure until the decimalization of 1971 (although gold ceased to be current after 1917). The dies for the gold coins were made by an Italian engraver, Benedetto Pistrucci. Strongly neoclassical in design, they are both elegant and economical, and the reverse type of the sovereign, St George slaying the dragon, has proved so popular that it has been in use ever since. Pistrucci also produced a design for a great medal celebrating the victory of Waterloo in 1815. Commissioned in 1819 the design was not completed until 1849 and it was never produced in medallic form as the dies could not be sufficiently hardened. However, electrotypes have been made from the dies and the magnificence of the design can be appreciated from

12 ELIZABETH I. MESTRELL'S SIXPENCE

13 CHARLES I AND HENRIETTA MARIA. MEMORIAL BADGE

14 CROMWELL. PATTERN CROWN

15 GEORGE III. PISTRUCCI'S SOVEREIGN

16 WATERLOO MEDAL

16 WATERLOO MEDAL

17 VICTORIA. JUBILEE MEDAL

18 JAMES III OF SCOTLAND. UNICORN

19 MARY, QUEEN OF SCOTS. TESTOON

20 GEORGE II, FOR IRELAND. 'VOCE POPULI' TOKEN

16 these. On the obverse are the heads of the four allies, the Prince Regent, Francis II, Emperor of Austria, Alexander I, Emperor of Russia, and Frederick William III, King of Prussia, enclosed within a classically inspired frieze. On the reverse, the two commanders, Wellington and Blücher, are shown in classical costume on horseback with their horses held still by a winged Victory; above them is Jupiter in his chariot and all around them are the fallen giants. The allusion is a nicely turned reference to Napoleon's defeat and the medal is a splendid climax to Pistrucci's achievements.

The coinages of George IV and William IV designed by William Wyon follow the established pattern and were produced with the same easy distinction of design which marks the first issue of Victoria's reign. The florid neo-Gothic coins of the late 1840s were also by Wyon. The most important of these was the florin, introduced in 1849 as a first step towards decimalization. In 1887 Victoria's jubilee was celebrated by a new coinage, showing the Queen as Empress of India with the Imperial Crown, Garter and Star of India prominently displayed and a long veil hanging down her back. These coins were not popular and were superseded by a further new coinage in 1893. These bore the 'Old Head' portrait designed by Thomas Brock. On the occasion of her diamond

17 jubilee in 1897 a medal was produced showing the portrait head of the Queen from the existing coinage by Brock on the obverse and on the reverse the portrait head from the coins of Victoria's first issue by Wyon. This was accompanied by the inscription 'Longitudo Dierum in Dextera Eius et in Sinistra Gloria', a reference to the book of Proverbs in the Bible conveying the fulfilment of the promise the young Queen had when she had ascended the throne. The sentiment of this sums up the proud achievement of the British Empire, and the design of the reverse has a delicacy of touch which is related strongly to the *Art Nouveau* movement, an appropriate reminder that 'Change is inevitable. In a progressive society change is constant.'

The twentieth century has been notable for the replacement of gold and silver by a purely token coinage. Although gold has never been officially demonetized and has continued to be issued it has not been generally circulated since 1917. Its internal use, like that of the large silver denomination of the crown, has become restricted to prestige or commemorative issues, as at the Accession of a monarch. The silver content of coins was reduced in 1920 and was replaced in 1945 by cupro-nickel. The only coins actually made from silver since 1945 are the small denominations issued annually as Maundy money. In terms of design, the main movements of twentieth-century art are sparingly reflected in coins. Notable exceptions are the florin of Edward VII, which shows the influence of the Art Nouveau movement as clearly as any poster design by Mucha; the crown issued in 1935 to mark George V's Jubilee, and the dodecagonal threepenny bit of George VI. These last two have the staccato hardness of outline typical of *Art Decoratif*. Edward VIII is represented by two medals commemorating

his Coronation, even though he was never crowned, and his Abdication; he issued no coins for the United Kingdom. In addition to the crown issued in 1953 to commemorate Elizabeth II's coronation, showing the Queen seated on horseback, another crown was struck in 1965. This set a precedent by showing Sir Winston Churchill's head on the reverse; the first time since the Norman Conquest that the portrait of a person other than the monarch has appeared on the regular coinage. In 1971 the old structure of the English pound with its value of 240 pence was completely revised and the currency was decimalized. This has brought the English coinage into line with the currencies of Europe and has finally realized the proposal of a decimal currency of 1841.

A few examples of Scottish and Irish coins are displayed at the end of the English series. The medieval silver coins of Scotland show a strong English influence but the gold coins are closer to continental prototypes. Of particular interest is the

18 unicorn of James III: it is said that some of these were made from a gold chain which the king wore around his neck and had melted down to provide bullion for this issue when he had no other source of gold left. The groat issued by him shows the use of a continental type of portrait bust in Scotland some time before it was adopted by Henry VII in England. The style of this and more particularly the bonnet piece of James V, which shows a strong similarity in portraiture with the paintings of Clouet, bear witness to the Scottish alliance with France. This is further attested by the testoon of Mary of 1561 bearing the monogram FM, which are the initials of her husband, François, King of France, and Mary herself. In her widowhood and

19 sole reign was issued a testoon which bears one of the few reliable representations of her.

James VI of Scotland issued an extensive series of coins with even more varieties of type than the series later issued in England. Good examples are the gold lion-noble, hat-piece and sword-and-sceptre piece. The design of these is good, their execution often weak. Nicholas Briot struck coins for Charles I in Scotland which show a broader sense of design than his English series. With the bawbie of William III the issue of independent types of Scottish coins ends. A Scottish shilling based on the design of the gold lion-noble of James V was, however, issued in honour of the Scottish wife of George VI, Elizabeth Bowes-Lyon, daughter of the Earl of Strathmore and Kinghorne.

Unlike the Scottish and the English series the Irish series is not continuous. Evidence of the strength of Norse contacts is shown by the coins of Sihtric and their contemporary derivatives; they are derived from an English penny of Aethelred II. John issued coin as Lord of Ireland from about 1185. These have his name upon them, unlike the coins he issued in England which have the inscription 'Henricus Rex'; they also show a curious full-face portrait which has been aptly called 'moon-like'. To prevent confusion with his English series Edward I issued an Irish penny with his portrait enclosed within a triangle. Apart from these and brief issues in 1339 and 1425 no main issues of coin appeared in Ireland from about 1307 until 1460 when a distinctive type with a large crown on the obverse instead of a royal portrait was brought out by Edward IV. The coinage was specifically produced at a lower weight standard than English coins of the same denomination, so that, for example, an Irish groat was worth three English pence. This was intended to prevent the mass export of Irish silver which had been current practice in the reigns of John, Henry III and Edward I.

An active policy of issuing debased coins for Ireland like the billon placks and bawbies issued in Scotland by James V and Mary was pursued by Henry VIII. His first Irish issue of 1534 introduced the harp to the coinage and as a symbol of Ireland this has been current ever since. Henry's later issues of 1540 and 1544 were still further debased. Despite the efforts in England to improve the standard of the coinage, Irish coins remained more or less debased throughout the rest of the Tudor period. The troubles of Charles I's reign are echoed in the coinage; first an emergency silver currency was issued by the Lords Justices, currency with just the weight stamped upon it, then under the Lieutenancy of Lord Ormonde coins were produced with the denomination clearly marked on the reverse and the royal cypher crowned on the obverse. No coinage was minted specially for Ireland under the Commonwealth, although the Irish harp was included among the symbols on the current coin of the period. At the Restoration Charles II granted a patent to Sir Thomas Armstrong for coining farthings, but these proved unpopular and the Irish produced their own token coinage, of which the St Patrick halfpennies and farthings issued about 1673 are representative examples. After fleeing from England in 1688 James II landed in Ireland in the following year in an attempt to regain his throne. The Catholic element in Ireland provided him with some support but as he did not have enough money to provide for the war he was forced to produce a token money made of a brass alloy which it was intended should be exchangeable for silver after his victory over William III. This ambitious plan was never realized as he was defeated and the so-called 'gun-money' was withdrawn by William in 1691, although some coins were countermarked for use as halfpennies.

In 1722 William Wood was granted a patent by George I for minting copper coins for Ireland and the American colonies. These coins were struck at Bristol but were so unpopular that in 1724 he was forced to stop production and his Irish coinage was shipped off to America. In 1760, because of a chronic shortage of copper coins of low denomination a large number of tokens were produced by Roche, a button manufacturer. These have a laureate bust of the King in very crude style with the inscription 'Voce Populi' which can be freely translated 'by popular demand', on the obverse, and on the reverse Hibernia seated. Formal union with England came in 1800 and in 1821 the two currencies were amalgamated; the final issue of separate coins for Ireland was of copper pence, halfpence and farthings in 1822 and 1823; these were withdrawn in 1826 and since then the coinage of the United Kingdom has been uniform.

20

Egyptian antiquities

Main floor

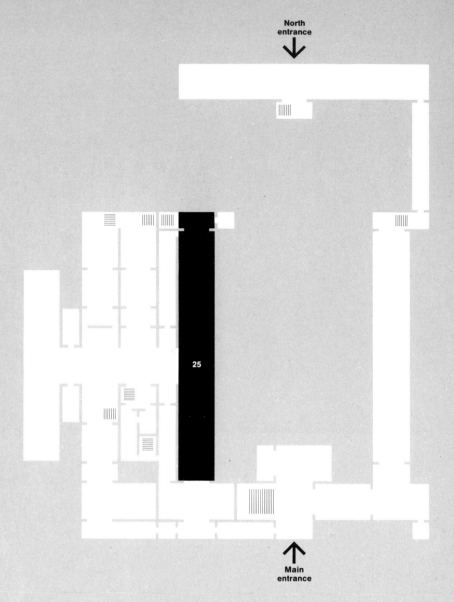

25

Main
entrance
↑

25 Egyptian sculpture

Upper levels

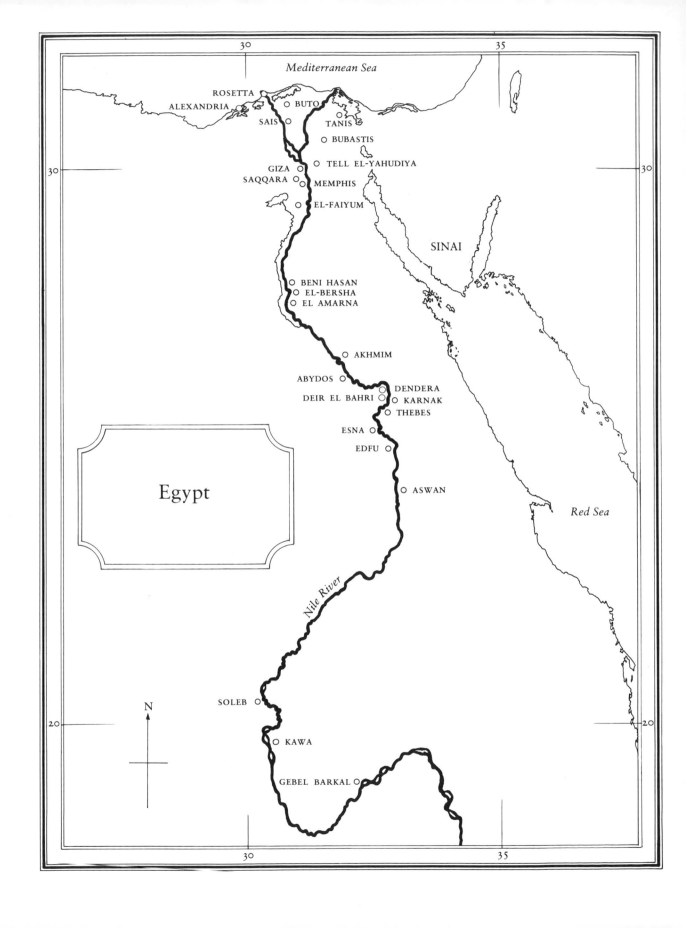

The collections of the Department of Egyptian antiquities number nearly 70,000 objects which illustrate every aspect of ancient Egyptian civilization.

The first Egyptian objects entered the Museum in the eighteenth century, but it was not until the early nineteenth century that serious collecting began. After the collapse of Napoleon's Egyptian campaign in 1801, the antiquities gathered by the French expedition were ceded to the British and presented to the British Museum. Among them was the Rosetta Stone, a monument which from the first promised to provide the means by which the secrets of ancient Egypt might be revealed. At that time it aroused great excitement among scholars, and stimulated a general curiosity among the public; it has remained an object of continuing interest, and would in itself provide sufficient reason for a visit to the Egyptian Galleries of the Museum. It is now, however, nobly supported by many outstanding monumental sculptures and a wealth of smaller antiquities, both works of art and objects representative of the religious and secular life of the peoples of ancient Egypt. By the end of the nineteenth century well-documented objects from excavations, especially those conducted by the Egypt Exploration Fund (later Society), were beginning to swell the collection. Excavations, gifts and purchases have continued to add to it until the present day.

Although the great number of objects in the collection allows the public exhibition of only a part, those exhibited comprise all the most important pieces, and a representative selection of the most interesting antiquities from every period of ancient Egypt's history. Large sculpture and other stone monuments are shown in the Egyptian Sculpture Gallery on the ground floor; other objects may be seen in a range of rooms on the first floor numbered in sequence from the First Egyptian Room to the Sixth Egyptian Room, with antiquities from the latest period covered by the Department being shown in the Coptic Corridor.

25 EGYPTIAN SCULPTURE GALLERY

Approached from the Museum's main entrance, the south end of the Egyptian Sculpture Gallery is marked by two colossal granite figures of King Amenophis III of the Eighteenth Dynasty (1417–1379 BC), imposing monuments from the king's mortuary temple at Thebes, conceived and executed in the traditional manner of Egyptian royal sculpture. Beyond them, and forming the limit of the introductory area of the gallery, are two further colossi made in the same reign for the temple at Soleb in the Sudan. These are two monumental sculptures of recumbent lions in red granite nobly exemplifying the Egyptian artist's ability to represent animals with sympathy and understanding. The one on the right was completed and inscribed in the reign of Tutankhamun (1361–1352 BC).

1 RED GRANITE LION FROM A TEMPLE AT SOLEB

The introductory area between these four monuments of Amenophis III consists of two sections dealing with the history and the scripts and language of ancient Egypt. The historical section on the right contains an outline of Egyptian history illustrated in particular by the substantial remains of a list of kings from the Temple of Ramesses II at Abydos on which the names of the rulers who controlled Egypt during the 'heretical' period introduced by Akhenaten are omitted. Expunged from the record, they ceased to have reality in history. The Rosetta Stone dominates the language section on the left. It is the surviving part of a great basalt formal monument or *stela* bearing an inscription dated to year 9 of Ptolemy V (196 BC) which is repeated in two languages – Egyptian (in both the hieroglyphic and demotic scripts) and Greek. With the help of the Greek version scholars were able to find the key to the decipherment of hieroglyphs. The subsequent study of the Egyptian language and of the scripts in which this language was written (hieroglyphic, hieratic and demotic) made it possible for the inscribed objects, and texts written on papyri, which have survived in such large numbers from antiquity, to be read and understood.

Inscriptions play an important part in establishing the purpose and significance of most Egyptian sculpture, for there are very few pieces of ancient statuary from Egypt which are not provided with texts. Almost all sculpture was produced for religious purposes, to

3 FALSE DOOR FROM THE TOMB OF KAIHAP

2 THE ROSETTA STONE WITH REMAINS OF A TEXT IN HIEROGLYPHIC, DEMOTIC AND GREEK

promote the worship of deities, to glorify the power of specific kings, to serve as intercessionary instruments in obtaining benefits for private persons, or to act in a more specific funerary role, representing the person of the dead individual. Some sculpture was monumental in the strictest sense of the term, forming part of the arhitectural embellishment of temples, like the four pieces of the reign of Amenophis III which are placed at the beginning of this gallery; but most pieces were conceived in private roles, to be consigned to the darkness of the tomb or to the unfrequented courts of temples. All these kinds of statue may be seen in the display in the Egyptian Sculpture Gallery.

Beyond the introductory area, objects are displayed in the gallery according to a chronological arrangement beginning with the Old Kingdom (2686–2181 BC) and proceeding northwards until the Graeco-Roman Period (330 BC–400 AD) is reached at the north end of the gallery. Much of the Old Kingdom collection of the Museum consists of fragments from the mastaba-chapels of tombs in the Memphite burial grounds of Giza and Saqqara. Passing between the two monumental false-doors of the royal official Tjetji the visitor is confronted by the fine, near life-size, statue of Nenkheftka, a tomb-sculpture of the Fifth Dynasty (2494–2345 BC) which shows its subject in one of the great traditional poses for the standing person. In figures of this kind in the Old Kingdom the conventional is dominant, the only originality usually being found in the presentation of the head. Here the execution is masterly, though the conception is commonplace. To the right of Nenkheftka is the great false-door of Ptahshepses, a prime historical document of the Fifth Dynasty, and a shallow flight of steps leading to a raised area and an entrance to a small side-gallery. Behind the Ptahshepses false-door has been reconstructed the mastaba-chapel of Urirenptah, which contains scenes illustrating many aspects of daily life in the Egypt of about 2350 BC, including the ploughing of fields, the harvesting of crops, a musical entertainment, the slaughtering of cattle and the making of the tomb-owner's bed. The moderate quality of the carving of these scenes is more than offset by the charm and interest of the details depicted.

The false doors, already mentioned, represented the focal points in the mastaba-chapels; before them offerings were placed, and through them the dead men's souls could emerge to enjoy the offerings and revisit the world. The texts on these false doors contain prayers for offerings and also long lists of the titles and honours of the deceased. Artistically the
3 finest in the collection is that of Kaihap which faces the visitor as he enters the side gallery which runs on the east side of the main Sculpture Gallery.

In the side gallery, which is in all respects small in scale, objects are displayed which would be for the most part rather lost in the great space of the main gallery. In the area to the right of Kaihap's false-door are small sculptures, reliefs and a selection of fine metal, wooden, terracotta and other objects of Old Kingdom date. One of the earliest royal representa-
4 tions from Egypt is the small ivory figure of a king wearing a short cloak, a garment in later times associated with the festival of royal renewal called the Sed. At the end is the fine granite seated statue of the boat-builder Ankhwa (also known as Bedjmes), one of the earliest stone sculptures to have survived from ancient Egypt. It displays the squat, somewhat compressed form of Third Dynasty sculpture (2686–2613 BC) but lacks the conventional treatment of detail which renders much later sculpture rather academic. Even more striking, aesthetically, is the ebony figure of Meryrehashtef (c. 2200 BC), which shows the subject as a slender, naked, striding young man.

Continuing along the side gallery to the left of Kaihap's false-door, the visitor passes through a small room containing provincial reliefs of the First Intermediate Period (2181–2140 BC) and fragments of brightly coloured scenes from the mortuary temple of King Mentuhotpe II of the Eleventh Dynasty (2133–1991 BC), presided over by a striking sandstone head of the king, also from the temple at Thebes. To the
5 right is the *stela* of Tjetji, one of the most important historical monuments in the collection. It belongs to the early Eleventh Dynasty, a period of scanty records, when two rival royal lines fought for the control of Egypt. This room also contains some Twelfth Dynasty sculpture (1991–1786 BC) including the group of three *stelae* and a statue from the sepulchral monument of Inyotef at Abydos; the statue is notable for its representation of Inyotef as unusually thin, with promi-

nent ribs. A small vestibule beyond provides a setting for three typical small sculptures of private persons of Middle Kingdom date, the finest of which is the standing cloaked figure of an unnamed official in granite, the carving of which is unusually subtle. Beyond this vestibule lies another small area devoted to the Middle Kingdom (2050–1786 BC), with a fine painted wooden coffin of Seni and three painted relief scenes from the necropolis of El Bersha in Middle Egypt. Of particular note also is the limestone block statue of Sihathor, displayed within its original niche *stela* carved with representations of himself and his wife. This piece is of great interest both for its setting and as one of the earliest examples of the block statue which became one of the most characteristic forms in the repertoire of Egyptian sculpture.

At this point the visitor may return to the vestibule and pass once more into the main gallery where he will

4 IVORY FIGURE OF KING OF THE 1ST OR 2ND DYNASTY

[29]

5 STELA OF TJETJI

6 GRANITE STATUE OF KING SESOSTRIS III

be faced immediately by a granite torso of Sesostris I, second king of the Twelfth Dynasty (1971–1928 BC), beyond which on the far side of the gallery in Bay 21 stand three exceptional life-size figures of Sesostris III of the same dynasty 1878–1843 BC. These statues, of which the central one is a true masterpiece of Egyptian sculpture, are splendid representatives of the individuality of royal portraiture in the Twelfth Dynasty. In all the king is shown wearing the head-dress known as the *nemes* and his attitude of stepping forward with his hands laid flat on his kilt, becomes one of the standard postures for the representation of royalty. The approach to this group of statues passes down a ramp leading from the raised platform on the east side of the gallery, and between two further royal portraits of the Twelfth Dynasty, the colossal granite heads of Sesostris III and Ammenemes III. The latter, with deep-cut sockets to receive inlaid eyes, is particularly powerful. The bottom of the ramp is flanked by two columns which recall the massive nature of Egyptian temple architecture. One has a palm capital and comes from the funerary temple beside the pyramid of King Unas of the Fifth Dynasty (2494–2345 BC); the other, a papyrus-bundle column, is almost certainly of Middle Kingdom date, although it is inscribed with royal names of the Eighteenth (Amenophis III), Nineteenth (Merneptah), and Twentieth (Sethnakhte) Dynasties.

The remaining part of the south end of the Sculpture Gallery is occupied mainly by sculptures of the Eighteenth Dynasty (1567–1320 BC), in many cases set against a background of royal and private inscriptions most of which come from tombs, and seek the provision of food, drink and other offerings on behalf of the respective tomb-owners. The dominant sculpture, set in the middle of the gallery is a colossal red granite head of an Eighteenth Dynasty king, formerly thought to be Tuthmosis III, but now generally considered to represent a later monarch, possibly Amenophis III. It comes from the Temple of Mut at Karnak, where its torso still lies; but its vast right arm rests beside it in the gallery. Just in front of this great head, to the right and left, facing into the gallery, are two further royal statues. The seated statue of King Sobkemsaf I of the Seventeenth Dynasty (c. 1650 BC) is the largest of the very small number of royal sculptures surviving from this shadowy period. It is notable both for the unusual decoration on its base and also for the technical details of how the inlaid eyes were fixed. Opposite in Bay 17 is the impressive colossus of a king, striding, as it were across the gallery towards Sobkemsaf. This statue although bearing the names of Ramesses II and Merneptah, both kings of the Nineteenth Dynasty, almost certainly possesses the facial features of Tuthmosis III (1504–1450 BC). Beyond this colossus and to the left of the great head, four statues of the lioness-headed goddess Sakhmet occupy the last bay in this part of the gallery. Two show the goddess standing and two show her seated, and they come, like the great head, from the Temple of Mut, where about 600 statues of Sakhmet were set up in the reign of Amenophis III (1417–1379 BC). She was a fierce, bloodthirsty deity whose nature is much belied by the benevolent appearance of these statues.

7 COLOSSAL ROYAL HEAD OF THE EIGHTEENTH DYNASTY

To the right of the great head an opening leads again into the side gallery, the Old and Middle Kingdom parts of which have already been visited. Fine small sculpture and tomb paintings are exhibited in the part allotted to the Eighteenth Dynasty. Three contrasting statues of important officials face the entrance from the main gallery: Menkheperresonb, high-priest of Amun in the reigns of Tuthmosis III and Amenophis II, Senenmut, steward of Queen Hatshepsut, and Kamose, an army officer during the reign of Amenophis III. Of these, the finest, and most unusual is that of Senenmut, who is here shown in his role of
8 tutor of the princess Neferure, whom he holds on his lap. He is shown wearing an all-enveloping garment of a kind most common in the Middle Kingdom, from which the princess's head emerges. To the left, flanking the entrance to the room where wall-paintings are shown, two further private statues are placed on pedestals; both are block statues made of quartzite and show how, by the Eighteenth Dynasty, the Egyptians exploited the large, relatively flat, surfaces of this form of sculpture, for the use of inscriptions. One is of the scribe Tetity, and the other a second representation of Senenmut, very different from the one exhibited nearby. Beyond stands one of the finest royal heads in the collection, a schist portrait either of Queen Hatshepsut or of her nephew King Tuthmosis III. The difficulty of identifying with confidence royal portraits is strikingly exemplified by this head. Its royal attributes are equally possible for king or queen; its facial features are sufficiently characteristic to be dated to the mid-Eighteenth Dynasty, but not adequately differentiated for precise identification.

The three wall-paintings exhibited in the side gallery are artistically the finest in the collection. Two, from the tomb of Nebamun (about 1400 BC) show a banquet scene and a hunting scene. The former is
9 remarkable for the inclusion of two musicians with their faces shown frontally, contrary to the common Egyptian artistic convention by which faces are shown in profile; equally unconventionally, two dancers have their bodies shown in profile. The second scene shows
10 Nebamun hunting birds in the marshes from a flimsy papyrus skiff, accompanied by admiring wife and child. Here the Egyptian artist has been particularly skilful in exploiting his rather limited palette to represent texture and shading in the painting of birds, fish and Nebamun's retriever cat. The third scene, from the Tomb of Sobkhotpe, shows the bringing of tribute to the Egyptian king by emissaries from the Near Eastern countries under Egyptian influence.

8 STATUE OF SENENMUT AND NEFERURE

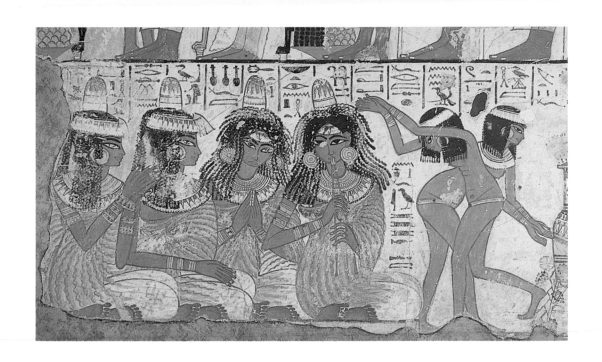

11 OINTMENT BOX

12 GOLD AND SILVER FIGURE OF AMEN-RE

Between the southern and northern parts of the Egyptian Sculpture Gallery lies a more open area known as the Central Saloon. It has been made the setting for colossal royal sculpture, a few choice pieces of private sculpture and, in the centre, a complex of show cases containing fine small objects mostly of New Kingdom date, such as a wooden figure of a 11 swimming girl pushing before her an ointment box in the shape of a duck, a splendid gold and silver figure of 12 the god Amun and a glass cosmetic bottle in the form 16 of a fish. On the right-hand (eastern) side two sculptures from the mortuary temple of Amenophis III at Thebes can be seen. They are carved in mottled brown conglomerate quartzite, in a manner which falls outside the conventional forms of the period, and indicates a change in artistic approach which foreshadows the eccentricity of sculpture of the reign of Akhenaten. A few examples of Amarna sculpture are displayed in the floor-cases in the centre of the Central Saloon. A colossal white limestone bust of Amenophis III, also from Thebes, is placed between these floor-cases looking north. Of the sculptures on the west side of the 14 Central Saloon, the most interesting is a pair statue showing an unnamed noble and his wife carved in the refined style of the late Eighteenth Dynasty (c. 1350–1320 BC). They are shown sitting in a relaxed manner, hand in hand, awaiting the eternity of their posthumous existence.

Entering the northern part of the Sculpture Gallery, the visitor finds himself first in an area devoted principally to sculptures of the Nineteenth Dynasty (1320–1200 BC) and dominated by the massive gran-17 ite bust of Ramesses II (1304–1237 BC) which was given the misnomer 'the Younger Memnon' soon after it reached the Museum in 1817. This statue, extraordinarily sensitive in its carving in spite of its size, comes from the Ramesseum, the vast mortuary temple of the King at Thebes; it is cut from a block of two-coloured granite skilfully exploited by the sculptor to differentiate the head from the torso. In front and to the right are four further royal sculptures, two granite colossal torsos of Ramesses II (Bay 14) and a contrasting pair of life-size figures of Ramesses II and Sethos II (1216–1210 BC) in Bay 12. At this smaller scale Ramesses is shown kneeling, holding before himself an offering-table, while Sethos, represented in a fine, hard, quartzite, sits on a throne holding a small ram-headed shrine on his lap – a cold, but immensely competent sculpture of great technical accomplishment. On the other side of the gallery Bay 13 contains inscriptions for the tomb of Horemheb at Saqqara and two sculptures of Horemheb after he became king in about 1348 BC. In one the Nile god is shown ostensibly with the features of the reigning king; it is inscribed for Horemheb but the portrait is almost certainly of Tutankhamun under whom Horemheb served as a military commander. It is an exceptional portrait containing more than an echo of the fine style of the later part of the reign of Akhenaten. Another remarkable sculpture, in the adjacent Bay 11, is a standing statue of Khaemwese, at one time the crown-prince of Ramesses II. Carved from breccia, a very hard, conglomerate, stone, it makes a striking memorial of a

13 GRANITE RAM BEARING AN INSCRIPTION OF KING TAHARQA

14 FUNERARY STATUE OF A NOBLE AND HIS WIFE

man whose reputation in life was so great that in subsequent ages he was revered as a sage and a magician. Two fine private funerary inscriptions occupy the bay behind this statue.

Beyond the great bust of Ramesses II rises a ramp leading to a raised area, and to a second side gallery. The way from the ramp into the side gallery is flanked by a number of sculptures of gods in animal and bird form dating from the New Kingdom to the Late Period (1250–600 BC). Two pieces on the left date from the reign of Taharqa, a King of the Twenty-fifth Dynasty of Nubian origin (690–664 BC): a fine recumbent ram 13 supporting between its front legs a figure of Taharqa, and a small sphinx with a head representing the king. Both sculptures come from a temple built by Taharqa at Kawa in the Sudan. The entrance to the side gallery is flanked by two life-size wooden royal figures – guardian figures of Nineteenth Dynasty kings from their tombs in the Valley of the Kings at Thebes; and the view through the entrance reveals the fine gilded inner coffin of the priestess of Amun, Henutmehit, more of whose burial equipment can be seen in the Second Egyptian Room, upstairs.

Turning to the right within the side gallery, the visitor enters an area in which, for the most part, smaller objects of the New Kingdom are exhibited. At the far end, however, stands one of the most individual of private monuments in the collection, the black 15 granite *stela* of the two architects Hor and Suty (1400 BC). It carries a hymn in which the sun god is adored as the universal creator – an idea which was developed and enlarged in the religious revolution of King Akhenaten about thirty years later. This area also contains a group of inscriptions made by the workmen who constructed the royal tombs of the New Kingdom. These lowly but talented craftsmen made for themselves monuments of great interest, incorporating prayers to unusual deities, very often of foreign origin.

15 STELA OF HOR AND SUTY

16 GLASS VESSEL. EL-AMARNA

17 UPPER PART OF A COLOSSUS OF KING RAMESSES II

The larger part of this northern side gallery contains material dating from the last centuries of Pharaonic Egypt and from the Graeco-Roman Period, a time which, in spite of a momentary renaissance of Egyptian culture in the Twenty-fifth (747–656 BC) and Twenty-sixth (664–656 BC) Dynasties, witnessed the gradual decline and extinction of native power. In a group of three sculptures in different materials on the right as the visitor enters this part of the side gallery, the most interesting artistically is a very large bronze figure of a priestess, and historically, the block-statue of Iti which is dated in the highest known regnal year of King Shabaka of the Twenty-fifth Dynasty. Many of the objects shown in this area illustrate the lives and careers of the Divine Votaresses of Amun and their senior officials. At this time, the Divine Votaress was virtual ruler at Thebes which had become a semi-independent city-state within the land of Egypt. The most remarkable official, who served under several Divine Votaresses at the end of the Twenty-fifth Dynasty and early in the Twenty-sixth Dynasty, was Mentuemhat, of whom a fine granite statue is displayed flanked by a circular offering basin, dedicated for himself, and a granite offering table dedicated for his son Nesiptah.

On the other side of the gallery, further on, are monuments of Ankhnesneferibre, daughter of King Psammetichus II of the Twenty-sixth Dynasty (595–589 BC), and also Divine Votaress of Amun. The great lid from her schist sarcophagus is carved with a splendid figure of the princess. This lid is so placed as to be observed at a distance through a narrow doorway in the wall of the main Sculpture Gallery.

Returning to the raised area in this gallery, the visitor will see that the view of the sarcophagus lid is made through a small monumental doorway belonging to a Theban shrine built by Ankhnesneferibre. Near-by, at the edge of the raised area, is the chest of her sarcophagus, carefully carved with religious texts. A second, even bigger, sarcophagus stands alongside. It was made to hold the body of Nectanebo II, the last native Egyptian king (360–343 BC), and is splendidly decorated with sections taken from a composition known as *The Book of what is in the Afterworld*. Sadly, Nectanebo was never, apparently, buried in it, and it was subsequently used as a public bath in Alexandria. One more piece on the raised area requiring special mention is in Bay 8, the Shabaka Stone. It is a huge, black basalt block, inscribed with a copy of a very ancient dramatical text concerned with the theological system associated with the god Ptah of Memphis. The inscription was commissioned by King Shabaka who found the existing copy of the text badly damaged by worm holes.

In the main body of the Sculpture Gallery, in the angle formed by the two wings of the raised area, a fine and instructive royal head has been placed. It illustrates the difficulty of establishing the identity and date of uninscribed sculptures. On stylistic grounds it has been identified as Amasis of the Twenty-sixth Dynasty (570–526 BC) and also as Nectanebo I of the Thirtieth Dynasty (380–362 BC). A convincing identification is rendered difficult by the general tendency of Egyptian royal sculpture to be governed by conventions of style and a strong archaising tendency. Near this head, in Bay 7, stand two contrasting sculptures,

18

18 SARCOPHAGUS OF NECTANEBO II

both inscribed with the name Sheshonq, borne by a number of kings of the Twenty-second Dynasty (945–715 BC). One shows the benevolent deity, Hapi, the god of the inundation of the Nile; the very fine features of the head and the exquisite carving of the multifarious offerings which the god carries as his bounty, demonstrate how the high traditions of Egyptian monumental sculpture were maintained even in periods when the country was politically at a low ebb. The second Sheshonq statue (inscribed for the first king of that name) is one of those Sakhmet statues carved by Amenophis III for his temple of Mut at Karnak, of which other, unsurped, examples are shown in the New Kingdom area of the gallery.

Moving northwards along the axis of the gallery the visitor passes between two more vast granite columns from Egyptian temples and finds the largest scarab carving in existence. The scarab beetle was identified with Khepri, the sun at its dawn appearance, and this great granite figure must have come originally from an Egyptian temple. In modern times it was brought to this country from Constantinople by Lord Elgin. At this point, on the east side of the gallery in Bay 4, steps lead through the wall back into the side gallery, where another huge sarcophagus, made from Nesisut, is exhibited. To the left, in a showcase, four divine figures are shown to represent some of the unusual aspects of Egyptian religious iconography in the later periods: a large, lion-headed, seated bronze figure of the goddess Edjo (Wadjet), a spare limestone statue of the jackal-god Anubis, a charming painted wooden statue of Thoth as a baboon, and an extraordinary limestone representation of Horus, falcon-headed, but dressed as a Roman emperor. Heads from private sculptures exhibited near this showcase, demonstrate the strength of monumental portraiture in the later periods of Egyptian history. It is more than probable that Roman portraiture in stone was considerably influenced by the techniques and conventions practised by Egyptian sculptors at this time.

The way out at the north end of the Sculpture Gallery passes between two small obelisks of Nectanebo II, which were found in Cairo, but were originally placed in a temple dedicated to the god Thoth, possibly at Hermopolis in Middle Egypt. The exit itself is flanked by a pair of limestone sphinxes from a Ptolemaic temple in Upper Egypt, so far unidentified. These sphinxes are in no way Egyptian, but wholly Greek in style and inspiration; they are female, and winged, and sit up. The typical Egyptian sphinx is male, without wings, and couchant.

By mounting the north-western staircase the visitor reaches the first floor where the rest of the Egyptian antiquities on display can be seen.

60/61 THE FIRST AND SECOND EGYPTIAN ROOMS

These rooms are devoted to a display of mummies and coffins which illustrate the different funerary customs which prevailed at various periods. The earlier coffins are exhibited in the Second Egyptian Room, whilst those of later date are in the First Room.

19 STATUE OF THE NILE-GOD HAPI

20 RECONSTRUCTED PREDYNASTIC BURIAL

The graves in Egypt in the Predynastic period (before 3100 BC) consisted of shallow pits in the sand, containing a contracted body surrounded by a few 20 grave-goods, as shown by the reconstructed burial in the Second Egyptian Room (Floor-case A). The preservation of this body has been caused by the desiccating effect of the sand which formed the filling of the grave. At a slightly later date, small coffins began to be used, constructed of basketwork or wood, examples of which are also on exhibition. The use of coffins took the body out of contact with the dry sand and consequently it tended to decompose rapidly, with the result that artificial methods of preservation were introduced. The Egyptians believed that it was necessary for the body to be preserved for the next life, and they went to great lengths to achieve this preservation by the process of mummification.

During the latter part of the Early Dynastic Period and the beginning of the Old Kingdom, the practice of contracted burials gradually fell out of use, to be replaced by extended burials in full-length coffins. Wooden coffins, of simple rectangular shape, were used throughout the Old and Middle Kingdoms, and there was a tendency for the decoration of the coffin to become more elaborate. This is well illustrated by the simplicity of the Sixth Dynasty coffin of Nebhotpe, exhibited in the Second Egyptian Room (Floor-case I), as compared with the painted coffins of the Middle Kingdom, a number of which are on display in the same room. Particularly fine examples of the latter are those of Gua (Floor-cases E, J) and Seni (Floor-case F) which come from El-Bersha in Middle Egypt. Each had two coffins, intended to fit one within the other, but Seni's inner coffin is in the southern side gallery of the Sculpture Gallery. Notice how each coffin is constructed from narrow planks jointed together by means of dowels. At each end of the lid there is a circular mark, where a projecting boss of wood, used for lifting the lid into position, has been sawn off after completion of the burial. These coffins are painted both inside and outside; the scenes show objects which were included in the funerary equipment, such as weapons and stone vessels for the use of the deceased. On the interior of the coffins are extracts from magical texts written in black ink, their purpose being to safeguard the deceased in his passage through the underworld and to ensure his continued existence.

In the Twelfth Dynasty (1991–1786 BC) masks of plaster and linen were sometimes placed over the faces of mummies, a custom which led to the use of completely anthropoid coffins in the Second Intermediate period. Large anthropoid coffins of the Seventeenth Dynasty are displayed in the Second Egyptian Room. A particularly interesting coffin of this type is 21 that of King Inyotef (Wall-case 79), consisting of gilded wood with surface decoration in the form of feathers. The latter motif is common at this period, and is usually referred to as *rishi*-decoration, from the Arabic word for feather.

21 WOODEN GILDED COFFIN OF KING INYOTEF

22 PORTRAIT ON THE ROMAN MUMMY OF A BOY

The remaining wall-cases in the Second Egyptian Room contain coffins of the Eighteenth to Twenty-first Dynasties, made of wood or cartonnage (a mixture of plaster and linen). These coffins are anthropoid and are, in most cases, covered with religious texts and scenes on both the interior and exterior surfaces. Rich burials were frequently equipped with more than one coffin, contained one inside the other. The priestess of Amun, Henutmehit, who lived during the Nineteenth Dynasty (1320–1200 BC), had two splendid wooden coffins, each of which was gilded and fitted with inlaid eyes of glass. In addition, the mummy was overlaid by a cover of cartonnage, which fitted within the inner coffin (Wall-cases 67–69; the inner coffin is exhibited in the Sculpture Gallery). The painted decoration of coffins of this period is largely concerned with scenes showing the deceased praising the gods, typical examples being found on the Twenty-first Dynasty wooden coffin of Djedhoriufankh, in Wall-case 58. On the floor of the coffin is painted a large figure of Amenophis I, the second king of the Eighteenth Dynasty, who by this date had been deified and had become a popular god of the Theban Necropolis. The inner surfaces of the sides are covered with offering scenes and the interior of the canopy bears a painting of a vulture goddess hovering protectively over the deceased.

The art of mummification, which had been practised since the Early Dynastic period, reached its height in the Twenty-first Dynasty, to which age belongs the
23 finely bandaged mummy of a priestess displayed in Wall-case 86 in its original coffin. The majority of mummies in the Museum, however, are exhibited in the First Egyptian Room, and they range in date from the Late new Kingdom to the Roman period. Basically, the process of mummification involved the drying of the body with natron (a naturally occurring form of sodium carbonate), and the removal of the internal organs for separate treatment, after which they were either returned to the body or preserved in special containers called canopic jars, examples of which can also be seen in the First Room (Wall-cases 9, 10). A number of the mummies on display are still enclosed in body-cases of cartonnage, which are covered with painted scenes and funerary inscriptions. After the Twenty-first Dynasty the standard of mummification declined down to the Roman period, but the bandaging became more elaborate, shown by the intricate
22 arrangement of the wrappings on the mummy of a boy of about the first century AD (Wall-case 44). The face of this mummy is covered by a portrait of the deceased, executed in coloured wax upon a wooden panel. Such portraits became common in the Graeco-Roman period, and other fine examples can be seen in the Third Egyptian Room. Together with many of the mummies in the First Room there are displayed X-ray photographs, which reveal information about the presence of amulets or other objects beneath the wrappings. Of particular interest are the X-rays of the mummies of an unnamed young man (Floor-case D) and Thentmutengebtiu (Floor-case E) which show the presence of artificial eyes in the former and a winged scarab amulet on the feet of the latter.

23 MUMMY OF A PRIESTESS OF THE 21ST DYNASTY

The coffins of the Late period, displayed in the wall-cases of the First Egyptian Room, are made of wood and are more massive than those of the New Kingdom. The decoration is entirely composed of religious texts and scenes but the quality of the representations is rather poor compared with the earlier work. Large wooden outer coffins continued to be used down to the Ptolemaic period, such as the ponderous coffin of Hornedjitef (Wall-cases 24–25), which was originally fitted with inlaid eyes of glass. Another kind of coffin used in Late period and Ptolemaic times is constructed in the form of a rectangular chest with corner posts and a vaulted top, as examplified by the coffins of Hor, of the Twenty-sixth Dynasty (Floor-case G) and of Nebudjat, of about 200 BC (Floor-case F). The carton-nage body-cases and linen shrouds of the Roman period continued to be decorated with traditional Egyptian scenes down to the third century AD, but the style becomes increasingly debased, as can be seen on the painted linen shrouds from mummies of this age in the First Room, and at a slightly later date the practice of mummification and the use of coffins ceased.

The First Egyptian Room also contains examples of mummified animals, birds, fish and reptiles, the extra-ordinary relics of cults of the Late period in Egypt, which revived the worship of ancient deities in their animal forms. The carefully wrapped bodies deposited in the great cemeteries at places like Saqqara, Bubastis and Abydos, probably represented the formal ac-knowledgement of the power of intercession possessed by these deities, and invoked by visitors to their shrines (Wall-cases 1–4).

62 THE THIRD EGYPTIAN ROOM

In the divisions of this room are exhibited tomb paintings, religious and secular papyri and objects connected with the burial cult. The Museum's collec-tion of papyri is the largest in the world, and its examples of tomb painting provide a fine conspectus of what the ancient artist could produce.

During the formative early period of Egypt's history (c.3000 BC) artistic conventions were formulated which survived virtually unchanged throughout dynas-tic times: thus in two-dimensional art, exemplified in the wall-paintings in this room, the eye is always shown frontally in a profile face, shoulders shown frontally are joined without incongruity to torsos in profile, and both sets of arms and legs are represented in profile.

By magical enactment the activities of daily life reproduced in carved relief or, as in this room, in tempera painting on the walls of tombs of important persons, were intended to reproduce the earthly en-vironment after death. The scenes of counting of cattle and geese are particularly fine illustrations of life on a large estate. For the Egyptians cultivation of the land made fertile by the annual inundation was the basis of economic prosperity and of daily existence itself. The agricultural nature of Egyptian life is reflected in their concept of the next world, as illustrated by the scenes in the Book of the Dead of Anhai (c. 1150 BC), which shows the deceased cultivating the land in the Field of Reeds, a utopian abode in which the dead were supposed to dwell. One posthumous activity which the Egyptians attempted to avoid was conscription for the work connected with rehabilitation of the land after the annual inundation of the Nile – a form of forced labour which might operate in the after-life. Deputies were provided in burials from the Middle Kingdom onwards in the form of *shabtis* (Wall-cases 98–102, 105), generally mummiform figures equipped with hoes, mattocks and baskets. They could come magically to life through the spell written on them and 'dig the fields and irrigate the river banks' in the name of their dead owners. Fine examples in the section of the room devoted to tomb equipment are those of Amenophis II (c. 1425 BC), Sethos I (c. 1304 BC) and Taharqa (c. 664 BC).

25

24 GOLD-MOUNTED SCARAB OF KING SOBKEMSAF

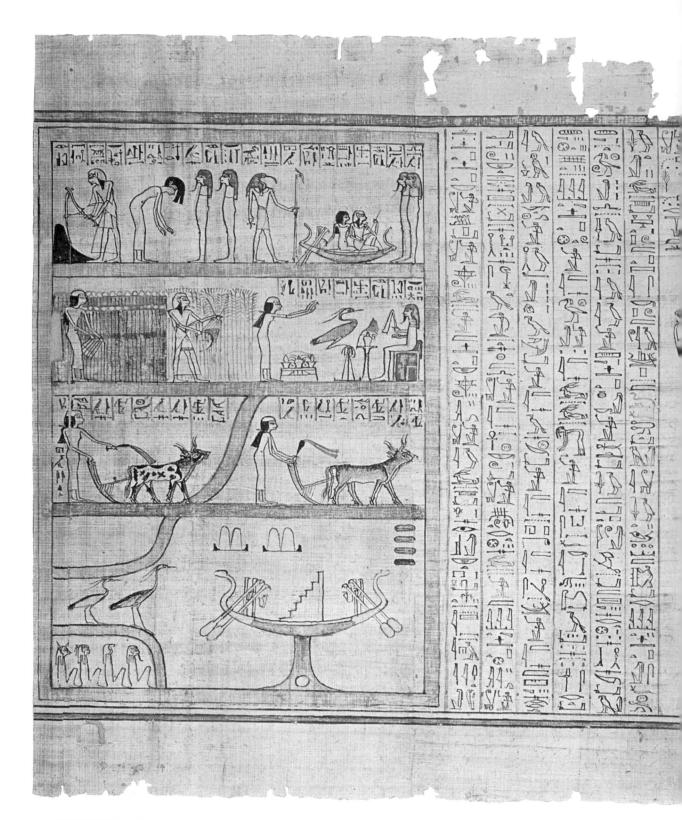

25 AGRICULTURAL SCENES FROM THE BOOK OF THE DEAD OF
ANHAI

The content of the tomb-paintings illustrates vividly the quality of life in Eighteenth Dynasty Egypt. The bounty of the Nile and the land provided all the necessities of daily life. What Egypt's flora and fauna could not provide came by trade or as tribute from Africa and the Near East: dark Nubians are depicted bringing gold and leopard skins, bearded Syrians lead horses for Egyptian chariots. The horse-drawn chariot was a Hyksos innovation which revolutionized the Egyptian army and led to great chariot battles during the expansionist campaigns of the New Kingdom Pharaohs. The battle of Kadesh (*c.* 1299 BC) in which Ramesses II almost lost his army but saved the day against the Hittites through his personal valour is recorded in a literary composition on a hieratic papyrus (Wall-case 129). The chariot was also popular during the New Kingdom as a peaceful means of transport. In one wall-painting the restless energy of the horses in one chariot's team is well contrasted with the placid grazing of a mule-team.

A rare survival of the Second Intermediate Period (Dynasties XIII–XVIII) is the gold-mounted green
24 jasper heart scarab of King Sobkemsaf (*c.* 1650 BC), a Theban ruler and a Hyksos vassal which is shown in Wall-case 96 along with many other amulets used by the Egyptians to protect themselves in life and in death. In the Abbott papyrus (Wall-case 133), a record of investigations into robberies of royal tombs at Thebes during the reign of Ramesses IX (*c.* 1125 BC), the robbing of Sobkemsaf's tomb is specially mentioned. The underside of the scarab is engraved with a spell (later Chapter XXXB of the Book of the Dead) designed to prevent the heart giving adverse evidence at its dead owner's judgement before entry into the Kingdom of Osiris. The weighing (judgement) of the heart episode is beautifully illustrated in many copies of the Book of the Dead, displayed among the religious papyri; note especially a vignette of the Book of the Dead of Ani (*c.* 1250 BC). Among other amulets on display originally inserted within the wrappings of mummies and intended to give further protection to the dead, are faience figures of the four Sons of Horus, guardians of the viscera which were removed from the body and embalmed separately during the process of mummification (Wall-case 97). Protection in the underworld could also be afforded by invocation of
26 Ahmes-Nefertari, wife of Ahmose the liberator who founded the Eighteenth Dynasty (*c.* 1567 BC), who together with her son Amenophis I was deified as a patron of the Theban Necropolis and is thus depicted in a wall-painting from a Theban tomb. The black colour used for her flesh does not imply negroid blood but a connection with death and resurrection.

The founding of the First Dynasty in about 3100 BC by the legendary Menes, King of Upper Egypt (the Nile valley south of Cairo) when he conquered the delta kingdom of Lower Egypt was followed closely by the first appearance of true writing in the form of hieroglyphs and cursive hieratic. The former is a monumental script specially suitable for incising in hard materials or painting on a large scale; its adaptation for brush on papyrus, pottery and wood is called hieratic. The earliest known written papyrus dates

from the late Fifth Dynasty (*c.* 2400 BC) and contains temple accounts in both scripts (Wall-case 125). The Middle Kingdom (Dynasties XI–XII) marked the golden age of Egyptian literature, represented in this room by papyri bearing texts in various states of completeness. The *Satire on other trades* by the scribe Achthoes (Wall-case 129), famous didactic and pessimistic literature, medical treatises on diseases of animals as well as humans (Wall-cases 130–33), hymns and poems, all originated at this time even if, as in the case of the *Rhind Mathematical papyrus*, dated to year 33 of the Hyksos king Apophis, our copies date to a later period. Interesting non-literary works include private letters and military despatches from frontier posts (Wall-cases 126–28). The hieratic papyrus recording the *Instructions for kingship given by Ammenemes I*, founder of the Twelfth Dynasty (*c.* 1991–1786 BC), to his son Sesostris whom he pessimistically counsels to trust no man (Wall-case 129) and the New Kingdom account of the taking of Joppa are unusual quasi-historical compositions.

The keen sense of humour of the Egyptian illustrator when released from religious subjects is evident in the
27 Satirical Papyrus vignettes which depict animals engaged in such human activities as beer-making, herding animals and playing chess (Wall-case 116). To the Ptolemaic dynasty (304–30 BC), whose rulers were the successors of Alexander the Great, belongs the bulk of the collection's demotic documents (Wall-case 135); letters, recipts, medical papyri, legal documents and romances are all represented in this cursive script which replaced hieratic during the Saite period (seventh century BC). Of special interest is the papyrus dated to the first century AD recording in demotic script some of the adventures of Setne Khaemwese, who was a son of Ramesses II; his statue in the Sculpture Gallery has already been noted. His later reputation as a wise man and magician caused him to become the hero of a whole cycle of adventure stories, in this instance written 1300 years ater his death.

63 THE FOURTH EGYPTIAN ROOM

A vital factor in the growth of Egyptian civilization was the almost complete self-sufficiency of the country in basic natural resources. The exploitation of these resources gave rise to a wide range of techniques and industries, many of which were already at an advanced stage of development by the time of the founding of the First Dynasty in about 3100 BC. The skill and ingenuity of the Egyptian craftsman are demonstrated by the displays in the Fourth Room, which are devoted, in the main, to themes from daily life. Topics illustrated include rope-making, basketry, toilet articles, dress, weaving, music, magic, food, navigation, hunting, warfare, building, stone-vessel production, mensuration, writing, and furniture. Only a selection of these can be mentioned here.

The woven-fibre industries, such as rope- and mat-making, basketry, and textile weaving, were known in Egypt from the earliest times, the principal materials employed being palm leaf, reed, rush, papyrus, flax and various kinds of grass. Baskets, after clay pots, were the most common form of household container. The several on display (Wall-cases 136–38) are known to have contained fruit, seed, linen cloth, and bronze tools. These baskets were all made by the same method – that of coiling a fibrous core spirally into the shape required and then sewing together the different layers. A closely allied, though more advanced technique, is that of textile weaving. The woven cloth of Egypt was invariably of linen thread, the source of which was flax. The cultivation and preliminary processing of this crop are often illustrated in painted vignettes on funerary papyri. It can be seen from a vignette on the papyrus of Nakhte (Wall-case 144) that flax was not cut with the sickle, like cereal crops, but was pulled up by the roots. Shown in the same case are some of the tools employed in the subsequent processes, among them sharp-toothed 'hackling' combs, which were used for separating the valued fibres from the woody tissue, and wooden spindles in the form of slender sticks weighted towards the top with a whorl, by means of which the thread was finally spun. Egyptian looms were hand operated, and of two types – a horizontal ground loom, which was used from the Badarian period (before 3100 BC) to the end of the Middle Kingdom (c. 1760 BC), and a vertical loom, first attested in the New Kingdom (c. 1550–1085 BC). The vast majority of woven fabric from the Dynastic Period consists of mummy wrappings and bandages, or lengths of cloth which were placed in the tomb to serve the deceased in the after-life (Wall-cases 144–45). Few actual garments have survived, and most of these are extremely fragmentary. A fine exception is the large linen tunic or shirt (Wall-case 141) which may have been worn as an undergarment. Silk and cotton were not known until the Graeco-Roman period (after 330 BC), and wool, though available, seems to have been accounted ritually unclean.

26 WALL PAINTING SHOWING QUEEN AHMES-NEFERTARI

27 ANIMALS PLAYING DRAUGHTS, FROM A SATIRICAL PAPYRUS

28 WOODEN MODEL

The concern of the Egyptians with bodily cleanliness and appearance is reflected in the large number of cosmetic vessels and toilet implements which have survived (Floor-case A). Apart from their utilitarian value, these small objects, which were made from a variety of materials, offered the craftsman an opportunity to show his individual artistic abilities in a manner which was denied to the artist who worked in the strictly circumscribed field of Egyptian funerary art. The result of this freedom is a wealth of imaginative and delicate forms and designs; among the more striking is a bronze toilet implement in the form of a rider on horseback. However, the ornamentation of such domestic articles was not always simply decorative in purpose; often it had a religious or magical significance. The belief in magic as an efficacious force for good against evil was prevalent in all levels of Egyptian society. In consequence, the images of protective deities were commonly represented in beds, head-rests, amuletic wands, mirror handles and other domestic objects. Two of the most popular deities in this respect were Thoeris, a goddess shown as a pregnant hippopotamus standing on its hind legs, who was particularly revered as a protectress of women in childbirth, and Bes, a dwarf with the features of a lion, who was thought to bring happiness to the home and to protect it against harmful creatures like snakes (Wall-cases 146–47).

The annual inundation of the Nile, which fertilized the land, provided a firm and continuing basis for agricultural prosperity. The various activities carried out on the land are vividly brought to life by wooden tomb models of the Old and Middle Kingdoms (*c.* 2300–1760 BC), showing workers digging and ploughing (Wall-cases 156–57). In the same cases are displayed many of the actual tools used by the farmer. The principal crops grown were flax (already mentioned above), emmer and barley. The primary use of the cereal crops was for bread-making. In addition beer was made by fermenting barley-bread; a wooden model of the Middle Kingdom represents a woman straining the mash from this bread into a beer vat (Floor-case D).

Another important aspect of Egypt's self-sufficiency was its rich resources of animal and bird life. The Nile teemed with fish and the marshy areas of the delta and the Faiyum abounded with wild birds. Fowling and fishing were commonly represented in tomb paintings (see Sculpture Gallery). A favourite sport was to hunt birds with throw-sticks or boomerangs – examples of these are exhibited in Wall-case 161. Larger animals, like the antelope, the oryx and wild bull, were hunted in the desert by means of the bow and arrow (Wall-cases 161–62). The bow was not only a hunting weapon but also played an important part in warfare. It was used mainly by Nubian auxiliaries in the Egyptian army who were valued for their traditional skill as archers. The main weapons of the native Egyptian infantryman were the axe and shield, which were supplemented by the dagger and spear (Cases 162 and F). The warlike period of the New Kingdom, when Egypt established an empire in Asia, saw the introduction of more advanced military equipment,

28

30 SCRIBES' WRITING PALETTES

29 STONE VESSELS OF VARIOUS PERIODS

including coats of mail made of small bronze plates riveted to leather jerkins (Floor-case F) and a curved scimitar-like sword with blade and handle cast in one piece (Wall-case 160).

The rapid growth in the material culture of Egypt, which coincided with the founding of the First Dynasty, may to a great extent be attributed to the increasing availability of copper and its use for making tools. It is thought that the use of tools like metal stone-workers' chisels (Wall-case 166) in the quarrying and dressing of large slabs of stone was greatly instrumental in the development of large-scale stone architecture from the First Dynasty onwards. However, the traditional skill of the Egyptian worker in stone is already evidenced by the great quantity of beautifully worked stone vessels from the Predynastic Period (before 3100 BC). In Wall-cases 168 to 177 there is arranged, in chronological order, a selection of the finest and most characteristic stone vessels from all the main periods of Egyptian history. The period of highest achievement was probably the Early Dynastic Period (c. 3100–2600 BC); for it was then that the greatest variety of materials was used and the widest range of shapes fashioned. Stones employed included basalt, breccia, alabaster, granite, limestone, diorite, schist and serpentine. From the Old Kingdom onward alabaster was by far the most popular material. The hollowing out of these vessels seems to have been effected by means of a crank drill, consisting of a stone boring bit fixed in a forked shaft and weighted with stones at the top (Wall-case 167).

Undoubtedly, among the greatest treasures of the Egyptian Collection are the inscriptions written in ink on papyrus, which we have already encountered in the Third Egyptian Room. In Floor-case K of the Fourth Room the forms and development of the various scripts are illustrated, while in Floor-case J may be seen a collection of the equipment which the scribe used in the writing down of these scripts. The most important part of this equipment was the scribe's palette which consisted of an elongated piece of wood of rectangular shape. At one end, one or more holes were carved for holding the ink. Brushes, made of rush, were kept in a slot carved out of the middle of the palette. Exhibited in Floor-case J is a palette bearing the name of Amosis I, the first king of the Eighteenth Dynasty (c. 1567–1546 BC). Papyrus was not the only material employed for writing; the scribe might also use wooden boards which were usually overlaid with gesso and painted white, and flakes of white limestone and potsherds (called *ostraca*). These secondary writing materials were commonly used in scribal schools for writing out various exercises. One of the most popular exercises seems to have been the copying out of excerpts from well-known literary works. It is an ironic fact that much of our knowledge of some of the greatest works of Egyptian literature is derived from imperfect copies made by ancient Egyptian schoolboys.

This room contains small sculpture in various materials and figures of Egyptian gods.

Proof that the belief in life after death was established at an early period is provided by baked mud female figurines (Floor-case G), intended to ensure fertility in the after-life, from burials of Egypt's prehistoric cultures (before 3100 BC). No less early there existed a respect for the forces of nature and the special attributes of animals which led the Predynastic Egyptians to worship inanimate objects and certain creatures as repositories or expressions of divine power. Although by the Early Dynastic Period most gods came to be represented with at least human bodies, animal forms of deities existed throughout the Pharaonic Period. This room contains a large display of both forms of divine representations.

The dead man's soul to whom offerings were made was thought to reside for part of its existence in a tomb statue of stone or wood in the likeness of the deceased. The early Fourth Dynasty limestone tomb-group of Katep and Hetepheres (c. 2600 BC) combines the seated figures of man and wife (Wall-case 193). Hetepheres's flesh is coloured yellow, pointing the contrast between her secluded indoor life with that of her active husband whose skin is brownish-red. In contemporary male statues the left leg is usually advanced and the hands clenched at the sides. In spite of these attempts to contrast the strength and controlled power of the male with the submissiveness and fragility of women the figures remain static and conventionally posed; the features are idealized. A fine example of a male sculpture is the wooden statue of Tjetji (Floor-case A) who is shown, unusually, nude. His eyes are strikingly inlaid with obsidian and crystalline limestone.

One of the greatest kings of the Twelfth Dynasty, Sesostris III (1878–1843 BC), both soldier and administrator, has left statues which are among the few examples of Egyptian royal sculpture which can be called true portraits. Life-size statues of this king have been seen in the Sculpture Gallery. The weary mouth and sad eyes are unique and instantly recognizable here again in a small royal head and torso of schist without other means of attribution (Wall-case 194). During the Thirteenth Dynasty Egypt suffered disruption and decline which ended in the domination of most of the country by foreign elements, mostly Asiatic. The power of a king like Meryankhre Mentuhotpe V, represented by a schist statuette (Floor-case B), was largely restricted to the southern part of Egypt. The north, included Memphis, became the domain of the Hyksos, so called by historians writing in Greek from the ancient Egyptian designation 'rulers of foreign countries'.

Theban royal ladies seem to have played an influential part in the struggle for independence from the Hyksos and its aftermath. Ahmose the liberator's grandmother, Tetisheri, is depicted as a young girl in a charming painted limestone statuette which certainly predates the Hyksos expulsion (Floor-case C). The limbs are exceptionally slender and the head with its

31 FUNERARY STATUE OF KATEP AND HETEPHERES

32 FLINT KNIFE WITH CARVED IVORY HANDLE

distinctive vulture headdress (much favoured by later queens of the New Kingdom), is carved with great delicacy. The freshness of approach which characterizes this statuette was undoubtedly due to the breakdown of old artistic concepts during the Second Intermediate period (Dynasties XIII–XVII). Queen Hatshepsut (1503–1482 BC), one of the four queens in Egypt's history to reign alone as pharaoh has been identified with the exceptional black granite head exhibited in the open (Bay 200), but the identification is not certain, and the head may be of a slightly later date. The Eighteenth Dynasty was a time when many fine sculptures of officials and private persons were made; good examples are shown in this room. A popular new form of private statuary of the same period was the kneeling figure holding a cult-object or a *stela* carrying a text, exemplified by the unpretentious liveliness of a small painted limestone figure of a priest holding an offering-table (Wall-case 197).

Very remarkable heads of King Amenophis III (*c.* 1417–1379 BC) are shown in the Sculpture Gallery; a smaller, almost equally fine head of the king is shown here (Wall-case 199). The luxury and elegance of his reign are well represented by the finely observed wooden figure of a negro servant girl carrying a chest on her head, once part of a cosmetic container, now in the Sculpture Gallery. Amenophis III's son and successor changed his name early in his reign (*c.* 1373 BC) from Amenophis to Akhenaten in deference to the form of the sun god which he now elevated to be supreme. The Aten or sun's disk with its many rays ending in hands offering 'life' is a constant feature of royal scenes of the so-called Amarna Period (*c.* 1380–1350 BC). Akhenaten himself with his characteristically swollen hips and stomach, spindly limbs and elongated skull slouches beneath the Aten's caressing hands in part of a limestone relief from his new capital at El-Amarna (Case 1). Curiously, his father and mother are depicted in the same Amarna style in another such relief adjacent to the last. The impetus which Akhenaten's reign gave to naturalism in art is well illustrated in the feeding deer frieze on a stone manger shown below these reliefs. Although the boy-king Tutankhamun (*c.* 1361–1352 BC) embraced

The Sixth Egyptian Room is reached by the doorway on the south side of the Fourth Egyptian Room.

Amun as chief god once more and returned the religious capital to Thebes, the Amarna style in art persisted during his reign. This new-found suppleness and delicacy are evident in the small wooden figure of an official (Floor-case F). After the Amarna heresy the old gods re-established their dominance.

The troubled Libyan period was brought to an end by a king of the Twenty-fifth Dynasty (*c.* 710 BC), a line of Egyptianized Nubians (from the area of the modern Sudan) who inaugurated a revival in Egyptian art, religion and foreign policy. To this period belongs the Benson head from a statue of a high official, one of the best examples of the archaizing idealized style of Twenty-fifth Dynasty art, which is shown by itself in a floor-case. The Twenty-sixth Saite Dynasty (664–525 BC) continued the revival of the arts, particularly sculpture, deriving inspiration from Old Kingdom models. Men once more are represented wearing simple kilts or long plain garments, but the proportions of the body and the rather empty expression of the features are far removed from the best Old Kingdom work (Wall-case 203). The use of metal for figures of private persons becomes more common in the Late Period (Dynasties XXV–XXX).

The whole of the south wall of this room is occupied by a display of divine figures, mostly in bronze (Wall-cases 207–21). Most of the well-known deities are represented, many of them in their animal forms. Among the finest are a bronze Nefertum, one of the gods of Memphis (Case 210), a large cat, incarnation of the goddess Bastet (Case 213), and a splendid alabaster cow's head, from a statue of Hathor as a cow in the temple of Hapshepsut at Deir el-Bahari (Case 215).

64 THE SIXTH EGYPTIAN ROOM

On entering this room the first thing to be seen is one of the gems of the collection, the Pitt-Rivers' Predynastic knife, a finely flaked flint blade fitted with an ivory handle carved with rows of animals and other creatures. The artistic observation of the individual figures and the precision of the execution reveal the remarkably high standard of achievement reached in the years before Egypt emerged as a single historical state.

Three floor-cases on the west side of the room contain the finest pieces from the Museum's collection of Predynastic and Early Dynastic objects. In the

[53]

interpretation of many pieces from these early stages of cultural development, it is often difficult to decide what is ritual and what is domestic. The slate palettes which were used for the grinding of cosmetic eye-paint are objects which are open to many different interpretations. Shaped in many cases like animals, birds or fish (Floor-case B) they may embody divine representations or represent simply the creatures depicted. Many show the stains of eye-paint and were undoubtedly used as palettes; others are more elaborate and carry carved scenes which may reflect events of historical importance. The Battlefield Palette (Floor-case C) shows a lion attacking men, possibly an allegorical scene of the king slaying his enemies. A similar symbolic reference to a national struggle may be contained in the marvellous scenes on the Hunters Palette (Floor-case B) where men hunt lions and other wild animals.

Two-dimensional figures of Early Dynastic kings can be seen on a stone relief and a small wooden label in Floor-case C. An ivory label in the same case contains a scene and reference to a punitive act by King Den of the First Dynasty (c. 2950 BC) against an eastern enemy.

The early periods of Egypt's history are particularly well represented by pottery, and indeed much of the most interesting pottery ever made in Egypt comes from the Predynastic Period. A series of wall-cases (1–17, in reverse order), on the south side of the room contains a conspectus of Egyptian pottery from all periods, the Predynastic examples being shown in the first six cases. Of special interest are the pots of buff-coloured ware decorated in purple with representation of boats, human figures, deities and cult figures (Cases 13, 14). Of later pottery, the most striking are the painted vessels, often of extraordinary size and shape made during the Amarna Period (Case 9). With the gay

floral decoration of these pots in mind it is worth looking at the wall-paintings of the same period, from the palaces of El-Amarna, which are placed at both ends of the room.

Apart from pottery, the Egyptians used many other materials for receptacles both ritual and domestic, in particular, a glazed composition commonly called faience, glass and bronze (in early times copper). Objects of all these materials are on display in the Sixth Room. Two wall-cases (24 and 26) and Floor-case F contain faience objects of all periods. This material was not well-suited for the making of very fine ware like porcelain, but it was used by the Egyptians in a plastic manner to produce very attractive small sculptures, vessels, and inlays for decorative purposes. The range of colours achieved in the glazes was wide, and could be used with great effect, for example on the tiles representing foreign captives from the palace of Ramesses III at Tell el-Yahudiya (Wall-case 24). The animal figures in this medium are especially appealing; in particular the hippopotami in Wall-case 26 and the monkeys and cats in Floor-case F.

The same bright colours are found in the glass which is shown in Floor-case E. The Egyptians probably learned the craft of glass-making from the East, but they quickly developed a distinctive and highly skilled industry which reached its height in the late Eighteenth Dynasty (c. 1410–1320 BC). The virtuosity of the Egyptian glass-worker is also shown in the remarkable inlays and decorative elements of the Ptolemaic and Roman periods, on which the finest designs are carried out by the use of bundles of many-coloured glass rods fused together.

A remarkable collection of copper and bronze objects, mostly for ritual purposes, is displayed in the two Wall-cases 19 and 21. Many of the shapes used for metal vessels were derived from stone and pottery prototypes, but an independent development, which assumed great importance in later periods, was the situla. Vessels of this type, used for carrying liquids used in religious ceremonies, were often decorated with scenes and inscriptions. A particularly fine series of large situlae is shown in Case 21. They range in date from the Twenty-sixth Dynasty to the Ptolemaic period (650–150 BBC).

Faience and glass were both materials used by the Egyptian jeweller as substitutes for coloured hard stones in jewellery. Examples of necklaces, pendants, rings and other ornaments from all periods may be seen in Wall-cases 18, 20 and 22, and in Floor-case D.

33 HEAD OF THE LATE PERIOD

To reach the latest material exhibited the visitor should leave the Sixth Room by the door through which he entered and cross the Fourth Egyptian Room.

The clever ways in which very disparate materials were combined to produce pleasing results are specially well exemplified by the elaborate collars and necklaces made in the New Kingdom.

Egyptian jewellery often incorporated scarabs, those most characteristic small antiquities found in very large numbers in all collections. The large scarab already seen in the Sculpture Gallery is far removed from the many small examples displayed in Wall-cases 23, 25 and 27. The designs and inscriptions engraved on scarabs are often commonplace and of little interest; others represent some of the finest achievements of the ancient carver in miniature. Of those on display, the greatest interest attaches to the large scarabs issued by Amenophis III to commemorate important events and royal achievements: a lion hunt, a wild-bull hunt, his marriage to Queen Tiye, the digging of a lake, and the arrival of a foreign princess with her retinue. The Museum possesses the only complete series of these scarabs (Case 25).

THE COPTIC CORRIDOR

This gallery leads from the Fourth Egyptian Room to the King Edward Staircase, and it contains antiquities from Graeco-Roman and early Christian Egypt. The word 'Copt' was originally a designation for the indigenous population of Egypt, as distinct from foreign settlers, but it gradually came to be applied specifically to the Christian part of the population. Both pagan and Christian antiquities occur in Egypt during the third to sixth centuries AD, and it is not always easy to assign an object to one or the other culture.

Belonging to the first four centuries AD is an important group of mummy portraits, mostly coming from the extensive Graeco-Roman cemeteries in the Faiyum in Middle Egypt. The mummy of Artemidorus with its portrait in position stands in Wall-case 7 and further examples can be seen in the Third Egyptian Room. The portraits are executed in a naturalistic but idealized style, the subjects being shown in the prime of life and wearing typical costume of the period. Soft wax was used as a vehicle to contain the pigments; it seems probable that it was melted by the heat of the sun and applied to the wooden panel by means of a brush. Plaster masks for mummies were also used in the Roman period and a number of examples of the first to third centuries are exhibited with the mummy portraits.

The teachings of Christianity were written in a new form of script called Coptic, which is really the ancient Egyptian language written in Greek letters, with the addition of a few signs from demotic. This script had begun its development in the first century for the writing of magical texts, for which the pronunciation of the words was of prime importance, but it came to be the standard language of the Coptic communities by the third to fourth centuries.

The gravestones of Christian origin in the Coptic Corridor show the typical form of the funerary inscriptions, most of which consist of short formulae. Some

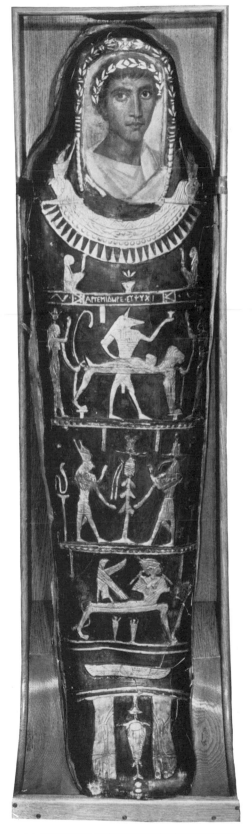

34 MUMMY OF ARTEMIDORUS WITH PORTRAIT

gravestones have crosses in the form of the Ancient Egyptian *ankh*, or hieroglyph for 'life'. They are highly decorated with floral and scroll designs following the Hellenistic tradition, whilst incorporating such symbols of Christianity as the dove.

The Hellenistic tradition may be seen also in the limestone statue of a seated goddess on the same wall as the Coptic stele and in the statue of a woman from Oxyrhynchus in Wall-case 1 opposite. Whilst the former is decidedly pagan, the latter probably comes from a tomb chapel of the early Christian cemetery and is a rare example of sculpture in the round of the late Roman period.

The Hellenistic influence is also apparent in the decorated textiles which occur from the fourth century. The early examples of these textiles are purely Hellenistic in character, depicting figures from classical mythology, such as the two cupids in a boat on a tapestry from Akhmim (Wall-case 5). Pagan subjects continue in later times, as on a large tapestry of the fourth or fifth century showing divine figures (Wall-case 4) and in the bands of decoration on a linen tunic from Akhmim (Wall-case 6). This tunic is typical of the garments of the Coptic Period, and the purple wool used for the bands is characteristic of the monochrome ornamentation of textiles in the fourth and fifth centuries; the use of several colours on clothing did not become common until the sixth. Subjects of purely Christian nature do not become common until the eighth century and they continue until the twelfth, when the textiles themselves disappear.

On the opposite wall, between the Coptic stele are two highly interesting woven woollen carpets from Nubia, dating to the fifth and sixth centuries AD.

Following the entry of the Arabs into Egypt in AD 641 Coptic culture gradually gave way to that of Islam and Coptic gradually ceased to be a living language. It survives only in the liturgy of the Coptic Church.

35 TAPESTRY SHOWING CUPIDS

Greek & Roman antiquities

Main floor

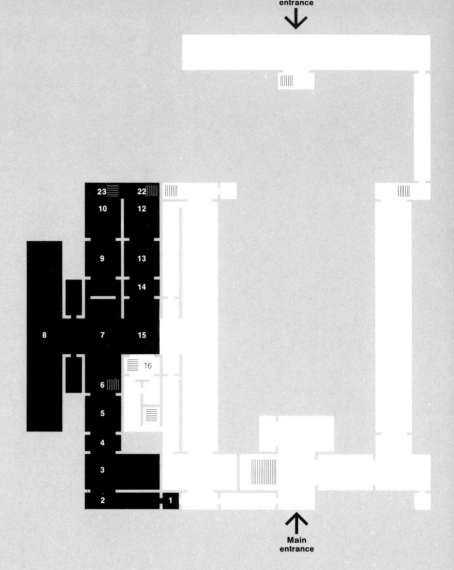

North entrance

Main entrance

Upper levels

68 Greek & Roman bronzes & terracottas
69 Greek & Roman life room
70 Greek mythology
71/72/73 Greek vase rooms

40

Caspian Sea

Black Sea

30

ANATOLIA

MESOPOTAMIA

Tigris River

Euphrates River

CYPRUS

O ASCALON

NDRIA

EGYPT

Nile River

Red Sea

The
Greek & Roman
World

Eastern Mediterranean

The British Museum possesses one of the finest collections of Greek and Roman antiquities in the world, covering almost every aspect of Greek and Roman art. The objects range in date from the Bronze Age civilizations of the Cyclades and Crete of the third and second millennium BC down to the late Roman Empire. (The antiquities from Britain during the Roman period are displayed in the galleries of the Prehistoric and Romano-British Department.)

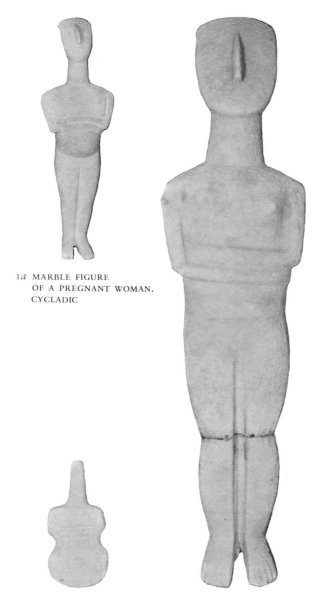

1*a* MARBLE FIGURE
OF A PREGNANT WOMAN.
CYCLADIC

1*b* STYLIZED MARBLE FIGURE
OF A WOMAN. CYCLADIC

1*c* MARBLE FIGURE
OF A WOMAN. CYCLADIC

1 THE CYCLADIC ROOM

In art the civilizations of Egypt and Mesopotamia at first outshone the achievements of the Mediterranean lands which were subsequently settled by the Greeks. The earliest known artefacts of striking quality from this area are the Cycladic idols which were made of the local marble during the third millennium by Bronze Age immigrants from Anatolia who had settled in the small islands of the Cyclades clustered in the Aegean between the Greek mainland and Anatolia. Most of these idols represent naked women and were found in graves, so it has been suggested that they were perhaps originally dedicated by the living as images of themselves to gain magical supernatural protection or some other benefit, and were later buried together with their owners so as to neutralize their powers. Similar superstitions are found among later primitive people, and such beliefs would explain

1*a* the considerable number of Cycladic idols representing pregnant women, which might have been dedicated in the hope either of inducing fertility, or of securing protection in the dangers of childbirth.

The idols show a progression from representing
1*b* women by a highly schematic 'violin' shape to forming a more naturalistic, although still stylized figure,
1*c* with a distinctive head, body and legs. (Compare exhibits A5, A6 with A15 and A25.) The extreme simplification of the parts of the body into abstract forms, especially the head, gained great admiration for these idols among early twentieth-century artists. We cannot explain the almost invariable position of the folded arms on these figures, which has some similarity to that of Anatolian female statuettes. The pose may have been chosen because it was simple to represent, or because this gesture seems to be instinctively self-protective.

Traces of colour remaining on the largest idol exhibited here (*c*. 2500–2000 BC Case 4) show that details such as hair, mouth, eyes and necklaces were originally added to some of these statuettes in red and black. The Cycladic idols to some extent foreshadow the later achievements of Greek sculpture in their use of marble, and in their development of a simple, elegant and disciplined style of representation.

Around 2000 BC the comparatively primitive culture
of the Cyclades was eclipsed by the spectacular Bronze
Age civilization of Crete, which was the product of a
much more highly organized society centred round the
courts and palaces of various priest-kings, that at
Knossos being the most famous. Memories of this
period survived in the later Greek world in the legends
of the Cretan King Minos and the Minotaur, a creature
part man and part bull who devoured Athenian maidens and young men. Archaeology confirms the connection of bulls with Cretan culture; a fine bronze
statuette shows a charging bull with a young man in
the act of somersaulting over its back, a feat which was
probably part of a ritual ceremony (Case 1). The
movement of both the bull dashing forward and the
athlete vaulting backwards is rendered with striking
grace and freedom, which is all the more surprising in
comparison with the static art of contemporary Egypt.

Fine gold jewellery, such as the pendant with a
prince or priest-king wearing a feather crown, flanked
by ducks, and standing like Pharaoh on a Nile boat
(*c.* 1700–1500 BC Case 1), emphasizes the luxurious
character of Cretan civilization, and shows a closer
connection with Egypt. Cretan art was remarkable
for its representation of animals, whether naturalistically and impressionistically rendered as in the
statuette of the bull-leaper, or heraldically displayed
in a more stylized manner, like the ducks flanking the
prince on the pendant, and the pair of goats on a
crystal seal stone (*c.* 1450–1400 BC Case 5).

Civilization was slow to develop on the Greek mainland, although it was apparently settled by Bronze Age
immigrants from Anatolia around 3000 BC, and by
several later waves of Greek-speaking invaders.
Around 1550 BC the city of Mycenae on the mainland
rose to prominence and power, and it appears that
Greek-speaking people overran Crete some time after
this, as inscribed clay tablets written in an archaic
form of Greek called Linear B have been found at
Knossos (*c.* 1400 BC Case 1). The precise relations
between the waning power of Crete and the growing
city of Mycenae remain obscure, but about 1400 BC
Mycenaean art ceased to be merely a derivative of
Cretan art and acquired an impressive character of its
own, and so it represents the first definitely Greek
culture to reach a high level of civilization and artistic
achievement.

Extensive remains of the city walls and beehive
shaped tombs can still be seen at Mycenae, and it is
distant memories of the splendour of the city in the
Late Bronze Age which appear to lie behind the stories
of the Homeric poems. Parts of the marble facing of
the largest of the Mycenaean tombs, the so-called
'Treasury of Atreus', are now in the British Museum.
This tomb is cut into the hillside and approached along
a long open passage way from which the domed tomb-
chamber is entered through a doorway 6 metres high.
This doorway was flanked by tapering columns of
grey-green marble decorated with rows of zig-zags,
which were alternately left plain and filled with a
running spiral. These columns have been reconstructed

2 BRONZE BULL AND ACROBAT. *c.* 1600 BC

3 MINOAN GOLD PENDANT

at the entrance to the Cycladic Room (Room 1). The lintel of the doorway was surmounted by slabs of grey-green marble cut into a row of plain discs with a spiral running above which was crowned by a band of fine red marble, or *rosso antico*, decorated with panels and a stylized floral ornament. Immediately over this lintel there were several rows of running spirals, fragments 4 of which can be seen on the wall in Room 2. A provisional reconstruction of the whole facade is on display beside them. This use of contrasting marbles in an architectural facade must have been striking.

The influence of Mycenaean civilization was widespread, for pottery apparently made in the Peloponnese has been found in many Mediterranean regions. A bowl found in Cyprus (*c.* 1400–1300 BC Case 3) is decorated with a procession of riders in chariots; this is probably the type of chariot in which the heroes of the Homeric poems rode, and this representation is one of the earliest Greek attempts to portray horse-drawn chariots and their riders, a motif which often recurs in classical art, and one in which we can trace the gradual mastery of realistic representation acquired by Greek artists.

4 MARBLE DECORATION FROM THE 'TREASURY OF ATREUS'

About 1100 BC further invasions of Greek-speaking Dorians appear to have obliterated more or less all traces of Mycenaean civilization; even the skill of writing was lost. Three or four hundred years known as the Dark Ages followed; towards the end of this period the shape and forms of Greek society and art which were to crystallize in the Classical Age began to emerge. In the late eighth century the Homeric poems, in the form in which we now have them, and those of Hesiod were composed, the Homeric poems looking back to the civilization of Mycenae as the vanished world of the heroes, and Hesiod laying stress on the present troubled state of Greece. 'Now truly is a race of iron, and men will never rest from labour and sorrow by day, nor from dying by night', said Hesiod.

The pottery of the Geometric Style produced during this period starts to lay the foundations for later Greek artistic achievements; many of the pots are finely proportioned, and are crisply decorated with geometric patterns which are often drawn with the aid of compasses. (See, for example, the clay toilet box in Case 2. c. 750 BC.) Decorated with a limited range of abstract patterns and with a scheme of closely related colours, they show the Greeks' skill in fully exploring any medium or motif which they took up. Figures were gradually introduced again into the decoration of pottery. At first they were mere silhouettes, but eventually more rounded, realistic figures were attempted, as in the plate from Rhodes of c. 600 BC which shows the fight between Hector and Menelaos for the body of Euphorbos. This is one of the earliest examples of the illustration of a scene from the *Iliad* which can be definitely identified, because the figures have their names written beside them, as on many later Greek vases.

In this early period of Greek art the influence of the East assumed great importance, as can be seen in the elegant bronze griffin head which originally decorated the rim of a cauldron (c. 650 BC Case 6). The griffin was a mythical beast of oriental origin which attained great popularity in Classical art. This bronze griffin is one of the earliest examples of a hollow cast bronze from the Greek world: Minoan bronze statuettes were cast solid. Hollow casting is a complicated process involving the fashioning of a core of clay or plaster surrounded by a layer of wax modelled in the shape of the required statue, which was in turn covered by an outer mantle of clay and sand. The wax layer was then heated so as to melt away, and was replaced by the molten metal which was to form the final artefact. From this both the inner core and the outer mantle were removed. The invention of hollow casting was to be important since it made possible the production of life-size statues and heads in bronze, a medium in which many masterpieces of Classical art were produced, such as the Chatsworth Head (Room 5).

Also dating from the Archaic period are a number of seated marble figures and lions which came originally from the Sanctuary of Apollo at Didyma, south of Miletus. Inscriptions show these statues were dedicated to the god by pilgrims, some apparently being representations of the donor. This is the earliest in

7 CAST BRONZE GRIFFIN'S HEAD

5 PITCHER WITH 'GEOMETRIC' DECORATION. c. 740 BC

date of the great groups of monumental sculpture which it is the good fortune of the British Museum to possess. The seated figures date from between 580–510 BC, and are made of beautifully grained white marble. The stiff dignity of these figures, which derives from their Egyptian prototypes, is tempered by the graceful folds of their long cloaks and tunics. The lion has a relaxed, recumbent pose.

During the sixth century BC the characteristically Greek art of vase painting made great advances. The finely shaped dinos, or bowl for mixing wine, and its stand date from c. 580 BC, and the bowl is signed by Sophilos, the first Athenian vase painter whose signature has survived. Much of the vase and stand is decorated with rows of animals and mythical beasts. The most interesting part is the top zone of the bowl which shows the Olympian gods and goddesses arriving for the wedding-feast of Peleus and Thetis. Both Poseidon and Zeus loved the sea-goddess Thetis, but they prudently decided she should marry the mortal Peleus in view of the prophecy that she would give birth to a son who would be more powerful than his father. Peleus stands at the door of his house greeting the gods and goddesses as they arrive in their chariots. The representation of the four-horsed chariots of Zeus and Hera, and of Amphitrite, is already far more skilled than that on the Mycenaean

bowl. (Room 2 Case 3.) The stance of many of the male and female figures is still rather stiff and Egyptianizing, but details of the painting, like the rows of animals on the goddesses' dresses which are picked out in red against a white ground, are highly decorative. Although the vase is executed in the technique known as black-figure, in which figures are depicted as black silhouettes against the natural colour of the clay with their details picked out by incision, there is here a greater admixture of red and white than is common later in the development of the black-figure style. These colours, together with the bright orange of the clay, combine to create a lively composition.

The famous amphora, or wine-jar, made and painted by Exekias (c. 540 BC Case 7) provides an example of the work of one of the greatest known draughtsmen of antiquity. In the drawing on this vase an amazing feeling for the volume of the figures has been achieved within the limitations imposed by the technique of rendering them as black silhouettes. On one side Achilles is shown plunging his spear into the throat of the Amazon Queen, Penthesilea, from whom realistically red blood squirts out. This is a closely-knit composition which is boldly drawn with convincing foreshortening of the shields, and great richness of detail in the tunic and panther skin worn by the Amazon Queen.

8

6 CLAY PLATE FROM RHODES

8 WINE-JAR SIGNED BY EXEKIAS

The other side of the vase shows Dionysos garlanded
9 as he receives a cup of wine from his son, Oinopion.
These figures are again drawn with sharp linear
accuracy, particularly the fine detail of the hair of the
two figures and the beard of Dionysos. The figures are
framed by sprays of ivy springing from the hand of
Dionysos, and by the names of the figures and the
signature of Exekias. Although some anatomical
details are still incorrectly rendered, such as the eye
drawn as if seen frontally instead of in profile, it has
been justly noted that in the bold and subtle drawing
of this type of work we see the rise of Western drawing.

The names of Achilles and the Queen, and the signature of Exekias appear on the front of the vase
together with the inscription 'Onetorides is handsome'; the inscription of such love names is found on
many Greek vases.

A finely shaped kylix, or drinking cup, signed by
Hischylos as potter and by Epiktetos as painter, shows
on the outside the development of a new technique of
vase painting, red-figure, which was invented towards
the end of the sixth century BC (Case 8). In red-figure
painting the figures are, as it were, reversed: instead of
being rendered in lustrous black glaze against a light
background they are left in the natural colour of the
clay while the background is filled in with black. This
new technique was to provide scope for much greater
development of freedom and elaboration in drawing
on vases.

The outside of the cup, decorated in the new red-
figure technique, shows palmettes and two pairs of
apotropaic eyes, which were a superstitious device to
avert misfortune, framing two satyrs. The satyrs
carry shields and are rather ludicrously armed with a
drinking horn, trumpet and wine jug, instead of spears
and swords – appropriate decoration for a drinking
cup.

The inside of the cup is decorated in the old-
fashioned black-figure technique; a young man with
10 two spears is shown mounted on a prancing horse.
The glossy black background of the inner side of the
cup surrounding the light clay-coloured medallion,
which frames the horseman, echoes and enhances the
decorative qualities of the central design.

The small bronze figure of a banqueter reclining on
a couch and holding a bowl for wine is a work of
11 exceptional quality (c. 520 BC, Case 8). Its slightly
curved base shows that it probably decorated the rim
of a bronze cauldron or tripod together with two other
similar figures. It is believed to have come from
Dodona, the great sanctuary of Zeus in northern
Greece, and it may, therefore, have formed part of a
dedicatory offering. As in the vase painting of Dionysos
by Exekias, the hair and beard of the banqueter are
shown in extremely fine detail. This lean, lithe banqueter with his alert look is one of the finest small
bronzes to have survived from antiquity; much of its
attraction derives from the contrast between the
wonderfully smooth surface of both the skin and the
drapery, which ripples gently round the raised knee,
and the elaborately decorative detail of the young
man's hair and beard.

9 WINE-JAR SIGNED BY EXEKIAS; DETAIL

10 CUP SIGNED BY EPIKTETOS; DETAIL. c. 520 BC

11 BRONZE STATUETTE OF A BANQUETER

12 The marble figure of the *kouros*, or young man, from Boeotia, dating from about 560 BC, exemplifies one of the most famous of Greek innovations in art: the large-scale representation of the nude young man. It is well known that the Greeks competed in athletic contests naked, and Thucydides (I.vi) draws attention to this as one of the significant differences between the Greeks and neighbouring barbarians. The production of these marble *kouroi* started in the seventh century, and derived from Egyptian statues. The Egyptian stone figures, however, unlike the Greek *kouroi*, were not entirely free-standing: they had a pier supporting the back, while the arms were nowhere detached from the torso, and the legs were not carved as separate forms. Moreover, Egyptian sculptors worked within strict canons of proportion, whereas the Greeks aimed constantly to achieve more anatomically correct, and more naturalistic representation, each generation of sculptors building on and advancing beyond the achievements of their predecessors. Something of this process can be seen in the two *kouroi* on display here. The *kouros* of *c.* 560 BC represents a fairly advanced stage of the development, for considerable liveliness and realism have already been achieved, although the forms of the body are still rather angular, and the transition from one member to another remains awkward.

The other *kouros* in this room shows, in spite of its fragmentary state, some of the advances which were made in representing the male nude in the later sixth century BC. The marble has been smoothly modelled to suggest the softness of flesh, and transition from one part of the body to another is now skilfully achieved.

Formerly all *kouroi* were thought to represent the god Apollo. However, as many statues of this type have been found in sanctuaries dedicated to gods other than Apollo, and in cemeteries – in fact the statue described above was found in a tomb – it is now realized that *kouroi* might have served as funerary monuments, or as dedicatory offerings to various gods, or as representations of Apollo.

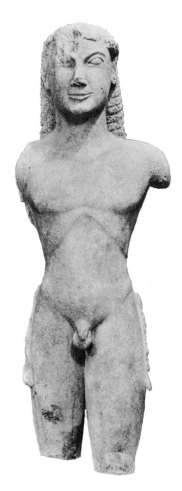

12 MARBLE STATUE OF A YOUNG MAN

Much of the sculpture in this room comes from Lycia in south-west Turkey. Together with the magnificent Nereid Monument in Room 7 and the Tomb of Payava in Room 10 these reliefs from tombs were brought from Xanthos in Lycia to England in the mid-nineteenth century.

Although not Greeks, and subject to the Persian King after 546 BC, the Lycians often employed Greek sculptors on their funerary monuments. The so-called Harpy Tomb now in the centre of Room 5 originally crowned a massive pillar standing outside the city of Xanthos. It was named after the two winged creatures with women's heads carrying off maidens previously thought to be the Harpies who, according to legend, carried off the daughters of Pandareos to be servants of the Furies. However, these creatures are now generally interpreted as sirens, who attained prominence in ancient funerary art as the conductors of souls to the world of the dead, rather like angels in Christian imagery.

The Harpy Tomb dates from c. 480 BC, and on three sides is thought to show the heroized male ancestors of one of the ruling families of Xanthos. On the fourth, originally the west side, three maidens appear as if in procession between two seated women. Two figures carry pomegranates which were associated with the cult of the dead, so this side too may represent heroized members of the Lycian family rather than Demeter and Persephone, as was once believed. The Greek historian Herodotus (*History*, I. 173) in fact says that Lycians reckoned their descent through the female line.

13 Displayed along one wall of Room 5 is a frieze of cocks and hens also from Xanthos, and dating from c. 480 BC. Although this frieze was taken from the city walls, it probably also originally decorated a tomb. It represents a less ambitious subject than the reliefs of the Harpy Tomb, but it is carved with much more life and vigour; the claws and feathers of some of the cocks are rendered with considerable realism.

13 LIMESTONE FRIEZE FROM XANTHOS, LYCIA

During the last years of the sixth century BC and the early years of the fifth, Greek artists finally set themselves free from the conventions and limitations of Archaic art, achieving complete mastery of the representation of the human figure in an idealized form, and yet endowing their compositions with a sense of movement and vitality, and at the same time creating harmoniously balanced designs. These developments in Greek art achieved their fullest expression in the sculptures of the Parthenon, but to some extent these trends in art can be discerned in many other more modest works of the fifth century.

14   A cup, or kylix, signed by Epiktetos provides a fine example of the new development in drawing made possible by the invention of the technique of red-figure vase painting (Case 1). In the central roundel of the cup a girl with castanets wearing a panther-skin is shown dancing to the music of a pipe player who is naked apart from a cloak thrown decoratively over one shoulder. Dancing girls and musicians were a traditional part of the Greek symposium or drinking party, and this vase probably illustrates some such entertainment. The figures are drawn with a lively grace and a simplicity of line which skilfully suggests the rhythm of the dance and the co-ordination of the figures' movements.

Towards the end of the sixth century we find an increasing interest in and aptitude for the rendering of more light-hearted and lyrical subjects, as in this vase, and an emphasis on satyrical and genre scenes, rather than epic subjects.

However, heroic myths were still represented, as on the austere black krater or mixing bowl by the Berlin painter (c. 490 BC, Case 3). The decoration round the rim of this vase shows two great victories achieved by Achilles in single combat in the Trojan War; that between Achilles and Hektor with their respective divine champions, Athene and Apollo (in fact Apollo deserted Hektor so Achilles finally killed him, the event which forms the climax of the *Iliad*, XXII. 131 ff.), and the duel between Achilles and Memnon, two mortals watched over by their divine mothers, Thetis and Eos.

15   The psykter or wine-cooler designed to float in a bowl of water, signed by Douris and inscribed with the words 'Aristagoras is handsome' is decorated with a finely drawn group of satyrs revelling, a scene pervaded by an air of cheerful lewdness. Satyrs were grotesque, bestial creatures, for the most part human in form, but with some animal characteristics such as horses' tails. The members of the chorus of Satyric dramas were dressed as satyrs, and some scholars believe that Satyric drama, which dealt with burlesque aspects of ancient legends, was the dramatic form from which Greek tragedy evolved. The scenes on this vase are perhaps connected with a Satyric drama, the figure in the elaborately patterned cloak being interpreted as the leader of a chorus of satyrs (Case 5).

14 CUP SIGNED BY EPIKTETOS; DETAIL. *c.* 510 BC   15 WINE-COOLER SIGNED DOURIS. 490–480 BC

A fragmentary cup of exceptionally delicate shape,
16 having a long thin stem, and elongated wish-bone
shaped handles, is decorated with the picture of a girl
reaching up to pick an apple from a tree (Case 7). Set
against a white ground obtained by covering the red
clay with creamy white clay, the drawing takes on a
modern aspect, appearing as if done on paper. This
cup appears to have been signed by the potter Sotades,
and dates from the middle of the fifth century BC. The
technique of painting on a white ground, which was
invented in the late sixth century, was never as widely
used as red-figure decoration since the white clay gave
a less durable surface, unsuitable for ordinary use.
Possibly the scene on this cup represents the Garden
of the Hesperides which was believed to be on
the western edge of the world and to possess a tree
with golden apples guarded by nymphs. For the
missing figure on the left of the tree is labelled Melissa,
a name which is ascribed to one of these guardian
nymphs on a vase now in Naples. We may note here
considerable advances in drawing; the girl's eye is
correctly rendered in profile, and the representation of
the form of her body beneath the swirling folds of
her transparent dress is beautifully done, distantly
recalling the still greater skill with which the masters
of the early Italian Renaissance, such as Botticelli,
painted young girls whose physical beauty was accentuated and enhanced by flowing drapery.

The visitor wishing to look at the Greek sculpture
in the British Museum in chronological order, so as to
follow its development in the middle and later fifth
century BC, should go straight to Room 8 (the Duveen
Gallery) to see the Parthenon sculptures, returning
later to Room 6 where the frieze from Bassae is displayed, and to Room 7 with the Nereid Monument.

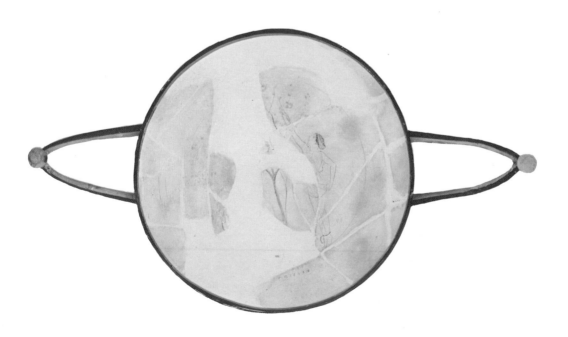

16 CUP SHOWING A GIRL PICKING APPLES

The great Temple of Athene Parthenos, the patron goddess of the city, was built on the Acropolis at Athens in the mid-fifth century BC as part of a plan for the beautification of the city initiated by Pericles, the famous Athenian statesman. Pericles induced the Athenians to divert for building purposes money collected from their Greek allies to form a fleet for defence against the Persians who had previously invaded Greece and sacked Athens itself, destroying the old temples on the Acropolis in 481 BC, before being decisively defeated at the battle of Salamis. There appears to have been considerable opposition to Pericles' building programme; according to Plutarch's account (*Life of Pericles*, XII) some Athenians complained that money contributed for war was being used to tart up the city, decking her out at vast expense with buildings, statues and thousand-talent temples, as if she were a pretentious woman flaunting her charms.

The great Doric temple of Athene was comparatively well preserved until 1687 when a magazine of gunpowder stored inside it exploded during the Venetian–Turkish war, blowing out the roof and many of the columns along the sides. During the early nineteenth century Lord Elgin brought a great part of the surviving sculptures from the pediments, metopes and

17 FROM THE WEST FRIEZE OF THE PARTHENON

frieze to London, to save them from still greater damage. The South Slip Room adjacent to Room 8 has a model of the Parthenon showing the original positions of the pedimental sculptures in the gables of the temple, that of the sculpted panels or metopes above the colonnade, and that of the frieze crowning the outer wall of the temple inside the colonnade, or peristyle.

The metopes were probably the first part of the programme of sculptural decoration to be finished as they were placed above the columns and framed by the triglyphs, or grooved panels, which were an essential feature of the Doric order. All the metopes in London illustrate the fight between the Lapiths and Centaurs. The Centaurs were savage creatures, part man and part horse who, having drunk too much at the wedding-feast of the Lapith king, attempted to carry off the Lapith women. Some of the metopes, which are carved in extremely bold relief, show the struggle with great vividness (see panel XXVII).

The frieze from the interior of the colonnade represented the Panathenaic procession held to celebrate the birthday of Athene. The famous sculptor Phidias was in charge of the whole building project, and it has therefore been suggested that his workshop produced the frieze, of which 247 feet are now in London. The frieze was designed originally to represent successively each stage of the procession, culminating in the presentation of a specially embroidered dress to Athene in the presence of other deities.

The design of the frieze starts off from the south-west angle, the procession being divided into two streams, one going along the west and north sides, and the other going straight down the south side. The two parts of the procession converge in the centre of the east side. Two groups of horsemen are shown preparing to set off, one group from each stream of the procession. One of these groups occupied the whole of the west side of the temple, and the final slab from this part of the frieze is shown immediately to the right of the entrance to the Duveen Gallery. The gradually developing momentum of the procession

17

18/19 FROM THE EAST PEDIMENT OF THE PARTHENON

[74]

is beautifully portrayed, and the marvellously realistic representation of the horses has often been admired. Progressing eastwards down both the north and south sides of the temple we find successively portrayed on the blocks of the frieze horsemen, chariots, old men and boys on foot, and finally the victims for the sacrifice with their attendants.

A slab from the south section of the frieze (now on the west side of the Duveen Gallery), in spite of its battered shape, shows the amazing skill Greek sculptors had now acquired in representing a four-horse chariot at full speed in the difficult medium of low-relief. Ruskin pointed out that the projection of the heads of the four horses, one behind the other, is not more than three-quarters of an inch from the flat ground, and that the one in front does not in reality project more than the one behind it. 'Yet', continues Ruskin, 'by mere drawing you see the sculptor has got them to appear to recede in due order, and by the soft rounding of the flesh surfaces and modulation of the veins he has taken away all look of flatness from the necks. He has drawn the eyes and nostrils with dark incisions, careful as the finest touches of a painter's pencil: and then, at last, when he comes to the manes he has let fly hand and chisel with their full force.'

The sculpture from the East Pediment is displayed at the north end of the Duveen Gallery. The sculpture of this pediment represented the birth of Athene, who sprang armed from the head of her father Zeus. The central figures have perished, and the surviving ones displayed here come from the angles of the pediment, or gable, of the temple. The identity of the individual figures is disputed, but it is evident even from the remnants of the composition on display that the whole design was suffused with a rhythm of turning and half-turning figures, as the gods and goddesses became aware of the dramatic event taking place in their midst. The magnificent reclining nude male figure, who perhaps represents Dionysos, has not yet seen what is happening, whereas the beautifully draped figures of Demeter and Persephone on his left seem just to have heard the news from the goddess advanc-

ing on their left. The rich drapery of the seated women is specially remarkable; the infinite care with which even the folds of their clothes at the back are executed is perhaps surprising, as these sculptures can never have been visible from the rear in antiquity once they were set in the pediment forty feet above the ground. However, such diligence seems in keeping with the success here achieved in giving all the figures of the pediment a strikingly three-dimensional quality.

The three remaining goddesses from the other side of this pediment have been variously identified: improbably as the Three Fates, and more plausibly as Hestia, goddess of the Hearth, and Aphrodite, goddess of Love, who lies back indolently against the knees of her mother, Dione. The luxuriant folds of the dresses of these two latter figures fall in rich patterns across the women's bodies, emphasizing and enhancing their curved forms. The sculptures from the West Pediment are much more fragmentary, but the fine figure of Iris, messenger of the gods, conveys a tremendous impression of energy and speed.

The Parthenon has long been admired as perhaps the greatest achievement of Greek art. Writing in the time of the Roman Empire, 600 years after it was built, Plutarch captured something of its timeless beauty. For Plutarch wrote of the works of art initiated by Pericles, of which the Parthenon was the chief 'They were created in a short time for all time. As each of them as soon as finished had the venerable air of antiquity, so now that they are old, they seem fresh and newly made. Such is the bloom of youth on them they look always untouched by time, as if they were suffused with unfailing life, and a spirit that cannot grow old' (*Life of Pericles*, XII).

18

19

We now return to Room 6 where the frieze from the Temple of Apollo at Bassae is displayed. This temple is spectacularly sited in the remote mountains of Arcadia. Early in the nineteenth century the frieze was excavated from the ruins and put up for sale; it was purchased by the British Government. In antiquity this temple was much admired: Pausanias, who travelled in Greece in the second century AD, describes it as second only to the temple at Tegea for the beauty of its stone and the symmetry of its proportions, and attributes it to Ictinus, one of the architects of the Parthenon, dating the building to 430–429 BC. Scholars have disputed this date, and it is now suggested that work on the temple was spread out over some time, beginning with the outer colonnade around 450 BC, and finishing with the interior and the frieze during the last years of the fifth century BC.

In Greek architecture the frieze usually decorated the exterior of the temple, but at Bassae the frieze ran round the interior of the cella, or main room of the temple. The frieze from Bassae represents two subjects: the fight between the Greeks, led by Herakles (who can be seen with his lion skin on Slab 21) and the Amazons, a legendary race of warrior women, and the fight between the Lapiths and Centaurs. The latter was a legend often represented in Greek art; it also appears on the metopes of the Parthenon (see p. 74). 20 Here the Lapith women are shown clutching their small children as they try to resist the Centaurs.

Although the execution of this frieze is uneven in quality, the design is everywhere shot through with dramatic life and violent movement. The exaggeratedly swirling drapery of the Amazon warriors and the Lapith women echoes and enhances the sense of movement portrayed in the figures themselves. We might say that in this frieze something of the baroque style has broken through into the sculpture of antiquity.

20 FRIEZE FROM THE TEMPLE OF APOLLO AT BASSAE; DETAIL

The Nereid Monument, remains from which occupy the whole of Room 7, is the largest of the tombs brought from Lycia to the Museum. It was in the form of a small Greek temple with columns of the Ionic order, that is crowned with capitals formed by volutes or spirals, and it was set on a high base which was surmounted by two friezes in low relief running all round the building. In the Museum only the front of the building has been reconstructed; this was originally one of the shorter sides, for there are four columns across the facade, whereas there were six along each of the long sides.

Between the columns of the monument stood life-size marble statues of sea nymphs who have been identified as the Nereids, daughters of Nereus, an old sea god. It is from these figures that the monument gets its present name. Some of the statues of these Nereids are displayed between the columns of the reconstructed facade as they would have stood in antiquity, while three others are set at ground level at the further end of the room. These statues show the extraordinary virtuosity attained by Greek sculptors at this date in both the representation of swift movement in life-size, three-dimensional sculpture, and in the skilful modelling of the forms of the female body beneath transparent drapery.

This impressive funerary temple has a mixture of Greek and Lycian elements in both the forms and imagery employed. The temple has Greek Ionic columns, but in setting a carved architrave directly above them it does not follow Greek architectural conventions. The high base crowned by two friezes is also not a part of the Greek architectural tradition, but seems to be of Lycian origin. The Nereids themselves are figures from Greek mythology, and the finest of these statues must have been the work of Greek sculptors. It has been suggested that around this time myths began to acquire a more personal symbolic significance, so that the Nereids would have been seen as promising to the dead a new life in the world beyond, acting as conductors of the soul to the world of the blessed.

On the other hand, some of the friezes of the Nereid Monument display events from the everyday life of the chieftain it commemorates, as when his soldiers scale the walls of a besieged city in the upper frieze on the monument, or where the dynast himself, sitting under a sunshade, appears to receive the surrender of the city. (This slab also comes from the upper frieze, but is now displayed on the left of the doorway leading from this Room into Room 15.) Although there are Greek elements in the carving of the frieze its choice of subject derives from the traditions of the Persian, and ultimately the Assyrian, monarchs, who commemorated their victories in sculptured reliefs.

21

21 MARBLE FIGURE OF A NEREID FROM THE 'NEREID MONUMENT'

22 One of the Caryatids, or statues of maidens, which were used instead of columns in the south porch of the Erechtheion, is on display in this room. The surviving accounts for the building inscribed on stone show that the building was completed between 409 and 406 BC, while Athens was involved in the Peloponnesian war against Sparta.

The Erechtheion is of an unusual form being on two levels, and having a projecting porch on each of the two longer sides, partly because it is sited on the north side of the Acropolis where the ground falls away steeply, and partly because it housed a number of ancient cults and their relics. There was an ancient image of Athene in the east end, and the tomb of Erechtheus, a mythical King of Athens, in the west end; access to some part of the western sanctuary seems to have been possible from the projecting south porch of the temple which was supported by Caryatids.

Like most of the building this Caryatid is of Pentelic marble, and is finely carved; the hair at the back of the neck is cunningly contrived to strengthen the statue at its weakest point so as to increase the load-bearing capacity of the statue. The carving of the dress of the maiden is beautifully done so as to fall in rich folds in some places, while being rendered so transparent in others that the forms of the girl's body show through.

22 CARYATID FROM THE ERECHTHEION, ATHENS

23 WATER-JAR SIGNED BY THE POTTER MEIDIAS

23 A hydria or water-jar signed by the potter Meidias and dating from *c.* 410 BC is a good example of a decorative, mannered style of vase painting current in Athens towards the end of the fifth century. The decoration of this vase is divided into two zones, the upper showing the abduction of the daughters of Leucippus by Castor and Pollux, twin sons of Zeus, and the lower showing Herakles in the Garden of the Hesperides, in search of the golden apples from the tree guarded by the snake.

Particularly remarkable are the richly drawn clinging draperies closely following the forms of the female figures; these swirling garments seem to echo the mannered and affected poses and gestures of the figures. Yet in spite of its exaggerations the composition of this vase has a charm and appeal which was soon to vanish from vase-painting.

Seals played an important part in many ancient civilizations, serving to a large extent instead of signatures on documents, and being used to secure letters, and even packages. From archaic times onwards Greek seals were often carved on the back in the form of a scarab beetle, in imitation of Egyptian 24 seals. A fine onyx seal of this type displayed in this room is decorated with a flying goose which is cut with extraordinary delicacy (Case 6). It has been suggested that this seal may have been the work of Dexamenos of Chios, the most accomplished gem engraver known to us, since he signed a seal decorated with a similar goose.

10 PAYAVA ROOM

This room is dominated by the Tomb of Payava which, like the Nereid Monument, comes from Xanthos in Lycia. The tomb dates from the earlier fourth century BC, and takes a form characteristic of Lycian tombs of this date which is perhaps derived from wooden prototypes. The damaged reliefs around the base and on the lid of the sarcophagus appear to show scenes from the life of Payava, the Lycian for whom the tomb was made.

25 A fine bronze head of a Berber dating from the later fourth century BC, which was discovered in the Temple of Apollo at Cyrene in North Africa, illustrates a comparatively early phase in the development of portraiture, an art which is often incorrectly taken to be an entirely Roman creation. Although representing a handsome young man, this bronze head still no doubt embodies some elements of idealization. Yet features such as the furrowed brow and slightly hollowed cheeks stamp this head as that of an individual, rather than an idealized male type. It is interesting to note that towards the end of the fourth century BC portrait heads are first found on Greek coins.

In the gallery of this room there is a newly installed exhibition of the finest objects from the Department's collection of Etruscan antiquities (Room 11). There are sculptures in stone, terracotta and bronze which date from the archaic period onwards.

25 BRONZE HEAD OF A BERBER
FROM THE TEMPLE OF APOLLO AT CYRENE

24 BANDED ONYX SEAL
MID 5TH CENT. BC

26 COLOSSAL MARBLE STATUE,
FROM THE MAUSOLEUM AT HALICARNASSUS

In this room considerable remains of the sculptural decoration from the Mausoleum at Halicarnassus are on display. The Mausoleum was known in antiquity as one of the Seven Wonders of the World; it was the tomb of King Mausolus of Caria, a state on the west coast of Asia Minor, nominally subject to Persia. Mausolus planned the tomb to stand at the centre of his new capital at Halicarnassus; uncompleted at the time of his death in 353 BC, the work was continued under the direction of his widow, Queen Artemisia, who was also his sister.

The exact form of this impressive monument (from which we get our word mausoleum used to describe a monumental tomb), is now uncertain, owing to the damage and destruction suffered in the intervening centuries. However, in the later fifteenth century the base of the monument was found buried, but largely intact, by the Knights of St John. The Knights carried away large quantities of stone to strengthen the fortifications of their great castle on the bay, as they tried in vain to halt the advance of the Turks. We know from the ancient writers Vitruvius and Pliny that the Mausoleum took the form in its upper part of a stepped pyramid set above a colonnade, and surmounted by a giant four-horse chariot; the forepart of one of the horses, together with part of its bronze bit and bridle can be seen here. We seem to have here an early example of a chariot being used as a symbol for apotheosis.

There is no evidence that the two colossal statues formerly identified as Mausolus and Artemisia do in fact represent them; these figures can only be identified as members of Mausolus's family, the Hecatomnids – the ruling dynasty of Caria. Probably portrait statues of the Hecatomnids, including the 'Mausolus' and 'Artemisia', originally stood between the columns of the Mausoleum, just as the statues of the Nereids stand between the columns of Nereid Monument 26 (Room 7). The fine head of 'Mausolus' with some orientalizing features, such as the long hair and cut of the moustache, is one of the earliest portrait heads to have survived.

Fifteen blocks of the frieze illustrating the battle between the Greeks and Amazons are on display. This frieze decorated the top of the base of the Mausoleum. Scholars disagree about attributing the various blocks to the famous sculptors Timotheos, Scopas, Bryaxis and Leochares, who are said to have decorated the building. The blocks vary both in style and quality of execution, but the finest sections convey a strong sense of energy and movement. Slab 1020 shows an intricate composition in which a Greek and Amazon lunge towards each other over another Greek who has been forced to the ground, and attempts to crouch beneath his shield; the bodies of the two assailants are represented with considerable, almost mannerist, elongation.

According to tradition, the huge archaic temple of Artemis at Ephesus in Asia Minor was burnt down in 356 BC, on the night of Alexander the Great's birth, by a certain Herostratus in the unworthy hope of the World, as was the Mausoleum at Halicarnassus (Pliny, *Natural History*, XXXVI. 95). The temple was of enormous size, the columns rising to almost sixty feet; following the precedent of the archaic temple, the lower parts of some of the columns were carved with reliefs, which was uncommon in classical architecture.

27   A surviving column drum, on which a considerable part of the sculptural decoration remains, can be seen here. Three life-size figures represent Hermes, the messenger of the gods with his herald's staff, the winged figure of Death, and a woman who has been tentatively identified as Alcestis, who volunteered to sacrifice her own life to save that of her husband, but was allowed to return from the underworld. Grouped and executed with great skill against the awkwardly convex surface of the column, the graceful nude figure of Hermes and the draped figure of the woman, particularly in the rich folds of her cloak, present carving of the highest quality.

27 MARBLE COLUMN DRUM FROM THE TEMPLE OF ARTEMIS AT EPHESUS

The sitting figure of Demeter from the sanctuary of the underworld deities at Cnidus provides another magnificent example of the work of fourth-century
28 Greek sculptors, *c.* 330 BC. The figure is life-size, and carved from marble, that of the head being more finely polished. The robes of the figure were probably originally covered by paint, as were many parts of ancient statues and reliefs.

Demeter, goddess of the corn, is seen here mourning the fate of her daughter, Persephone, who was carried off by Pluto, god of the underworld, as his bride. Since Demeter refused to let the corn grow, Persephone was allowed to return from the underworld for several months of each year, her appearance and disappearance being taken to symbolize the burying of the corn seed in the ground and the eventual growth of the crops. In time the rituals connected with the worship of Demeter and Persephone came to be associated with the hope of rebirth after death for those initiated into their Mystery Cults.

A bronze head representing Sophocles, the famous
29 Athenian dramatist, in advanced old age is a fine example of Hellenistic portraiture which dates from the third century BC. Sophocles' life spanned most of the fifth century, and he is said to have written one of his most famous plays, *Oedipus at Colonus*, shortly before he died in 406 BC. Although no contemporary portraits of Sophocles, nor of any other famous Greeks of the fifth century, survive, it seems possible on the evidence of literary accounts and of a Roman copy of an apparently original Greek portrait of the fifth century, that recognizable, although idealized, portraits of famous men were made at that time. The representation of Sophocles as an old man was perhaps a Hellenistic innovation, being an adaptation of an earlier likeness of him, whether or not it was merely a conventional one, which reflects the increasing interest of Hellenistic artists in subjects such as old age.

A glass bowl with gold-leaf decoration is one of a
30 pair of exceptionally decorative bowls found in a tomb in southern Italy, and dating from the third century BC. Glass-blowing was not invented until the first century BC but before that time glass bowls were made, as this one was, by casting the glass in moulds. This bowl consists of two layers of glass, each cast separately and fitting closely together with an elaborate floral pattern cut from gold-leaf sandwiched between them. At the centre of the bowl the gold-leaf decoration consists of an eight-petalled flower from which radiate leaves of the lily *Nymphaea caerulea* filled in with other plant designs, including ears of corn and stylishly rendered acanthus leaves.

It is likely that this bowl was made in Alexandria, particularly as we know from the ancient writer Athenaeus that glass vessels with gold decoration were among the striking exhibits displayed in the great festival processions of Alexandria, such as that held by Ptolemy Philadelphus, ruler of Egypt in the earlier third century, apparently in honour of his father, Ptolemy I (Athenaeus V, 30.199).

28 MARBLE STATUE OF DEMETER FROM CNIDUS

30 GLASS BOWL WITH GOLD-LEAF DECORATION

29 BRONZE HEAD OF SOPHOCLES

In this room works of art produced in the last years of the Roman Republic and the early years of the Empire are displayed. It is notoriously difficult to evaluate the contribution of the Romans to the development of the fine arts since in so many ways artists of the Roman period appear to have built on foundations laid by the Greeks.

31 The Portland Vase, which probably dates from the late first century BC or early first century AD, is one of the finest glass vessels to have survived from antiquity. It was apparently discovered near Rome in the sixteenth century, at that time in an excellent state of preservation, although perhaps lacking the lowest section, which may have tapered to a knob. Later the vase came into the possession of the Dukes of Portland, from whom it gets its present name. It was shattered into many pieces by a deranged visitor to the Museum in 1845, but it has been repaired. This vase is a fairly early example of blown glass, a technique which was probably invented in Syria in the first century BC. It was blown in two layers – an opaque white layer over one of cobalt blue, and the white layer was cut away like a cameo to leave a decorative frieze of figures against a background of trees and rocks.

The identification of the figures on the vase is uncertain. The most widely accepted view is that one, or possibly both sides, of the vase represent the wooing of the sea nymph, Thetis, by the mortal, Peleus. All the exponents of this interpretation agree that the young man advancing from the shrine or gateway is Peleus, but it is disputed whether the object of his advance, Thetis, is the seated woman with the sea-monster, who stretches out her arm to him, or whether this is merely Thetis's mother or grandmother, who encourages him to proceed towards Thetis, who lies asleep under a tree on the further side of the vase. Both these interpretations of the figures embody a version of the myth considerably altered from the original Greek form, in which a determined Peleus subdues a reluctant Thetis. In both explanations of the figures given here a rather diffident Peleus is encouraged to make his advances, either by Thetis herself, or by one of her relations. This romanticized version of the myth is also found in literature of the Roman period: Catullus describes Peleus and Thetis as falling in love at first sight, while Philostratus gives a version of the legend in which Peleus, having discovered that Thetis is immortal, is afraid to continue his love affair with her, and is induced to do so only after considerable encouragement.

Most surviving antique paintings come from the houses of Pompeii and Herculaneum, and the villas in their environs, which were buried by the eruption of Vesuvius in AD 79. Little is known of earlier Greek frescoes apart from some of the names of the artists. The small fresco panel shown here comes from a villa near Pompeii, and represents an idyllic
32 landscape with a tower-like building, perhaps a house, and a man on a bridge fishing in the foreground, and a sheet of water with boats on it beyond. Although

31 THE PORTLAND VASE; ROMAN CAMEO GLASS

this landscape, like other paintings of the period, shows an incomplete grasp of perspective, it has considerable charm, chiefly owing to its use of gently harmonizing colours.

A relief with a pair of portrait busts illustrates Roman developments in portraiture (*c.* 50 BC). The heads of the gaunt elderly couple are shown with an uncompromising, and rather unflattering realism.

15 SECOND ROMAN ROOM

This room contains Roman portraits and decorative sculpture as well as a splendid mosaic from St-Romain-en-Gal in southern France, which shows various deities of the countryside in an elaborate border. The marble portrait of Trajan (emperor AD 98–117) is particularly fine. The decorative sculpture includes marble reliefs (an excellent example from the villa of the Emperor Hadrian at Tivoli shows a youth with his horse and his dog) and copies made for Roman patrons of famous statues from earlier periods. The athlete binding a victory-band around his head, the so-called Diadoumenos, was copied from a bronze by Polykleitos of Argos, one of the finest Greek sculptors of the fifth century BC. The statue of Aphrodite crouching for her bath, one of many surviving versions of a type that was evidently popular in antiquity, formerly belonged to Charles I and is on loan from HM The Queen.

UPPER GALLERIES

In addition to exhibitions of Greek and Roman Daily Life and 'The Image of Augustus', the upper galleries contain temporary displays of Greek vases and of statuettes in bronze and terracotta. In the Life Room, objects of many kinds made from a wide variety of materials (including marble, clay, wood, ivory, bone and various metals) have been brought together to illustrate different aspects of life in Greek and Roman times, such as trade and industry, athletics, music and drama, warfare, home life, education, dress and religion. The exhibition, 'The Image of Augustus', shows how portraits of the Emperor played their part along with coinage and public proclamations in a propaganda campaign to establish his position as ruler of the Roman Empire.

New exhibitions are being planned for the adjacent rooms.

32 FRESCO PAINTING FROM A VILLA NEAR POMPEII

33 BUST OF 'CLYTIE'; PERHAPS A PORTRAIT OF ANTONIA,
DAUGHTER OF MARK ANTONY

82–5 THE WOLFSON GALLERIES

The corridor leading to Room 82 is lined with a photographic display of John Turtle Wood's discovery in 1869 of the Temple of Artemis at Ephesus. Opposite is a panorama of the Roman and Byzantine city found by Wood and more recently excavated by the Austrian Archaeological Institute. A map illustrates the findspots of sculptures displayed in the Wolfson Galleries.

Room 82 houses two Roman funerary reliefs found at Tomis (Constanta, Romania). The texts reveal in detail the rank of those who commissioned the tombstones. Small sculptures from the collection of Charles Townley are displayed in a showcase. Other showcases contain fragments of the sculptural decoration of the archaic Temple of Artemis at Ephesus, and small archaic sculptures from the island of Rhodes and the Greek trading post at Naukratis in Egypt. These reflect the powerful impact of Egypt upon Greek visitors.

Inside the entrance to Room 83 are sculptures from Cyrenaica (Libya). Many recall the legendary foundation of the city of Cyrene, and reflect the close ties with Greece maintained throughout the Roman empire. Two children's sarcophagi were found in a tomb near Benghazi; other objects from the tomb are displayed in an adjacent showcase.

A fine porphyry statue of a woman, made in the 2nd century AD, illustrates the technical competence of sculptors working an exceptionally hard stone. Beside this figure is a marble head from a colossal statue of Faustina, consort of the emperor Antoninus Pius (AD 138–161); this was found at Sardis (Asia Minor), where the emperor and empress were worshipped with the goddess Artemis. Only the extremities of this statue were made of stone. A similar technique was used to make a colossal statue, possibly a seated figure of the Graeco-Egyptian god Zeus Serapis, of which only part of one foot survives. The complete figures would have been over 18m high.

Also displayed here are marble sarcophagi, widely adopted by the Romans after the emperor Hadrian (AD 117–138) made Greece and its culture fashionable at Rome. A sarcophagus decorated with scenes from the life of Herakles is an outstanding example of the genre. The hastily recut portraits on two sarcophagi reflect urgent need occasioned by sudden death.

Room 84 is devoted to the remarkable collection of Roman sculpture made by Charles Townley (1737–1805). Mostly purchased at Rome, the sculptures were restored before shipment to London, where they were displayed in Townley's house. The collection represents the best of 18th-century taste and contains many works of great merit. Among these are Townley's 33 favourite sculpture 'Clytie', a statue of Venus found at Ostia, and a copy found at the villa of the emperor Hadrian of the discus-thrower by the Greek sculptor Myron. Townley purchased many outstanding examples of Roman funerary art, including a magnificent sarcophagus decorated with figures of the wine-god Bacchus and his followers. Roman portraits and heads of deities and heroes are displayed in Room 85. Also exhibited here is a part of the decoration of the stage building of the Great Theatre at Ephesus, constructed shortly after St Paul preached there in AD 56.

A choice selection of the coins of classical antiquity is displayed in the Greek and Roman Life Room. Greek coins form a distinct branch of ancient art and are often marked by designs of great beauty. The invention of coinage goes back to the seventh century BC and seems to have been made by the Greeks of Ionia on the eastern coast of the Aegean or by the Lydians in the nearby kingdom of Sardis. The Greek world at this time was composed of a number of separate cities all fiercely independent of each other, grouped mainly around the Aegean with offshoots in remoter areas such as the Black Sea, Italy and Sicily. The early coins were often stamped only on one side and had no inscription, but they were readily recognizable by the distinctive badge of the issuing city. Many of these badges were animal or plant designs – the tortoise of Aegina, the bee of Ephesos as well as mythological animals such as the griffin of Abdera, the Pegasus of Corinth or the chimaera of Sicyon. Other cities used as their devices the head of a god, and as designs began to appear on both sides of the coins, a regular formula became the god's head with the corresponding sacred animal, such as on the coins of Athens where the head of the goddess Athene has her owl for the reverses.

By the fifth century BC coinage had developed very widely and often became the vehicle for comparatively sophisticated artistic expression. This was specially
35 marked in Sicily with such masterpieces as the squatting Satyr of Naxos and the silver decadrachm of Syracuse with the head of Arethusa ringed by dolphins
36 (traditionally known as the 'Demareteion'); later decadrachms of Syracuse c. 400 BC were signed by the
37 artists Kimon and Euainetos and with their richly detailed female heads and lively horse chariots are among the most famous and prized of all ancient coins. Other aspects of Greek coinage are typified by an expressive head of Apollo from Amphipolis and by
38 a vigorous figure composition of Herakles killing the hydra from Phaistos.

Human portraiture does not appear on coins before the time of Alexander the Great (336–232 BC), apart from the occasional head of a Persian or Lydian notable. With the establishment of the Hellenistic kingdoms of Alexander's successors we find a whole gallery of realistic likenesses which give the coins great historical interest. One of the first is Alexander himself shown wearing an elephant scalp head-dress as conqueror of India; sometimes the ruler is shown with various attributes indicating that the king was worshipped as a god, but usually he wears only the royal diadem. Among the great variety of portraits visible on coins of the Hellenistic kingdoms may be mentioned specially
39 for their fine quality those of Antimachus of Bactria, Perseus of Macedonia, and the many gold coins of the Ptolemies of Egypt. The last of the Ptolemies, one of the most famous personalities of the ancient
40 world, Cleopatra VII, is shown on a silver coin from Ascalon.

Roman coinage began with large primitive bronze pieces of the fourth to third centuries BC. But by the time of the later Republic a complete monetary system had evolved in all metals.

From the time of the Roman conquest of Britain in AD 43 the currency in circulation in the provinces was provided by the Roman coinage in use throughout the Empire. Roman gold coins (aurei) did not circulate extensively in Britain and only a few hoards of Roman gold are on record. The earliest of these was the Treasure Trove found at Bredgar, Kent, in 1957 and consisting of 34 aurei from Julius Caesar to Claudius I. This is historically a most important hoard for its find spot and latest coin, dated to AD 42, suggest that it was buried during the initial advance of the Claudian invasion of AD 43. The Roman practice of recording contemporary events on the coinage was well illustrated by the reverse of one of the coins of Claudius. When Caligula was assassinated in AD 41 the Praetorian Guards escorted his elderly uncle, Claudius, to their camp and proclaimed him emperor. The reverse of one of Claudius' earliest coins shows the Praetorian
41 camp at Rome, and is inscribed IMPER RECEPT (the reception of the Emperor).

Although the Greek coinage of the Hellenistic kingdoms produced a whole range of regal portraits, the contemporary coinage of the Roman Republic virtually eschewed portrait coins of living persons. In the civil wars, however, towards the end of the first century BC, the chief protagonists such as Julius Caesar, Brutus, Antony and Octavian used the coinage to publicize themselves, and subsequently in the imperial coinage the portrait of the ruling emperor almost invariably appeared on the obverse, and occasionally this privilege was extended to other members of the imperial family. By comparison with the splendid portraits of Hellenistic monarchs portraiture on late Republican coins is rather crude. Realism is often carried to the point of caricature, as
42 on the posthumous portrait of Julius Caesar on an aureus issued by his great-nephew and successor Octavian in 44 BC. A marked improvement, however, is evident in the range of fine portraits, particularly on the gold coins, from Augustus throughout the first two centuries AD up to the Severan dynasty. The portrait of Augustus, the first emperor, shows the retention of an effective degree of realism, combined now with greater aesthetic sensitivity, while the bold, heavy-jowled portrait of Nero on a late coin about AD 64 shows something of the character of an emperor whose name became a by-word. The serenity of the spacious days of empire in the earlier second century AD is reflected by the calm urbanity of the portrait of
43 Hadrian, the emperor who spent himself in visits of inspection to most provinces of the Empire, including Britain. Hadrian's bearded portrait, in contrast to the shaven chin of earlier emperors, marks a change in fashion and may reflect his Hellenism. The portrait of
44 Marcus Aurelius, even more heavily bearded, is an apt representation for the nearest approach to Plato's concept of the philosopher-king.

35 NAXOS. SQUATTING SILENUS.
TETRADRACHM

36 SYRACUSE. 'DEMARATEION'.
DECADRACHM

37 SYRACUSE. DECADRACHM BY EUAINETOS

38 PHAISTOS. HERAKLES AND THE HYDRA.
STATER

39 ANTIMACHUS OF BACTRIA.
TETRADRACHM

40 CLEOPATRA VII.
TETRADRACHM

41 CLAUDIUS. IMPER RECEPT.
AUREUS

42 JULIUS CAESAR, AUGUSTUS, NERO.
AUREI

43 HADRIAN.
AUREUS

44 MARCUS AURELIUS.
AUREUS

Medieval & Later antiquities

Upper levels

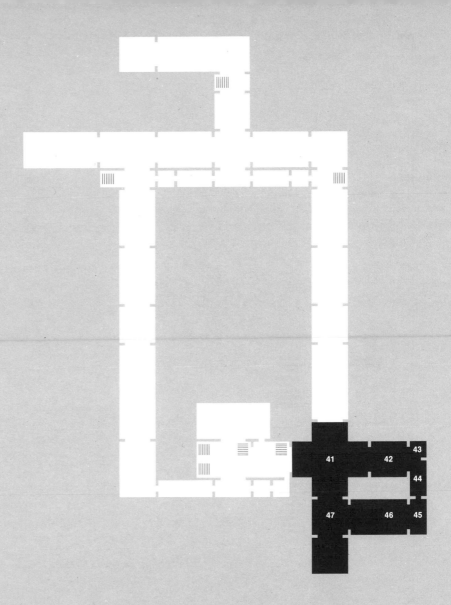

41 Early medieval art
42 Medieval art
43 Medieval tiles & pottery
44 Clocks & watches
45 The Waddesdon Bequest
46/47 Renaissance & Later antiquities

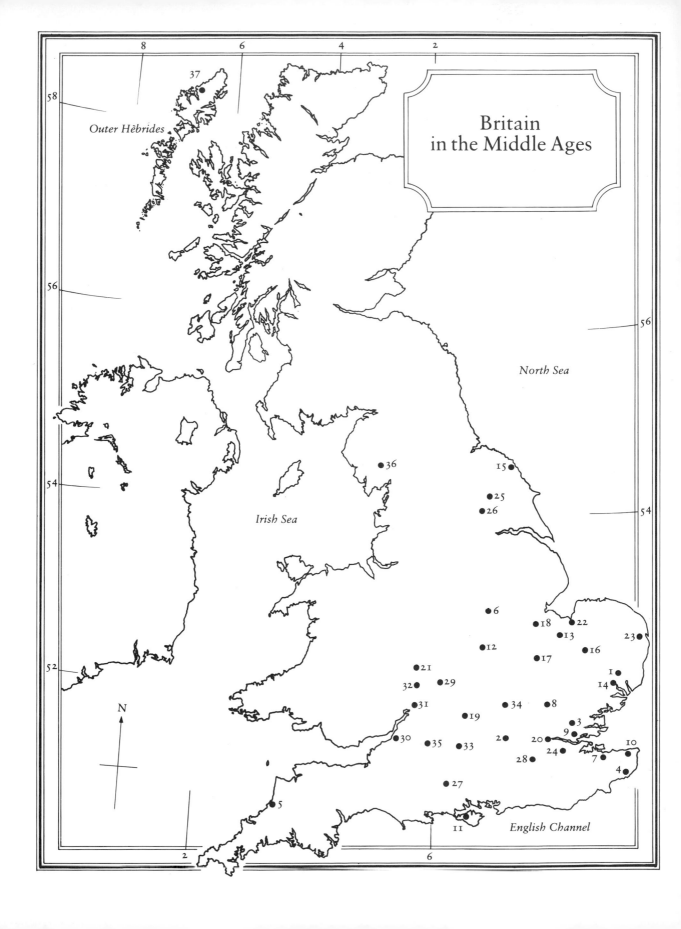

Britain
in the Middle Ages

Outer Hèbrides

North Sea

Irish Sea

N

English Channel

Medieval & Later antiquities

The principal medieval objects in the Department of Medieval and Later antiquities are displayed in a suite of three rooms entered from the Roman Britain Room. In the Early Medieval Room, which is in process of reorganisation, the archaeology and art of the British Isles will be represented by objects which span the years between the beginning of the fourth and end of the eleventh centuries, whilst developments of the Early Christian, Migration and somewhat later periods elsewhere will be shown in counterpoint to the British material; the new room will display the objects described overleaf, though in different cases. In the Medieval Room are exhibited secular and religious works of art beginning in the ninth century in Europe, in the tenth century in the Byzantine world and ending about 1500. In the Medieval Tile and Pottery Room, there is a selection from the Department's rich collection of English decorated tiles of the thirteenth to the sixteenth century together with a representative display of the pottery produced in England between the seventh and fifteenth centuries.

1 SUTTON HOO
2 TAPLOW
3 BROOMFIELD
4 DOVER
5 TINTAGEL
6 HOLME PIERREPONT
7 FAVERSHAM
8 WHEATHAMPSTEAD
9 MUCKING
10 SARRE
11 CHESSEL DOWN
12 DESBOROUGH
13 WILTON
14 IPSWICH
15 WHITBY
16 THETFORD
17 ST NEOT'S
18 STAMFORD
19 OXFORD
20 LONDON
21 WORCESTER
22 GRIMSTON
23 DITCHINGHAM
24 LESNES ABBEY
25 RIEVAULX ABBEY
26 BYLAND ABBEY
27 CLARENDON PALACE
28 CHERTSEY ABBEY
29 HAILES ABBEY
30 BRISTOL
31 GLOUCESTER
32 GREAT MALVERN
33 SAVERNAKE FOREST
34 DUNSTABLE
35 LACOCK
36 LOWTHER, (WESTMORLAND)
37 LEWIS

The display has as its focal point the material found in the celebrated ship burial at Sutton Hoo. This material reflects a wealth of different cultural and artistic traditions which are further illustrated in the adjacent bays; these contain displays of Early Christian material from the Mediterranean region and Migration period grave goods from northern Europe.

In the earlier part of the period covered by this room, the principal historical developments of direct relevance to the display are, first, the conversion of the Roman Empire to Christianity and, secondly, the collapse of the western half of that Empire under pressure from within as well as from outside, and its replacement by a series of kingdoms peopled by tribes of Germanic origin, the majority of whom were pagan. Under the terms of the Edict of Milan, promulgated by the Roman Emperors Constantine and Licinius in AD 313, Christianity was recognized as one of the official religions of the Empire. Not until AD 380 did it become the sole official religion and throughout this intervening period, therefore, social customs and religious practices originally associated with paganism continued to be tolerated. This was one of the factors which gave to the art of the period a curiously hybrid quality. In the context of the future development of medieval art, however, a more important one was to be the reliance of contemporary artists and craftsmen on existing classical models when the need arose for a new category of image suited specifically to the depiction of Christian themes. Throughout the figurative

1 THE LYCURGUS CUP. LATE ROMAN GLASS CAGE-CUP

art of the Middle Ages there runs a strong classical current which has its origins in the attempts made by artists of the Early Christian period to reconcile their classical inheritance with the demands of the new religion.

1   The Lycurgus Cup (Case 9), a rare survivor of the luxury cage-cups produced for the rich of the Late Roman Empire, is a fine example of the unashamed flaunting of pagan culture at a time when the Empire had already accepted Christianity as its sole official religion. Cut from a single block of pea-green glass, which possesses the unusual quality of changing to deep ruby-red in transmitted light, it carries on its side a technically remarkable representation of the murder of the legendary Thracian king, Lycurgus, at the hands of the pagan god Bacchus and his retinue. It was probably made in either Italy or Egypt in the years around AD 400.

The Esquiline Treasure (Cases 7 and 8), named after the Esquiline Hill in Rome, where it was discovered in 1793, is also a reflection of the continuing wealth of the Roman patrician class in the late fourth century.

2   On the Marriage Casket of Projecta, however, which is the single most important item in the treasure, a token gesture to Christianity makes its appearance: set alongside the traditional imagery of a Roman marriage there is an inscription which exhorts Projecta and her husband, Secundus, to lead a Christian life. Secundus is possibly to be identified as the Roman patrician, L. Turcius Secundus Asterius, who is known to have married a Christian woman by the name of Projecta in AD 379, but was a widower four years later.

2 EARLY CHRISTIAN MARRIAGE CASKET

3 EARLY BYZANTINE IVORY PLAQUE

The final collapse of the western half of the Roman Empire in AD 476 did not extinguish the legacy of the classical past. Already in AD 330, the first Christian emperor, Constantine, had founded a new capital for the eastern territories on the site of the former Greek colony of Byzantium, and had given it the name of Constantinople. The works of art that were produced here during the sixth and seventh centuries, at a time when these eastern territories, now more generally known as the Byzantine Empire, were at the height of their power, reflect the persistence of artistic ideals which had their origins in the art of Greece and Rome. That these ideals were in no way incompatible with the demands of Christianity may be seen in the fine carved ivory plaque representing the Archangel Michael (Case 5), probably executed in Constantinople sometime between AD 519–527, and in the dish from the silver treasure found in Cyprus in the late nineteenth century with a representation of either Saint Bacchus or Saint Sergius in the centre (Case 4).

Byzantine works of art of this period were treasured not only by those who lived within the confines of the Empire. Many pieces found their way as far afield as the Germanic tribal kingdoms of northern Europe, whose artistic traditions were of a totally different character. After the major invasions of the south of England in the fifth century, the Anglo-Saxons had gradually established their supremacy throughout lowland and eastern England; Wales, Cumbria (north-west England), Scotland and Ireland remained separate. The only royal Anglo-Saxon burial thought to survive almost in its entirety is the celebrated ship-burial excavated at Sutton Hoo in Suffolk in 1939 (Cases 10–22). The burial, believed to be that of King Redwald of the East Angles (d. 625/6), illustrates the quality and variety of objects available at the highest level of society. It included Early Christian and Byzantine silver objects from the Mediterranean world, Merovingian coins from the Continent, which enable the date of the burial to be fixed at about AD 625, hanging bowls of Celtic origin and a helmet and shield from Sweden, which was probably the original home of the East Anglian royal house. The most striking pieces, however, which are the jewels and sword-fittings set with garnets, the purse, shoulder-clasps and pyramids set with glass mosaic and the great gold buckle, are of East Anglian manufacture, and vividly illustrate the distinctive artistic traditions of the Germanic kingdoms (Case 16).

Before 1939, the only graves of comparable status were those of noblemen buried at Taplow, Buckinghamshire, and Broomfield, Essex (Cases 23 and 30). Parallels with the range of prestige goods found at Sutton Hoo are evident at Taplow in the lyre, the gold jewellery and the drinking-horns. Both sites, however, were inadequately excavated in the nineteenth century, and poorly recorded. A current display, on the left-hand side of the Early Medieval Room shows material from an Anglo-Saxon cemetery at Dover which was the result of a controlled modern excavation of the 1950s (Cases 37–41). This has yielded much detailed information about an ordinary village-type community. The finds, typical of east Kent, date from

4 HELMET FROM THE SUTTON HOO SHIP-BURIAL. EARLY 7TH CENT.

the fifth to the late seventh century and cover a spread of different social classes. One of the richest graves, containing a quantity of gold jewellery, is Grave 29 (Case 39), while bronze and ironwork is typical of more ordinary burials. The cemetery is rich in warrior graves, as the display of swords and other weapons indicates (Case 38).

The corresponding area on the opposite side of the gallery displays Anglo-Saxon weapons (Case 34), pottery and glass from Anglo-Saxon sites (Cases 36 and 35), and objects found in England but imported from the Continent (Case 33). Contemporary vessels from Continental sites, including the Bingerbrück glass horn are in Case 32. Together with the wheel-turned pottery from the site of a Celtic monastery at Tintagel, which is of Mediterranean origin (Case 29), these cases illustrate the closeness of the trading links which existed at this period. For example, many of the glasses in Case 35 are Frankish imports into England, as is much of the wheel-turned pottery from Kent in Case 33. The glass fragment from Holme Pierrepont, Nottinghamshire, on the other hand (Case 35), which has a Latin inscription, was imported from Egypt, as were such metal vessels as the Coptic bowls from Faversham, Kent (Case 33), Sutton Hoo (Case 13) and Taplow (Case 30) and the ewer from Wheathamp-stead, Hertfordshire (Case 33).

A rich series of personal and dress jewellery current among the tribes of the European Germanic kingdoms is exhibited in Cases 24, 25 and 26, opposite the contemporary Anglo-Saxon and Celtic material in Cases 27, 28 and 29. Anglo-Saxon and Continental jewellery shows a taste for the glitter of gold and gilding and for lavish effects of polychrome decoration which has already been noted in regard to the rich, garnet-set jewellery from Sutton Hoo. Among the Germanic tribes of northern Europe, motifs employing animal themes, often highly stylized, were in common use; such motifs were partly derived from late Roman ornamental designs and there are numerous local versions, as, for example, on the gold stamped pendants from Gotland (Case 25). In southern Europe, on the other hand, direct Byzantine influence on jewellery design is particularly noticeable; the Castellani Brooch, which has cloisonné enamelling on gold and a circlet of pearls, is the most remarkable example of this influence, but a more typical fusion of Germanic and Byzantine elements may be seen in the gold treasure from Domagnano, Italy (Case 26).

Mediterranean and Germanic motifs are also intermingled in the jewellery of the Anglo-Saxon settlers in England. The persistence of Roman decorative traditions may be seen by comparing the Late Roman military bronze belt fittings and early Anglo-Saxon gilt-bronze saucer brooches from the south of England with their chip-carved scrollwork ornament (Case 27);

5 FRANKISH GLASS DRINKING-HORN

in the remarkably complete belt set from Mucking, Essex, which has silver inlay, and in the quoit brooch from Sarre, Kent, with animals and human masks. The great square-headed brooch from Chessel Down, Isle of Wight, is a fine example of an Anglo-Saxon development of the Germanic animal style in the early sixth century (Case 27).

During the seventh century a change in jewellery fashions spread throughout Anglo-Saxon England, of which the most striking features were the decline in the use of brooches and a growing fondness for pins and pendants as in the rich cemetery at Faversham, Kent (Case 28). Some of these are among the latest objects from graves. To this group belong the gold and garnet necklace with a pendant cross from Desborough, Northamptonshire, and the Wilton cross-pendant from Norfolk, both of which are explicitly Christian. With the re-introduction of Christianity into England in the late sixth century, however, the pagan practice of burying goods in graves was forbidden and gradually died out. By about AD 700 the deposition of grave goods in England and most of Western Europe had come to an end.

Although Christianity had been introduced into Britain many years before the final departure of the Romans in the fifth century, it had survived the Anglo-Saxon invasions only in those parts of the country which had not been overrun by the invaders. In 597,

however, the conversion of the Anglo-Saxon settlements to Christianity began with the arrival in Kent of a mission headed by Augustine, prior of the monastery of St Andrew in Rome. From this period onwards, the pattern of the material evidence assumes a different form: grave goods become increasingly rare and, with their disappearance, chance finds, hoards and settlement site material become the principal sources of information.

The re-establishment of close links with the Mediterranean in the years following Augustine's mission has left its imprint on the art of the period. One of the major innovations associated with the spread of Christianity was the erection throughout the areas of missionary activity of stone preaching crosses and, in the shaft from one of these, from Lowther in Westmorland, three different types of classical vine-scroll decoration are represented. References to classical antiquity are also apparent in one of the most celebrated works of art of the period, the Franks Casket, a Northumbrian carving in whale's bone of the eighth century, named after Sir Augustus Wollaston Franks who presented it to the Museum in 1867. Alongside runic inscriptions and lively representations of Germanic folk lore are scenes from Roman history and the Bible which cast a revealing light on the culture of eighth-century Northumbria, one of the principal centres of English Christianity and the home of the Venerable Bede.

6 BROOCHES OF THE MIGRATION PERIOD

7 ANGLO-SAXON GOLD AND GARNET PENDANT

The exhibition runs more or less chronologically in a series of island cases down the centre of the room, a few large-scale sculptures and other objects being mounted on the walls. The earliest of the European works of art date from the ninth century AD and the latest from about 1500, taking in on their way the Carolingian, Ottonian, Late Anglo-Saxon, Romanesque and Gothic periods. There is also at the very beginning a case devoted to Middle Byzantine Art drawn from the provinces of the Eastern Christian Empire.

The removal of the seat of administrative government from Rome to the new capital, Constantinople, in the course of the fourth century AD (see the Early Medieval room) did not end with a collapse of central imperial control as it did in the West between the fourth and sixth centuries. A number of periods of strong government interspersed with times of disorder and with external threat from beyond the frontiers finally ended beneath the walls of the great city on the Bosphorus in 1453 in capitulation to the Turkish Sultan. Most of the works of art in Case 1 were made between the tenth and the thirteenth centuries for use in connection with the liturgy of the Eastern Christian church: low relief carvings, precious ivory panels, 8 smallscale works in hard stones and coloured glass, and fine examples of gold and enamelled jewellery. Cloisonné enamelling on gold, in which narrow strips of gold wire (called *cloisons* in French) are attached to a base plate to form a design which is then completed by firing coloured glasses into the resulting cells, was carried to a high point of accomplishment by Byzantine artists. Other examples of cloisonné enamelling and a small display of the techniques of early medieval enamel can be seen in Case 4.

8 IVORY BYZANTINE BORRADAILE TRIPTYCH

Case 2 presents three small groups of works of art, Carolingian ivories and rock crystals, Ottonian ivories, and ivories from the last period of Anglo-Saxon rule in England. Under the great Frankish ruler Charlemagne, who on Christmas Day in the year 800 had himself crowned by the Pope as the first Holy Roman Emperor, the arts and learning enjoyed a remarkable 'renaissance'. The extent to which Carolingian art was indebted to Late Antique sources and to the ideal of Early Christian Rome is well illustrated by an ivory *pyx* (small box), which is exhibited alongside a pyx of the sixth century. Less overtly classical in character is the Lothar Crystal, so-called after the Carolingian ruler whose name appears in an inscription around the centre of the disk: he is probably the Emperor Lothar II, a successor of Charlemagne who ruled from 855 to 869. The rock-crystal is engraved with a fine point in a dramatic and vigorous style; it is a technical *tour de force*, reviving the antique art of crystal engraving. The story of Susanna and the Elders is shown in a number of episodes around the outside of the disk and culminates in the centre with the judgement of the Elders.

The Ottonian dynasty, which succeeded the Carolingians, also inspired a remarkable artistic revival in the late tenth and early eleventh centuries, to some extent influenced by the import into Europe of a number of the best Byzantine works of art. Some of these may have come as part of the dowry of the Byzantine princess Theophano who married the German Emperor Otto II in 972. The hieratic and nobly austere qualities of Middle Byzantine art were apparently much admired; a case in point is provided by the ivory of the Raising of the Widow of Nain's Son, which was probably part of a lost altarpiece given by the Emperor Otto I (962–73) to the cathedral at Magdeburg.

The patronage that the German emperors extended towards the cathedrals and other religious foundations within the Empire reflected their overall policy of reforming the Church as an instrument of imperial administration; this, in its turn, was one aspect of the much wider reform of ecclesiastical and particularly monastic institutions which took place throughout Europe around the year 1000. In Anglo-Saxon England a movement of monastic reform gave renewed impetus to the arts in the later tenth and early eleventh centuries. The precious group of ivory carvings with which the display in Case 2 ends bears witness to the exuberant and highly dramatic style of this period, a period which saw the creation of some of the highest achievements of English art. The tau-cross (T-shaped handle for a bishop's or abbot's staff) from Alcester, Worcestershire, shows Christ on the cross among richly carved acanthus leaves. A crozier-head from Beverley, Yorkshire, provides evidence of the flourishing conditions of the arts in England on the eve of the Norman Conquest of 1066.

Romanesque is a term which was first applied in the late eighteenth century to the round-arched architecture of Europe in the eleventh and twelfth centuries, to distinguish it from the 'pointed style', Gothic, which succeeded it. Hence by association the word Romanesque began to be applied to the sculpture and small-scale works of art of the same period. The term is not a happy one, for in reality European art of the eleventh and twelfth centuries differed markedly from one

9   THE LOTHAR CRYSTAL. A CAROLINGIAN ENGRAVED ROCK-CRYSTAL

10 KNIGHT FROM THE
LEWIS CHESSMEN.
WALRUS-IVORY CARVING.
12TH CENT

11 ENAMELLED PLAQUE SHOWING SAMSON. 12TH CENT

region to the next. This is to be expected of a time when political and economic power was seldom concentrated in real terms in the hands of a central ruler and administration; the structures of feudalism rested firmly on the local lord or ecclesiastical landowner. In Cases 3 and 4 are displayed outstanding examples of ivory carving, enamelling and metal-working dating from the eleventh to the first half of the thirteenth centuries. Elephant ivory was scarce and many of the ivories from Northern Europe in Case 3 are carved from the tusk of the walrus. Apart from the ivories with religious iconography, there is an important collection of decorated Romanesque gaming-pieces, including table-men (like modern draughtsmen and used for board games of the type of backgammon or draughts) and chessmen. The Lewis Chessmen were found on the Isle of Lewis in the Outer Hebrides in 1831, although they are now considered to be the work of a Scandinavian artist. With their simple solid forms and air of brooding strength, they represent one of the high points of twelfth-century art in Northern Europe.

At this time metalworkers in the Low Countries, Germany and England were also producing outstanding works of art for the performance of the church liturgy, for instance altar- and processional crosses and censers for the burning of incense (Case 4). What is more, the cult of relics, which had grown in strength since the earlier Middle Ages, led to the creation of reliquaries shaped after the bones which they enshrined, as with the head-reliquary of St Eustace from the Cathedral of Basle, Switzerland (also in Case 4). Here the artist has sheathed a carved wooden head with plates of gilt-silver; the wooden core is displayed alongside its metal sheathing. Thus the relic of St Eustace's head which was hidden within the core was given a tangible presence to the worshipper, who could by contemplating the reliquary be moved to feel close to the benign influence of the saint.

One of the major technical accomplishments of the Romanesque period was the revival of the ancient art of enamelling on copper. In Case 4 a small display of the techniques of early medieval enamel introduces the collections of twelfth- and thirteenth-century champlevé enamelling from the Low Countries, England, Germany and France. Champlevé enamelling, in which the areas to be filled with colour are gouged out of the copper plate, was little used before the twelfth century. One of its principal centres of revival was the area around Liège in the valley of the Meuse and the enamels from this region, which are known as Mosan enamels, are among the most technically accomplished of the period. A particularly fine example is the plaque showing Samson carrying away the gates of Gaza, where Samson's stockings are decorated with a detailed diaper pattern which is a *tour de force* of the enameller's craft. The same technique was known in England, as is indicated by the two plaques associated with one of the greatest of twelfth-century English churchmen, Henry of Blois, King Stephen's younger brother, Bishop of Winchester. In the second half of the twelfth century and on into the following century, a large production of these champlevé enamels was also concentrated in south-western France and northern Spain. At the time these brilliantly-coloured enamels were already known as 'Limoges work' and they have been so-called ever since, although it is clear that by no means all of them were made in the town of Limoges itself. The earliest Limoges coppersmiths were responsible for a number of masterpieces, such as the two plaques with the mourning figures of the Virgin and St John from a big crucifix of which the central Christ is lost, or the remarkable box with secular scenes of music and amorous dalliance (both in Case 4). By the thirteenth century the Limoges enamellers were working on a semi-industrialised basis; their high quality pieces are rare. Nevertheless the Museum's collections are exceptionally rich and illustrate the wide range of Limoges, for liturgical usage or for everyday purposes, such as the dishes for washing the hands during meals (gemellions). Limoges was not only bought by rich patrons of the time but again avidly collected in the eighteenth and nineteenth centuries by connoisseurs of the Medieval Revival.

The production of Limoges enamels continued long after certain new tendencies, generally referred to by historians as 'Gothic', had begun to make their appearance in medieval art. Although this term is a misnomer, in that it stems from the period when medieval art in general was held to be rude and barbarous, (i.e. like the art of the barbarian Goths), it is still universally applied to the art and architecture of the thirteenth to fifteenth centuries in Europe. The essential characteristics of this phase of European art are a delicacy and lightness of form which are quite at variance with the derogatory implications of the epithet, but are already well represented in a magnificent gilt-bronze Mosan crozier with foliage decoration (Case 4); it is in the manner of one of the greatest known medieval metalworkers, Hugo of Oignies.

From Case 5 onwards to the end of the Gallery, all the objects on display would normally be given the label 'Gothic'. Yet the story of Gothic is not a simple one. Nor do the Museum's collections represent except in a few rare examples the monumental sculpture and stained glass of the great cathedrals (for this the collections of the Victoria and Albert Museum should be visited). Case 6 is devoted to the theme of Gothic ivory carving. Particularly to be noted here are the statuettes of the Virgin and Child, with which the display begins, each one a devotional group from a small altar tabernacle of which the frame and other figures are lost. These ivories were brightly coloured with pigments. Here there are a number of small masterpieces to be set above the more ordinary run of plaques with standard scenes from the Gospels. The visitor is advised to browse and select his own favourites among these minute examples of the ivory carver's craft.

Mention has been made of Hugo of Oignies and it is only in the Gothic period that the names of individual artists begin to be known with some regularity, in contrast to the standard anonymity of the preceding centuries. For instance, among the Gothic metalwork exhibited in Case 5 will be found an early fourteenth-century Sienese chalice signed by the two goldsmiths,

12 BISHOP'S CROZIER OF GILT-BRONZE. 13TH CENT

Tondino di Guerino and Andrea Riguardi, while a silver cross with the enamelled arms of the important Hungarian family of the Hedervari was commissioned from a travelling Sienese enameller, probably a certain Peter Gallicus who is known to have worked for Charles I of Hungary around 1330. The Sienese were masters of the technique of translucent enamelling, an Italian innovation of the later years of the thirteenth century which remained fashionable throughout Europe during the rest of the Middle Ages. The champlevé technique is now employed with precious metals, gold or silver, so that the grounds beneath the fired glass inlays reflect the light and create a translucent effect.

Italian art was much admired in Northern Europe, following the remarkable artistic innovations of the late thirteenth and early fourteenth century in central Italy, which included not only the first translucent enamels on silver but also the great paintings on wall and panel by such artists as Duccio, Giotto and Simone Martini. The exquisite fragments of wall-paintings from St Stephen's Chapel, Westminster (Cases 7–8), executed between 1350 and 1363, bear witness to the respect of contemporaries for Italian Art; a detail such as the Muting of Tobit owes to Italy its modelling, its spatial arrangement and its delicacy of line and tone. St Stephen's Chapel, the private royal chapel within Westminster Palace, was almost completely destroyed by fire in 1834, but these paintings had already been rescued during rebuilding works in 1800. They are displayed with the scenes of Job in Case 7 and of Tobit in Case 8, facing each other as they did across the original chapel, which was of course far larger in scale. On the wall opposite the St Stephen's cases are grouped the celebrated thirteenth-century floor-tiles from Chertsey Abbey in Surrey, with scenes of battle and Romance, including a combat between Richard Coeur de Lion and Saladin.

Although it was in the realm of religious art that the Middle Ages left their most characteristic imprint, the display in the Medieval Room also includes many of the Department's more important examples of medieval secular art. A striking illustration of the care and attention that were lavished upon objects intended for royal use is provided by the silver seal-die of Isabella of Hainault, Queen of France from 1180 to 1190 (Case 5), where the standing figure of the Queen is worthy of comparison with the best of late twelfth-century monumental sculpture. Most royal seals were broken on the death of their owner to avoid being put to fraudulent use, but it seems to have been customary in France in the late twelfth century to bury them in the tomb, which is where Isabella of Hainault's seal-die was discovered.

Music was an important feature of medieval courtly life. The late thirteenth-century English gittern in Case 14 is the most notable musical instrument of the period to have survived and was the forerunner of the modern guitar: although now designed to be bowed, it was originally plucked. The date of its conversion is not known, nor is the manner in which it was played when, in the years around 1578, it belonged to either Queen Elizabeth I or her favourite, Robert Dudley, Earl of Leicester, the badges of both of whom appear on a silver plate attached to the peg box. About its qualities as a work of art, however, there can be no uncertainty since the carved decoration along the sides, with its grotesques, huntsmen and foresters and vigorous naturalistic foliage, is as lively and accomplished as the best of contemporary sculpture.

The forests of medieval England are also evoked by the Savernake Horn, named after the forest of Savernake in Wiltshire of which it was traditionally regarded as the tenure horn (Case 9). It consists of a single elephant tusk, which was probably fashioned into its present form in western Europe during the twelfth or thirteenth century, decorated with four silver mounts, two of which are eighteenth-century replacements. The two silver-gilt mounts embellished with translucent enamel are, however, of early fourteenth-century origin and are among the few English examples of this type of enamelling which have survived. Both are engraved with hunting dogs and beasts of the chase, but, in addition, the mount around the mouth of the horn bears representations of a king, a bishop and a forester. The reasons for the appearance of these three figures side by side are uncertain, although the presence of the king is clearly to be explained by the fact that the great forests of medieval England were protected by law for the king's sport. Associated with the horn is a baldric or carrying strap which, although not original, is of only slightly later date: the enamelled roundels with which it is deco-

13 SEAL DIE OF ISABELLA OF HAINAULT

rated bear the arms of the fourteenth century Scottish Earls of Moray, the first of whom was Regent of Scotland after Robert Bruce's death in 1329.

The translucent enamels used on the Savernake Horn are characteristic of the Gothic period, during which the brilliant effects of transmitted and reflected light were much admired. A better preserved example of this type of enamelling can be seen in the Holy Thorn pendant, a reliquary intended for personal use and decorated on the inside with scenes from the Life of Christ (Case 5). An alternative technique was developed in Paris towards the middle of the fourteenth century and consisted in the firing of opaque enamel onto gold objects in the round (*en rondebosse*). A particularly fine example of this is the Swan Jewel which was found at Dunstable in Bedfordshire in 1965 (Case 9). Many noble families in the fourteenth and fifteenth centuries used the swan as a badge to indicate their descent via the House of Boulogne from the Swan Knight of medieval romance, but in this case what was originally an emblem has been transformed into a jewel of the highest quality. Other outstanding examples of medieval jewellery can be seen in Cases 9 and 10.

Translucent enamelling is used extensively on one of the greatest treasures of the Department, the Royal Gold Cup of the Kings of France and England (Case 16), a cup of solid gold decorated in red, blue, brown

and green enamels with scenes from the life of St Agnes. Although it came to light only in the late nineteenth century, this is one of the best documented of medieval objects and can be traced back through James I, Elizabeth I, Henry VIII and John, Duke of Bedford and Regent of France, to Charles VI of France, to whom it was given in 1391 by the Duc de Berry, one of the greatest patrons of the age. It may have been intended originally as a birthday present for Charles V, who was born on St Agnes day but died in 1381 before the cup had been completed.

Despite its conspicuous use of religious iconography, the Royal Gold Cup does not seem to have had any liturgical function. Rather it was probably an item *de luxe*, intended for the royal table. A further indication of the wealth and luxury to which the great courts of Europe were accustomed in the later Middle Ages is provided by the Lacock Cup, which, although still used on occasion as a communion cup at the parish church of Lacock in Wiltshire, was similarly designed for secular purposes when it was made towards the middle years of the fifteenth century. Not even the arms and armour of the age were excluded from this love of ostentation, since there are among them certain purely ceremonial objects which were created by craftsmen of the highest calibre. One example is the Sword of State (displayed on the wall next to Case 17), a large sword carried before the Prince of Wales on

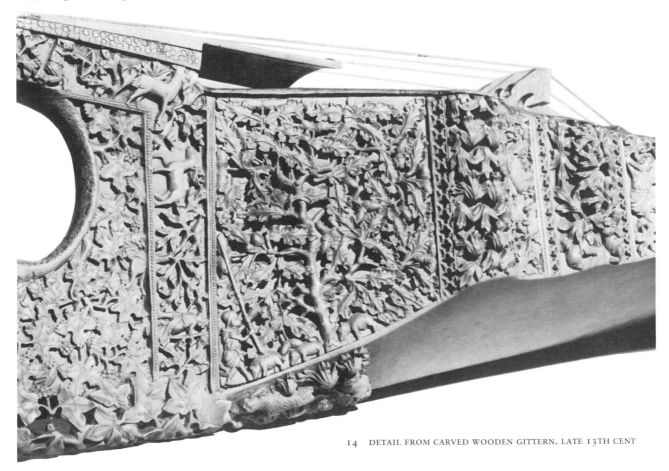

14   DETAIL FROM CARVED WOODEN GITTERN. LATE 13TH CENT

formal occasions. This may have been made for Edward, son of Edward IV and one of the Princes in the Tower, or for his namesake, the son of Richard III, both of whom died in their youth. Another example is the fifteenth-century Flemish Shield of Parade, which was intended for display at a tournament and is the only one of its kind to survive (Case 17). This is painted with the figures of a lady and a knight, behind whom stands the figure of Death and above whose head is a scroll with the words '*Vous ou la mort*' (You or death). This illustration of the knight's choice evokes in a characteristic way the romantic, fairy-tale world of late medieval chivalry.

Great works of art represent only one aspect of the displays at the end of the Medieval Gallery. Popular religion is a theme which is treated in Case 10 through the exhibition of carved alabasters with devotional imagery, jewellery and lead pilgrim badges, while Cases 11 and 12 are given over to everyday life in the later Middle Ages; they take in aspects such as measuring instruments (Astrolabes and weights), diplomatic (seal-dies for the authentication of documents) and table utensils (knives, spoons and jugs). The Flemish Shield of Parade with its evocation of the world of Courtly Love, already enshrined for us some decades earlier by English Chaucer, presents an idealised vision. The realities of everyday life were no doubt very different.

16 SHIELD PARADED AT TOURNAMENTS. 15TH CENT

15 GOLD CUP OF THE KINGS OF FRANCE AND ENGLAND. 14TH CENT

The display of medieval pottery begins with the seventh century, when wheel-made pottery replaced hand-made pottery in England (Case 1). The earliest centres of manufacture were Ipswich and Whitby, but, from the end of the ninth century, more developed forms began to appear: the three main types were Thetford ware, St Neot's ware (Case 3) and Stamford ware (Case 2). The last was of particular importance since it was the earliest glazed ware to be produced in England, the use of glaze on pottery deriving ultimately from Mediterranean sources, perhaps by way of France. The pitcher from the Angel Inn, Oxford (Case 2) is a notable example of Stamford ware.

At the end of the twelfth or beginning of the thirteenth century, the manufacture of yellow glazed globular pitchers was replaced by tall jugs with a bright green glaze (Case 3). Medieval jugs were often decorated elaborately, as is indicated by the jug from Cannon Street, London (Case 5), with its dragons in applied slip contrasting with the brown and green glazes. Also popular were the 'face-jugs', such as those from London, Worcester (Case 5) and Cambridge (Case 6), with their amusing appearance comparable to the effect of gargoyles in medieval churches. Certain shapes derived from external sources, as is the case with the aquamanile from Ditchingham, Norfolk, which may be compared with the bronze aquamanile from the River Tyne (Case 5). Despite their appearance, these have a purely practical purpose: to be used at

17

17 MEDIEVAL POTTERY FACE-JUG

19 PAVEMENT FROM A MERCHANT'S HOUSE. LATE 15TH CENT.

table for the serving of water. The puzzle jug from Oxford was intended for entertainment, since the hollow handle leads to a false bottom emptied by the stag's mouth; the puzzle was to drink from the jug without being drenched by the subsidiary spouts

Throughout the Middle Ages, pottery continued to to be imported into England from the Continent. The pottery from Lesnes Abbey, Kent, for example, includes a fine example of polychrome pottery from south-western France, doubtless associated with the wine trade, and fragments of a tin-glazed cover from Spain, the occurrence of which was probably associated with the import of delicacies (Case 7). In Case 9 a chimney pot and roof finial show the decorative fittings that would have stood above the crested ridge-tiles and glazed roof-tiles of the medieval roof. The methods of producing medieval tiles – the decoration of the surface, the keying of the back of the tile, and the ways of stacking the tiles in the kiln – are shown in Case 10 which also includes the only known wooden stamp for decorating tiles.

Decorated medieval tiles were manufactured in England from the thirteenth to the sixteenth century. They formed part of the decoration of Gothic buildings and were used to pave cathedrals, churches and important rooms in monasteries, palaces, castles, manor-houses and merchants' houses. The earliest examples are mosaic shapes, glazed dark green or yellow in imitation of Italian marble pavements:

18 mosaic panels and borders from Rievaulx Abbey and part of a circular pattern from Byland Abbey, both Cistercian houses in Yorkshire, are displayed (Panels 12 and 13). Mosaic shapes were sometimes decorated with inlaid white clay, and the circular pavement from Henry III's chapel at Clarendon Palace, Wiltshire, is a particularly fine example of this technique (Panel 15). Beneath are the remains of the kiln in which the tiles for the pavement were fired.

The development from elaborate mosaic to squares of uniform size is demonstrated by tiles from Chertsey Abbey in Panel 19. Square tiles decorated with motifs related to those at Clarendon and Chertsey are displayed in Panel 20 which also includes heraldic tiles from the chevet at Hailes Abbey, Gloucestershire, completed in 1271.

19 Late medieval inlaid tiles of the Malvern school are shown in Panel 18, including wall tiles dated 1457–8 and a design with the date 1456 from Malvern itself. Designs from Malvern and Gloucester occur in the Canynges pavement in the centre of the room. This complete pavement probably dated from *c*. 1461 when William Canynges, a wealthy merchant who became Lord Mayor of Bristol and a Member of Parliament, is known to have entertained Edward IV in his house.

18 MOSAIC TILES FROM RIEVAULX ABBEY. 13TH CENT.

The specially designed exhibition in this Gallery (opened 1975) presents the major developments in the history of mechanical time-keeping in Europe from the Middle Ages to the beginning of this century, in so far as the clocks and watches in the Museum will allow. For this purpose, as many of the movements as is practicable have been displayed alongside their cases and many of the movements are kept going so that the actual performance of the mechanisms may be closely observed and studied. To help the non-specialist, large-scale models demonstrating the action of the main inventions have been devised and these, together with the explanatory drawings and information, enable each development in this story of the clock-maker's quest to achieve an ever greater accuracy in time-keeping to be followed step by step through the twelve main areas of the exhibition.

The display itself is divided into three distinct 'rooms', each having its own colour scheme:
Red: clocks made *before* the invention of the pendulum was introduced into clockmaking (AD 1657).
Blue: watches arranged in two sequences: one concerned with the decorative forms of the outer cases and the other concerned with the technical developments, which are, of course, independent of the story of the pendulum.
Green: clocks made *after* the introduction of the pendulum (1657) and concluding with an example of the last major invention in mechanical time-keeping, Riefler's escapement (invented in 1891).

At the beginning of the exhibition, a small area is devoted to medieval clockmaking, but because so little survives and so little is recorded – for example, neither the inventor nor the date of the first mechanical clock is known – the display concentrates on the typical weight-driven 'great' clocks (or church-tower clocks), which had probably been introduced into most of the principal cities of Western Europe by about AD 1300. The large, hour-striking iron clock, formerly at Cassiobury Park, Hertfordshire, which is kept going, illustrates the extreme simplicity of the earliest form of escapement (the mechanism for slowing down the speed at which the weights drop and evening out the spending of the power created by the weights). This earliest form of escapement has come to be known as the 'verge' escapement; indeed, it remained the only form of escapement generally used in all clocks and watches until about 1670, approximately four centuries after its first successful, but unrecorded, application by some anonymous Gothic inventor. Both in this area of the display and at the beginning of the watch display, the verge escapement is explained with drawings and a moving model.

The second area of the exhibition is a direct continuation, for all the clocks in it have verge escapements and are weight-driven but they were all made for domestic use and date from the post-medieval period, *c.* 1500–*c.* 1660. All these clocks are constructed on the same basic design, using an open 'four-poster' frame to support the mechanism. The earlier clocks are made of iron and steel, with painted decoration, whereas the later examples are of brass, with engraved ornament. The mechanisms, all of which are visible and kept going, range from the simplest alarm-clock to the elaborate carillon clock made in 1598 in London by Nicholas Vallin. More elaborate still is the finely engraved astronomical clock with moving figures which stands in the centre of this area. Made in 1589 by Isaac Habrecht of Strasbourg, probably for Pope Sixtus V, it is believed to be the earliest surviving carillon clock on this relatively small scale.

The third area is concerned with the introduction of the spring, in place of the weights, as the source of power in clockwork. The successful application of the spring was made possible by the invention of the fusee to even out the motive power of the spring and, again, neither the date nor the inventor is known; it revolutionized clockmaking, for without the necessity for

20 CARILLON CLOCK BY ISAAC HABRECHT. 1589

weights hanging down, table-clocks, instead of wall-clocks, became a practical proposition. There is evidence to show that by the middle of the fifteenth century, probably in Burgundy or Flanders, clocks were being made with a spring-driven mechanism – one of the only two known surviving examples is here exhibited, along with a working model demonstrating the method of construction.

Area 4 contains a selection of the finest sixteenth- and seventeenth-century examples of these spring-driven clocks, all constructed on the same open 'four-poster' frame principle as the contemporary weight-driven clocks (in Area 2). One example is shown completely 'stripped down', so that every part of the mechanism can be studied. All these clocks have verge escapements except for the extremely rare example with the 'cross-beat' escapement, the only successful alternative to the verge escapement discovered before the introduction of the pendulum. Jost Burgi, working in Germany, invented it about 1600 and achieved with it a remarkably high degree of accuracy for a time standard uncontrolled by a pendulum. In this display, the inventor is represented by one of his own spring-driven posted-frame clocks; there is also a weight-driven example made at Arnstadt about 1640 and a demonstration model.

In the next area of the exhibition, the three main aspects of the striking mechanism of a clock are explained: how the mechanism is 'released' at the correct moment; how, with the count-wheel, it then causes the correct number of blows to be struck on the bell and, finally, how the mechanism is then 'locked'. An important mid-sixteenth century astrolabic clock from Dresden with a very rare feature, a second, or subsidiary, count-wheel, is displayed in this area.

The last area of this first 'room' presents the evolution of spring-driven clocks with a totally different form of construction – the so-called 'plated' movement. Its earliest appearance occurs in the second half of the fifteenth century, but its great significance is that it freed timepieces from a static position and led to the creation of the watch. The movement is placed horizontally, with the dial – at least, at first – placed on top, and all the mechanism, except the balance-wheel, contained between the two plates. The plates are used as a basis on which to build the mechanism with the wheels pivoted in the plates themselves. Consequently, there is no frame in which the movement is suspended; the plates are the bearing surfaces for the wheels and the mechanism, which could be compressed and laid out in curved lines to utilise every fraction of space between the plates. It thus became possible to create miniature time-pieces that weighed so little that they could be carried about on the person. Because the 'plated' form has no vertical axis and because the balance-wheel would continue to operate at whatever angle the mechanism was tilted, the 'plated' movement continued to function in any irregular or unpredictable position – and so truly portable clocks and watches became a reality in the sixteenth century. The display ranges from the simplest drum-shaped time-piece to the complicated astronomical clock made in 1620 by Thomas Starck, and the spectacular automaton *nef*, or ship-clock, probably made by Hans Schlottheim for the Emperor Rudolf II in Prague about 1580–1600.

The story of the watch is told in the next area, which is designed as a separate 'room' on an intimate scale. The highly decorative outer cases are grouped according to the material used (e.g. gold, silver, rock-crystal, enamels, etc.); perhaps the most exceptional is the French gold watch set with diamonds and enamelled with coloured flowers in low relief on a black enamel ground–a rare technique attributed to Henry Toutin, of Paris (1614–83); the London-made movement is signed: 'D. Bouquet, Londini'. The technical display, consisting of twelve cases, demonstrates the major steps in the development of the watch mechanism. Various escapements are displayed, their action being demonstrated with the aid of working models. Also explained with large-scale models are such inventions as the fusee and the stackfreed (for evening out the power of the spring) and the balance-spring, which, like the pendulum in clocks, has inherent physical qualities which greatly improved the accuracy of time-keeping. Both striking and repeating mechanisms are treated in detail and two cases are devoted to the methods of winding watches without a key and of maintaining accuracy despite changes in temperature. In each case a representative selection of watch movements fitted with the particular device or escapement are displayed–and a few are kept going.

22 GOLD ENAMELLED WATCH BY BOUQUET. *c.* 1650

21 EMPEROR RUDOLF II'S SHIP-CLOCK. LATE 16TH CENT

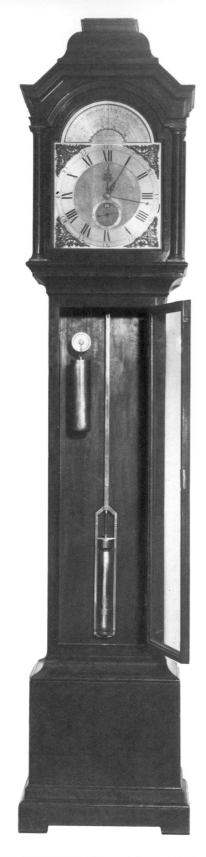

In the third 'room' can be seen the dramatic change brought to European clockmaking by Christian Huygens's brilliant discovery in 1657 of how to construct a pendulum clock. Because the pendulum is subject to the physical law of gravity, it has inherent time-keeping properties and is less dependent on variations in force within the clockwork mechanism itself. The result was the production of far more consistent timekeepers and, more obviously, of the long-case (or 'grandfather') clock. The first area, however, shows the application of the pendulum to table-clocks with spring-driven 'plated' movements, the earliest of which (about 1665) is by the most celebrated of early English makers, Edward East. In the next area, the simultaneous application of the pendulum to weight-driven clocks can be studied in the works by Quare, Fromanteel, Knibb and Tompion. The replacement of the verge by the 'anchor' escapement during the 1670s enables the arc of the pendulum to be greatly reduced and so improve the time-keeping. Then, in 1715, George Graham perfected the 'dead-beat' escapement and minimized the error even further; when combined with his temperature-compensated mercury pendulum
23 —as in his long-case equation clock (made about 1730)—a degree of accuracy was achieved in observatory clocks which was to remain unsurpassed for some 170 years.

In the field of portable clocks, much of the impetus for increased precision timekeeping arose during the eighteenth and nineteenth centuries from the need for accurate timekeepers at sea for navigational purposes. Several of these timepieces, known as 'marine chronometers', can be studied in the final area of this 'room'. Here, some of the most significant pioneering achievements are displayed, including Thomas Mudge's lever escapement (c. 1765), his constant force escapement of 1774, and John Arnold's invention of the spring detent escapement about 1780.

This final area concludes with a selection of pendulum clocks, in which are incorporated the most important developments in escapement design made in the eighteenth and nineteenth centuries. The earliest invention—the so-called 'grasshopper' escapement—was achieved by two brothers, John and James Harrison, about 1726, whilst the most far-reaching—Mudge's gravity escapement—was discovered in the middle of the eighteenth century.

Finally, in the centre of the 'room' is the 'rolling ball' clock, an ingenious invention by Sir William Congreve FRS, which was patented in 1808. Although intended
24 as a precision timekeeper, its performance was disappointing. Subsequently, domestic versions were made and are now enjoying increasing popularity. The attraction lies in observing the small ball moving in zig-zag grooves along an inclined plane which, every half minute, is tilted in the reverse direction. The ball is gradually worn down—it has been calculated that in a year the ball will travel 2,500 miles—and, eventually, has to be replaced to maintain the correct weight and speed. This particular clock, which was made by a London clockmaker named French within a few years of the granting of the patent, can still be seen in its original, elegantly designed glass and satinwood case.

23 EQUATION CLOCK BY GRAHAM. c. 1730

This room houses one collection, the finest single benefaction of Renaissance *objets d'art* ever received by the Museum. Bequeathed in 1898 by Baron Ferdinand de Rothschild, MP, on condition that the collection should be displayed in a room separate and apart from the other contents of the Museum, the Bequest comprises all the objects of art in the new smoking room at Waddesdon Manor, the house which he had built in Buckinghamshire (near Aylesbury) between 1874 and 1889, and, in accordance with his express wishes, the collection is known as 'The Waddesdon Bequest'.

Baron Ferdinand (1839–98) was the grandson of the founder of the Austrian branch of the great Frankfurt banking house of Rothschild and from his father, Baron Anselm, of Vienna, he inherited the nucleus of this great collection. At the age of 21, Baron Ferdinand settled in England and later developed an ambition to possess a cabinet of works of art of the highest quality, in the tradition of the Renaissance princes of Italy and Germany. So successful was Baron Ferdinand that the bulk of his Bequest consists of such objects as a German prince would have had in his *Schatzkammer* (or treasure-house) or in his *Kunst- und Wunderkammer* (or room of precious *objets d'art* and curiosities) and, for this reason, the Bequest, seen separately as a single entity, serves to evoke and illustrate a facet of Renaissance court-life, highlighting aspects of patronage, of ostentatious wealth and luxury, of virtuosity in craftsmanship and, even, of curiosity in the historic, the bizarre and the exotic. In Britain, the royal treasure-house of the English kings was dispersed at the time of Cromwell and the Civil War (1642–49) and, uniquely in this country, the Bequest now offers a tangible expression of a fashion in collecting which had been so favoured not only by the courts of Europe but, more modestly, by the merchant-princes of such great trading cities as Venice, Nürnberg and Augsburg.

24 CONGREVE'S 'ROLLING-BALL' CLOCK. *c.* 1810

The characteristic which unites the extraordinarily disparate elements of the Bequest is excellence of craftmanship, from the wood-carver to the glass-blower, from the painter of enamels to the damascener of iron, but above all—and dominating the Bequest—the ingenuity and skill of the goldsmith. His art in miniature can be marvelled at in the many Renaissance jewels, particularly in the hat-badges of the Conversion of St Paul (No. 171) and St George and the Dragon (No. 172), which demonstrate the combined use of repoussé work from beneath, delicate chasing on the surface of the low relief, enamelling in several colours, and setting with table-cut diamonds and other gems. The symmetrical architectural forms of some of the heavier pendants (Nos. 147–50, 153) contrast with the eccentric forms fashioned around an irregularly shaped (or 'baroque') pearl (Nos. 155, 157, 159, 188), whilst the highly imaginative use of large cabochon (or unfaceted) emeralds is strikingly demonstrated by two massive gold pendants, one in the form of a mermaid (No. 154) and the other a hippocamp or sea-monster (No. 156).Of the enamelled gold lockets in the Bequest, the most historic and the most beautiful is the 'Lyte Jewel' (No. 167), so-called because King James I of England and VI of Scotland presented it in 1610 to Thomas Lyte, of Lyte's Cary in Somersetshire, in appreciation of the pedigree he had prepared demonstrating that the royal ancestry could be traced back to the legendary founder of the British nation, Brut (or Brutus, the Trojan). Beneath the hinged cover of the locket, which has an openwork design incorporating the monogram, IR (IACOBUS REX), set with diamonds, was the king's 'picture', a particularly fine portrait of James I by the great English miniaturist Nicholas Hilliard (1547–1619); this miniature is now displayed separately. The Renaissance goldsmith's ability to work on a minute scale can be studied in the many other types of pendants, in the finger rings (Nos. 195–200), the enamelled handles of knives, spoons and forks (Nos. 201–15), and in the elaborate mounts for the vessels carved from rock crystal, agate, heliotrope, jade and other hard-stones.

Similarly, there are cups of rare stones such as chalcedony and onyx (Nos. 119 and 121), mounted in silver and gilded to look like gold. In each case a highly individual object has been created, none more so than the quartz cup (No. 122), which an Antwerp goldsmith has fashioned in the Mannerist idiom popularized by contemporary artists, such as Erasmus Hornick. The fascination of the bizarre led to the silver-smith making elaborate cups with ostrich egg-shells, nautilus-shells, even a nut from the Seychelles in the Indian Ocean and a horn that was thought to be the claw of a griffin (Nos. 102, 111–17, 125).

The Renaissance silver plate, which forms so impressive a part of the Bequest, is mostly German, though two very finely chased ewers and basins in the most developed Mannerist style (Nos. 89, 90 and 93, 94) were made in Antwerp about the middle of the sixteenth century. The ingenious variety of shapes and designs, even in the many versions of the 'standing cup and cover', is richly conveyed in the Bequest, which also contains a number of those rare table ornaments

25 THE LYTE JEWEL. PRESENTED BY JAMES I TO THOMAS LYTE IN 1610

fashioned in the form of animals and human figures (Nos. 131–42) – one of them, the huntsman by Christoff Ritter, of Nürnberg, still possesses its original clockwork mechanism to propel it along the table (No. 134). Perhaps the most remarkable survival is the complete set of twelve tazze (or wide shallow cups on stems), each elegantly embossed and boldly chased with allegorical figures (No. 97); they are the work of Paul Hübner, one of Augsburg's leading goldsmiths in the years around 1600.

In few fields of the decorative arts did the Renaissance prince show more interest than in the decoration of his arms and armour. This branch of the metalworker's craft, the art of damascening in gold and silver on iron, is illustrated with a few choice pieces, of which the finest is unquestionably the shield signed by Giorgio Ghisi of Mantua, and dated 1554 (No. 5). Only a close inspection of the frames surrounding the five main figures will reveal the extent of this craftsman's *finesse*, for they are crammed with minute scenes, some from the stories of the Trojan War (like the Trojan Horse), some from ancient mythology, and others, more light-hearted, from the repertoire of early Italian Mannerist ornament.

At Limoges, in France, the art of enamelling on copper was given a new dimension in the sixteenth century with the development of the 'painted enamel'. The Bequest contains some of the best products of the leading enamellers – the Pénicaud family, Leonard Limousin, Pierre Raymond, Suzanne Court, Jean Courtois and others – and perhaps the finest piece is the casket (No. 23) decorated with the five plaques of the Sibyls delicately painted in *grisaille* (a greyish-white monochrome on a black ground) attributed to Jean Poillevé, because, unlike most of these caskets, it has survived with its original silver-gilt mounts and enamelled finials.

Enamelling on glass was very popular in sixteenth-century Venice and the fashion spread north of the Alps to Germany, Bohemia and the Low Countries. Around the year 1500 a very curious kind of glass, an opaque pale-blue glass, was produced in Venice, and of the three examples known to have survived the goblet in the Bequest (No. 55) is the finest, both in form and in the masterly handling of the enamel painting in the roundels. Among the other rare glasses in the Bequest is an example of German enamelling dated 1518 (No. 59).

A related technique is polychrome painting on tin-glazed pottery, which in sixteenth-century Italy was known as 'maiolica'. The Bequest contains several spectacular examples, of which the most interesting are the two large vases (No. 61), made in Orazio Fontana's workshop in Urbino during the middle of the sixteenth century and then, some two hundred years later, superbly mounted in ormolu (gilt-bronze) in Paris, where they were purchased in 1765–6 by that great English writer and connoisseur, Horace Walpole, for his famous collection at Strawberry Hill, near London.

For a few decades around the end of the fifteenth and the beginning of the sixteenth century, microscopic sculptural wood-carving in three dimensions was

26 SILVER-GILT NAUTILUS-SHELL CUP. 1555

27 SHIELD OF DAMASCENED IRON. 1554

being produced in the southern Netherlands. Not very many examples have survived but each is a *tour de force*, the most daring of which is probably the miniature tabernacle in the Bequest (No. 233): the uppermost part opens in four petals, each with a scene in relief, to reveal the Virgin and Child, which, by means of a ratchet, is raised and lowered; similarly, the centre and lower sections are designed to be taken apart and each opens up to reveal numerous minutely carved scenes from the Passion with Latin inscriptions. The Bequest is particularly rich in these wonderful carvings (Nos. 232–41), four of which are beads from different rosaries and, unexpectedly, there is some evidence to show that such beads were being made in Kent, in south-east England, before the Flemish carvers attained their resounding successes in this field.

At about the same time, Conrad Meit, a gifted German Renaissance sculptor from Worms, was working at the court of Margaret of Austria, Regent of the Netherlands, and is thought to be the author of the two small, but strikingly fine, portrait busts, carved in wood in the round (No. 261). Other portraits, carved in low relief in wood or honestone (Nos. 242–58), are closely related to contemporary medals and some of them may have been made as models by the German medallists.

Two small wood sculptures of high artistic quality stand out from the rest: the Hercules and Antaeus (No. 262), which is by an unknown German artist of the mid-seventeenth century, and the seated Omphale (No. 263), which has been attributed to Artus Quellinus the Elder (1609–68), while he was working in Amsterdam in the middle of the century.

Finally, the Bequest contains, like every ancient princely *Schatzkammer,* some historic pieces of pre-Renaissance date. There are four beautiful Greek bronze heads in high relief (Nos. 1 and 2), an outstandingly fine medieval Limoges *châsse* (or reliquary casket), decorated with champlevé enamelling on copper depicting the Martyrdom of Ste Valérie, the patron saint of the city of Limoges, which was made about AD 1180 (No. 19), an Islamic mosque lamp of enamelled glass (No. 54) made in Syria in the fourteenth century, and a pair of elaborate late Gothic silver book-covers from St Stephen's in Bamberg (Nos. 87 and 88). But most precious of all, the Bequest contains the gold enamelled reliquary of the Holy Thorn (No. 68), which was made in France about 1400. The French goldsmith has created the scene of the Last Judgement with the Resurrection of the Dead below and God the Father at the apex; in the very centre, where Christ appears with the Virgin and St John and the Twelve Apostles, he has set the Holy Thorn upright in a large cabochon sapphire. This golden shrine, studded with gems and adorned with pearls, was made for Jean, Duc de Berry, that powerful French prince who was undoubtedly one of the greatest patrons of the arts in pre-Renaissance France.

28 ROSARY BEAD OF CARVED WOOD. EARLY 16TH CENT

30 TUDOR SILVER-GILT TAZZA

The present temporary arrangement allows for no more than a selection of the post-medieval collections to be shown, divided between two galleries.

In the Corridor (Room 46) the material is arranged chronologically, with the English material on the right-hand side and the Continental on the left. The English material commences with the reign of Henry VIII (1509–47) and includes the King's astrolabe, made by Sebastian Le Seney, a maker from Normandy, serving the King at eight pence a day. A remarkable pair of silver-gilt candle-snuffers bear the enamelled arms of the King and of Cardinal Bainbridge, Archbishop of York, who from 1509 was Henry VIII's ambassador in Rome where he was poisoned in 1514. To this period belong those distinctive drinking-vessels known as 'mazers' (shallow wooden bowls with wide silver rims and decorative silver bosses in the centre of the interior); perhaps the most interesting is the Rochester Mazer, made in London in 1532 and given by Brother Robert Peckham to the Priory at Rochester —only two years later his name appears in a document acknowledging Henry VIII's supremacy of the Church in England. Of the few pieces of English secular plate to have survived from this period, none is more 30 impressive than the two Rochester Tazze, one of which still has its cover. Made in London between 1528 and 1533, these pieces, which have been preserved in Rochester Cathedral, are probably all that survive from a grand set of twelve or more executed in the Renaissance style. The introduction of the Continental Mannerist style into England is illustrated by the silver-gilt 'Wyndham Ewer', made in London in 1554–5, the earliest piece known to survive of English goldsmith's work in this style. The accompanying basin was made to match the ewer in 1607–8 by Symon Owen, a prominent London goldsmith.

Among the outstanding pieces of Continental silver of this period are the German covered cup with elaborate nielloed decoration, mainly consisting of scenes of nude putti, and the French silver-gilt *nef* (or ship) table ornament, which are displayed with masterpieces of metalwork and enamelling like the Entomb- 31 ment Triptych by Nardon Pénicaud, of Limoges (*c*. 1510–20). Rare vessels of glass, pottery and Chinese porcelain were often mounted in silver by goldsmiths, both on the Continent and in England during the reigns of Edward VI (1547–53) and Queen Elizabeth I (1558–1603). Of these, Lord Burghley's Tankard is probably the most unexpected and graceful; made of glass, probably in Jacopo Verzelini's newly established glass-house about 1575, its silver-gilt mounts bear the enamelled coat of arms of the Queen's Chief Minister and Lord High Treasurer. The earliest surviving piece of English gold plate, the acorn cup from Stapleford Church, Leicestershire, is dated *c*. 1610–20 but the maker is unknown. The high quality of the workmanship of Continental goldsmiths, e.g. the potstone tankard by Marx Kornblum, of Vienna (died 1591), and the Trinity panel in low relief by the baroque goldsmith, Johann Andreas Thelott of Augsburg (died 1734), can be seen alongside objects made of other materials, such as enamels, ivory carvings and other small-scale sculpture, like the terracotta torso, which Michelangelo made as a preparatory sketch or model for one of the life-size statues intended for the tomb of Pope Julius II, probably about 1515–20.

The French Huguenot refugee goldsmiths, who during the last quarter of the seventeenth century settled in England with some encouragement from Charles II and from Mary II and William III, aroused strong opposition from the Goldsmiths' Company in London, but the excellence of their work in contrast with most 32 of the contemporary English silver can be readily appreciated in the Peter Wilding Bequest, which contains the first Duke of Devonshire's ewer and basin by Pierre Harache (1697) and two ambitious early works by Paul de Lamerie, a covered cup and an armorial dish, both made for the Rt. Hon. George Treby in 1723.

The impact of this Huguenot injection was gradually assimilated and its influence on English goldsmiths is illustrated by the set of silver-gilt communion plate on the opposite side of the Corridor, which was made by the London goldsmith Gabriel Sleath for presentation in 1731 by the Duke of Bedford to Hawksmoor's new church of St George's, Bloomsbury. It is on loan from the Rector and Churchwardens.

The display of English craftsmanship in the adjoin-

29 GOLD RELIQUARY OF THE HOLY THORN. EARLY 15TH CENT

ing cases shows the important and highly original contributions made by the English in the second half of the seventeenth century to glassmaking – lead-glass invented about 1675 by George Ravenscroft – and ceramics – the stoneware and proto-porcelain figures of John Dwight from about 1670: the combination of technical skill and sculptural merit in the life-size bust of Prince Rupert made at Dwight's pottery at Fulham about 1675 is unmatched on the Continent at this date. These cases also contain a number of examples of seventeenth- and eighteenth-century English 'delft-ware' (tin-glazed earthenware), many of which reveal strong Dutch influence: the potters were often immigrants from the Netherlands.

In the central domed area of the Corridor hangs a Swiss bird-cage clock of the late eighteenth century, and in the smaller showcases around the walls are gathered small-scale objects, jewellery, enamels, cameos and gems, gold boxes and scent bottles, etuis and especially items which are associated with famous and historical events or people, such as the magical and astrological items used by Dr John Dee, the mathematician, who on several occasions was consulted by Queen Elizabeth I, and the gold box bequeathed by the Emperor Napoleon I to Lady Holland. There is also a choice display of scientific instruments of the sixteenth to eighteenth centuries. The Department holds an outstanding collection of items reflecting the history of British heraldry, among which is one of the oldest sets in existence of the insignia of the Order of the Garter, made in 1628 for William Compton, 1st Earl of Northampton.

A few particularly fine medals (from the Department of Coins and Medals) have been included in the display in the Corridor. Despite the fact that commemorative pieces, coin-like in appearance, had been

32 SILVER-GILT EWER AND BASIN BY PIERRE HARACHE. 1697

31 PAINTED ENAMEL TRIPTYCH. c. 1510

produced in antiquity and in late fourteenth-century Italy, medallic art may be said to have begun in 1438 with Pisanello's portrait medal of John VIII Palaeologus. This piece was cast to commemorate the visit to Italy of one of the last Byzantine emperors, and it at once established the classic form of the medal as a work of art. The portrait was balanced by a reverse which could give further expression to the character of the person depicted, often by means of somewhat obscure symbolism. In the sixteenth century outstanding artists engaged in the development of the medal included Jacopo da Trezzo and Leone Leoni, both of whom are represented in the exhibition.

Northern Europe also made characteristic contributions to medallic art. In Germany there were artists such as Dürer and Hans Reinhardt, whose extraordinary and meticulously wrought medal of the Trinity executed in 1544 is exhibited.

The medal as originally conceived by Pisanello was a 34 work produced by the technique of casting and usually destined for very limited distribution in private circles. During the sixteenth century and later, increasing recourse was made to the production of medals by die-striking so that they took on more the appearance of a large coin, which could be made in quantity and widely circulated. Almost every country has produced such medals, of historical, commemorative and sometimes propagandist character.

Room 47 is devoted mainly to post-medieval ceramics and glass, and to the Hull Grundy collection of jewellery. Around the perimeter of the room is a display of ceramics arranged according to their method of manufacture. On the left-hand side of the entrance simple lead-glazed pottery is displayed together with slip-decorated earthenware. The techniques of decoration include moulding, incising, painting and transfer-printing as well as the use of a range of coloured glazes and liquid clay (slip). The large dish bearing the Arms of Charles II and signed by Thomas Toft is a late seventeenth-century example of this Staffordshire potter's skill in the use of trailed slips.

In the next case are examples of tin-glazed earthenwares from all over Europe. The technique, which creates a plain white surface like an artist's canvas, was developed in Spain under Islamic influence. The earliest pieces, which were made in Valencia about 1425–40, are painted in blue and decorated with gold lustre, often showing a characteristic combination of European and Islamic motifs. In Italy, where the technique was copied and elaborated from the fifteenth century, wares for ornamental use were made in many centres, such as Florence, Faenza, and Urbino.

Polychrome painting on tin-glazed pieces, especially of Biblical and mythological subjects, was practised in Italy; some had lustre decoration added: an example from the workshop of Maestro Giorgio in Gubbio is displayed. Emigrant Italian potters established workshops in France (at Lyons and Nevers), Holland and Germany. The inscribed dish made at Lyons in 1582 provides important early documentary evidence of this dissemination.

The stonewares exhibited are in the main utilitarian

33 STONEWARE BUST OF PRINCE RUPERT. c. 1670–5

rather than ornamental. Many are glazed with salt, which melts at a high temperature and coats the ware with a shiny film. Developed in Germany using rich local deposits of suitable clay from the Rhineland, where many potteries were established, such as those at Siegburg and Raeren, stoneware was fashioned into durable containers (often for wine) and was widely exported. The fine stonewares made in England by Dwight in London in the late seventeenth century have already been mentioned, but examples from Holland, Dresden and Staffordshire are also displayed.

The ability to fire a kiln to a high temperature is equally necessary for the production of porcelain. Porcelain imported from the Orient during the Middle Ages had aroused the admiration and envy of Europeans on account of its hardness and translucence. The first successful experiments made at the Medici Court in Florence (1575–87) only produced a 'soft-paste' porcelain (a glassy substance): examples of this extremely rare porcelain are displayed near the exit from the gallery. Over a century later in France soft-paste was made at Rouen and Saint-Cloud. Other factories, such as those at Vincennes and Sèvres (outside Paris), Bow and Chelsea (London) and Capodimonte (Naples, Italy), produced tablewares, ornamental pieces and also figures.

Like the Oriental porcelains, European hard-paste porcelain contained china clay and china stone. The first European to discover the formula was Johann Friedrich Böttger, who was working at the court of the Elector of Saxony in Dresden around 1710, and early examples of the first experimental period at the Meissen factory are displayed, together with products of its heyday, such as the elaborate figure-group by Kändler and Reinicke of a lady and girl pedlar. Early hard-paste porcelain from Du Paquier's factory in Vienna and from the short-lived factory established by Francesco Vezzi in Venice is represented by dated specimens of documentary significance. One of the earliest examples of English hard-paste porcelain is a coffee-can dated March 1768 and decorated with the arms of the city of Plymouth and the legend PLYMOUTH MANUFAC[Y]. This venture was the successful conclusion of some twenty years of persistent research by William Cookworthy.

A selection of European glass from the fifteenth to the eighteenth centuries illustrating various techniques of decoration is displayed beyond the porcelain. Examples of the earliest glass vessels from Venice, centre of glass-making in Europe, are included. The art of enamelling and gilding on coloured glass is illustrated by a blue goblet showing the Triumph of Venus made about 1450. Glass-making skills north of the Alps are represented by a large late-sixteenth century 'Humpen', or beaker, of Bohemian make, decorated with a lively hunting scene. Wheel-engraving on glass, developed in northern Europe in the seventeenth and eighteenth centuries, and stipple-engraving, at which the Dutch excelled, are used to decorate the goblets exhibited. Opaque-white glass was first introduced in Venice in the late fifteenth century. A rare surviving example made about 1509–10 is the two-handled vase which bears a portrait of Henry VII of England and his

badge. It may have been a diplomatic gift to the king. North of the Alps in the seventeenth and eighteenth centuries opaque-white glass was often gilded and enamelled in imitation of porcelain. The plate on exhibition, which is painted in red with a view of Venice copied from an etching, is a rare piece of this type. It was made at Miotti's glasshouse in Murano (Venice) as part of a set of twenty-four ordered by Horace Walpole in 1741 during his 'Grand Tour' as worthy souvenirs of his stay in Venice.

Room 47 also contains the magnificent gift of over one thousand pieces of jewellery which Professor and Mrs Hull Grundy made to the British Museum in 1978. This collection is rich with jewellery of the eighteenth, nineteenth and twentieth centuries. Examples include the English mid-eighteenth-century rock-crystal and painted enamel Badge of the Anti-Gallican Society, splendid late seventeenth- and early eighteenth-century gold piqué and tortoiseshell boxes and French and English coloured gems and pastes set in jewellery of baroque and rococo design.

34 JOHN PALEOLOGUS MEDAL BY PISANELLO. 1438–9

[119]

An important group of nineteenth-century 'historical and archaeological revival' jewellery includes pieces with rare signatures which are key documents in the study of the relationship between archaeological discoveries and the art of the jeweller. The collection is rich, for example, with the work of the Italian craftsman, Castellani, and Italian cameo jewellery of the nineteenth century is also well represented. Among the other 'styles' of this eclectic and historicist period is the neo-Gothic jewellery, including a magnificent gold pectoral cross and chain of about 1860 designed by the English architect, William Burges.

The aesthetic cult of 'Japonisme' is particularly well-represented in the form of jewellery in coloured gold by Tiffany of New York of *c.* 1870–80 and by an exquisite cloisonné enamel locket made by the French craftsman, Alexis Falize, in the late 1860s. The finest flowering of curvilinear Art Nouveau is displayed in all its varied forms, with an emphasis on delicate craftsmanship, vegetable and female forms, gems and colourful enamel. This was the innovatory style of the 1890s and 1900s.

The collection also includes a representative display of the light, bubbly Art Deco style of the 1920s and 1930s. More 'popular' jewellery is not neglected and the collection is very broad, ranging as it does from rare jewels such as the Spanish Renaissance gold pendant of about 1640 to those examples of naturalistic ornaments which probably appealed to the majority of our Victorian ancestors.

The Department of Medieval and Later Antiquities has extended its scope to include the nineteenth and twentieth centuries. An example of this is the ecclesiastical plate designed by A. W. N. Pugin in the middle of the nineteenth century, which is on loan from St Mary's Church, Clapham, and on display in this room.

35 MEISSEN PORCELAIN GROUP. *c.* 1745

36 ENAMELLED VENETIAN GLASS GOBLET. LATE 15TH CENT

37 CLOISONNE ENAMEL LOCKET BY FALIZE. LATE 1860S

Oriental antiquities

Main floor

North
entrance

Upper levels

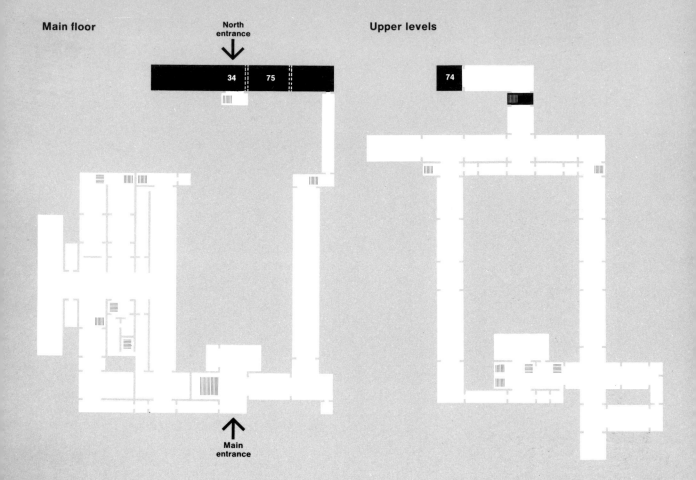

34

75

74

Main
entrance

34 Art of Islam, S & SE Asia, China & Korea

75 Art of Japan (lower gallery)

74 Oriental painting

Oriental antiquities

With the exception of the ancient civilizations of the Near East and Persia before the founding of the religion of Islam in AD 622, the Department of Oriental Antiquities covers the cultures of the whole of Asia from the Neolithic period to the nineteenth century AD. (The Palaeolithic period in Asia is the concern of the Department of Prehistoric and Romano-British Antiquities).

The Primary Galleries of the Department are Oriental Gallery I, which contains the collections from South and South-east Asia, the Lands of Islam, Central Asia, China and Korea, and Oriental Gallery III which contains the Japanese collections. Oriental Gallery II, apart from the permanent display of a small group of outstanding sculptures and paintings, is devoted to periodic exhibitions of paintings and prints mainly from Persia, India, China and Japan.

The reserve collections, both of antiquities and paintings, are available to holders of tickets of admission to the Students' Room.

The collections of the Indian subcontinent and of the countries of South-east Asia strongly influenced by Indian art and religion are exhibited in the west arm of Oriental Gallery I. In modern political terms this exhibition covers India, Pakistan, Bangladesh, Nepal, Tibet and Sri Lanka (South Asia); and Burma, Thailand, Cambodia and Indonesia (South-east Asia). The visitor is recommended to follow the arrangement in a clockwise direction.

Throughout the great period of her history from the sixth century BC to the thirteenth century AD the Indian sub-continent remained a group of separate states with shifting boundaries. Though partial attempts at political unity were brief and unsuccessful, the sub-continent, like medieval Europe, formed a cultural unit, held together by three closely inter-related religions (Hinduism, Buddhism and Jainism), a common literary language (Sanskrit) and common ideals of social organization. In art too there was a general mode of expression in which geographical and other factors distinguish three main stylistic provinces: North India, the region (including Pakistan and Bangladesh) from the Himalayas to the lesser barrier of mountains and rivers which cross India on a line roughly connecting Bombay and Calcutta; the Deccan, the high plateau from Bombay south to Mysore; and South India, the coastal plain from Madras to the tip of the peninsula, including the present states of Tamilnadu and Kerala.

Indian art, as it has survived, was almost entirely used to build, decorate and equip temples and monasteries. Since in the historical period the dead were cremated, there is no tomb furniture as in other cultures. Secular works of art are therefore rare and in the collections architectural fragments, images and ritual vessels predominate.

Prehistory of the Indian sub-continent

The Neolithic followed by the Chalcolithic cultures of the sub-continent together lasted from as early as the seventh millennium BC (at Mehrgarh in Baluchistan) to the late second millennium BC. By about 1000 BC iron technology began to grow in use and by the time of the Buddha (c. 563 BC to c. 483 BC) large walled cities were developing on the flat river plains of north India.

During the Chalcolithic period a great city culture grew up in the Indus Valley and adjacent regions. It is often called the Harappan Civilization after the name of one of the three major cities of the period (c. 2300 BC to c. 1750 BC). The others are Mohenjo-daro and Kalibangan, the latter now in the modern state of India. Cities were laid out on a regular grid pattern, often with a citadel placed separately from the lower town. Copper and bronze were worked and sculpted along with stone and shell. Numerous painted ceramic types were made, as were terracotta figures of mother goddesses and toy animals. Typical of the Harappans is their yet undeciphered system of writing usually found carved on beautiful steatite seals along with the figures of animals. Details of the origins and decay of this civilization are still obscure. Chalcolithic cultures

1 RELIQUARY. GOLD SET WITH RUBIES. AFGHANISTAN. 2ND OR 3RD CENT. AD

pottery was decorated with linear and animal designs. A particularly attractive polychrome ware from Nal seems to date from about 2500 BC.

Further east, in the basin of the River Ganges, and contemporary perhaps with the later stages of the Harappa civilization, was another quite distinct culture responsible for copper implements and weapons of unusual forms: barbed harpoons, swords with antennae hilts, strange human-shaped 'axes' and silver plates in the form of a bull's head. This so-called 'Copper Hoard Culture' is well represented.

NORTH INDIA

About 1500 BC North India was invaded by a people from South Russia related to our own European ancestors. They spoke an Aryan language, the parent of Sanskrit and the modern dialects of North India. In their religion man's relations with the gods were regulated by an elaborate system of sacrifice performed by a priestly caste, the Brahmins. This religion is called Vedic after their sacred texts, the Vedas. Slowly through the centuries this people settled in the whole of North India, intermarrying with the native population and absorbing many of its beliefs. By the sixth century BC one belief, that of reincarnation, was widespread, and with it convictions which have coloured all Indian speculation on the human condition: that a man's present state is due to his conduct in past existences and that some way must be found of release from this intolerable burden of continuous suffering. In the sixth century BC the two great teachers Buddha and Mahavira, founders of Buddhism and Jainism, preached the lonely path of non-attachment to this world and the negation of all desire. This austere doctrine could not be expected to appeal to the ordinary man and it was not long before both religions had elevated their founders to gods at whose hands release could be obtained by simple faith and devotion. The gods of the old Vedic religion survived but began to be superseded by the two great deities Siva and Vishnu and a supreme Mother Goddess who became Durga, the consort of Siva. In this new religion of Hinduism the gods were worshipped without the intervention of the Brahmin. It was a natural step in the first century AD for all the religions to render the gods more accessible to man's devotion by making images of them.

Early Buddhist Art (third century BC to first century AD)
In the third century BC North India was unified for a brief period under Asoka (about 269–232 BC), the greatest of all Indian rulers. Missionaries were despatched all over India and to Sri Lanka (Ceylon), and Buddhism entered upon its career as a world religion. Asoka proclaimed his own conversion by inscriptions carved on rocks and polished pillars – the earliest examples of writing in India – throughout his empire and beyond. The only known fragment outside India of such a pillar is exhibited. These pillars were usually associated with monastic establishments and stupas, solid hemispherical domes standing on a plinth and surrounded by a railing to form a processional path. The stupas contained relics of the Buddha or some great saint and were objects of worship. The most important early group of stupas in North India is at Sanchi (first century BC to first century AD). The figure of a dryad embracing a tree decorated one of the gateways to the processional path. Also from Sanchi is a rare group of beautifully turned relic-caskets in steatite and crystal.

The Kushan Empire (first to third centuries AD)
After the death of Asoka, North India suffered a series of foreign invasions through the one break in her land defences, the North-west Frontier Province. The first invaders were the Bactrian Greeks, descendants of Alexander the Great's colonists, who in the early second century BC occupied Afghanistan, Pakistan and part of the Panjab. Their finest heritage remains their magnificent portrait coins (see p. 131 below). They were followed about 50 BC by nomadic Scythian tribes known to the Indians as Sakas. The Sakas penetrated as far east Mathura, south of Delhi, whence comes a unique monument, the famous Mathura Lion Capital inscribed with the names of the rulers of the dynasty.

The Sakas were destroyed by a third invasion in the first century AD of another nomadic people called the Kushans, who for a time, under the great ruler Kanishka, controlled an empire from South Russia to beyond Delhi. There were two main artistic centres under the Kushans, one comprising the ancient region of Gandhara (the North-west Frontier Province) and Afghanistan, the other Mathura. In both centres the Buddha is portrayed for the first time not only in narrative scenes but as a cult figure. Moreover, in Gandhara, which lay close to the trade route across Asia from the Roman Empire to China, the powerful influence of the classical world is clear to see.

All aspects of the Buddhist art of Gandhara are represented here in one of the finest collections in the world: stone friezes to decorate stupas with vivid scenes of the main incidents of the Buddha's life and previous existences, small and large cult images in stone and stucco of the Buddha and the other benevo-

2 THE BUDDHA. BRONZE. CENTRAL INDIA. GUPTA: 5TH CENT. AD

lent deities (Bodhisattvas), a rare standing Buddha in bronze and a gold hair-pin in the form of a woman. One of the most celebrated of all objects from the Buddhist world is the cylindrical reliquary from a stupa at Bimaran; in East Afghanistan. Gold, set with rubies, it is decorated with arcaded figures of the Buddha and divine attendants. A rich series of gold Kushan coins is also exhibited.

The art of Mathura, which served the Buddhist, Jain and Hindu religions, is less well represented. Here the tradition remains predominantly Indian. The most important pieces are a group of Jain heads which show the development of the style during the second and third centuries AD and small railing pillars carved with figures of a boy piper and a dryad.

The Gupta Empire (fourth to sixth centuries AD)
During this period the whole of North India, for the second and last time in its history, was controlled by a native dynasty, the Guptas, ruling from Patna, the old capital of Asoka. This is by common consent the classical period of North Indian accomplishment in all the arts. Not only did it express with complete technical mastery an assured and integrated view of man's place in the world but also established forms of temple image on which all future development was based. All three religions were patronized.

There were two main schools of Gupta art, one centred on Sarnath, near Banaras, the other on Mathura. Sarnath created a type of Buddha image of warm and accessible spirituality which was to become the model for future Buddhist art. Two monumental figures splendidly represent this style. The Mathura style, stronger and more tense, is illustrated by one of the finest bronze figures known. A beautiful carved terracotta panel of a harpist shows a freer, more spontaneous handling. A magnificent series of Gupta gold coins, the finest to be struck in India, is also exhibited.

The break-up of the Gupta Empire in the sixth century AD led to the rise of numerous provincial dynasties. The Gupta heritage was common to all,

3 GANESA. SANDSTONE. WESTERN INDIA. 8TH CENT. AD

but developed into four parallel but distinctive regional styles: Western India, the modern states of Gujarat and Rajasthan; Central India, the modern state of Madhya Pradesh; Kashmir; and Eastern India, the modern states of Bihar and Bengal, together with Bangladesh. During this period (seventh to thirteenth centuries AD) the plan and decoration of temples and the representation of the gods increased in complexity.

Western India *(seventh to thirteenth centuries* AD)

The earliest sculpture from this region is a beautiful Mother and Child (seventh century AD), one of the mother goddesses of Hinduism. The eighth century AD is represented by a powerful image of the elephant-headed god Ganesa. A large pillar base carved with female figures (eleventh century AD) shows the ambi-

tious scale of the temples of this period. Many were built of marble which is used for a large panel of a rearing lion-headed monster (eleventh century AD). The predominant religions were Hinduism and Jainism.

Central India *(seventh to thirteenth centuries* AD)

The style of this region retained the weight and power of the Mathura school. The most notable early sculptures are a standing Siva and a magnificent large image of the Boar Incarnation of Vishnu, exhibited in Oriental Gallery II. Both images belong to the eighth century AD, together with an important group of Jain sculptures. As the style develops the cutting becomes sharper and the detail more abundant. The Candella dynasty, associated with the well-known group of erotic temples at Khajuraho, controlled most of Central

4 LOVERS. SANDSTONE. CENTRAL INDIA. CANDELLA: 10TH CENT. AD

India from the tenth century AD. In Candella style are a headless female figure typical of their smooth and summary treatment and a beautifully composed panel of two lovers. From the borders of Western India come two marble figures of Sarasvati, the Goddess of Wisdom, the larger of which was dedicated in AD 1034.

Kashmir (*seventh to thirteenth centuries* AD)

In the art of Kashmir and the surrounding region the Gupta style was modified by influences absorbed from the earlier Gandhara school and from Persia. The collection is exceptionally rich in this field and contains many important pieces. These include cast silver bowls, a group of delightfully modelled male and female heads (eighth century AD), unique examples of wood-carving (ninth century AD) and an ivory plaque delicately carved with a seated Bodhisattva with attendant adorers and musicians set in a wooden panel in the form of a miniature façade to a temple. This rare and beautiful object is perhaps the finest piece in the collection. The skill of the bronze-caster is shown in a group of elegant Hindu and Buddhist figures dating from the eighth to the eleventh centuries AD: this bronze style was carried to western Tibet where it survived into this century. Stone sculpture is also well represented, especially by the figure of a dwarf and by the large-scale head of a Boar Incarnation of Vishnu (ninth century AD).

Eastern India (*seventh to thirteenth centuries* AD)

The chief source of this style was the Gupta school of Sarnath which continued as an artistic centre after the fall of the empire. The main patrons were the Buddhist Pala dynasty (about AD 770–1050) and the Hindu Sena dynasty (about AD 1050–1220). The collection is the finest outside India and Bangladesh. The earliest pieces (eighth century AD) are a graceful Bodhisattva, closely following Sarnath models, and an exceptionally attractive dancing Ganesa. All stages of the later development of the style in its characteristic dark polished stone are shown. The superb craftsmanship and the confident handling of the large compositions save it from monotony. Bronze-casting was equally assured. Outstanding is an early image of Manasa, the Snake Goddess, with silver-inlaid eyes. A group of later bronzes can be securely dated to the middle of the eleventh century AD by inscribed dedications.

In the early thirteenth century AD North India was overrun by Muslim invaders from Afghanistan. Some artists and monks escaped to the security of Nepal and Tibet but the great Hindu and Buddhist art of North India was at an end. The Muslim Kingdoms and their successors dominated North India until the eighteenth century AD.

5 A BODHISATTVA WITH ATTENDANTS. IVORY AND WOOD. KASHMIR. 8TH CENT. AD

6 MANASA, THE SNAKE GODDESS. BRONZE INLAID WITH SILVER. EASTERN INDIA. *c.* AD 750

[125]

NEPAL AND TIBET *(ninth to nineteenth centuries* AD*)*

The early religious art of Nepal and Tibet owes everything to North India. The strongest influence on Nepal and southern Tibet came from the Pala style of Eastern India, while western Tibet followed the direction of her neighbour, Kashmir. Both countries soon expressed these influences in their own idiom, producing something if not original yet freshly interpreted.

The most creative period of Nepalese art, serving both the Buddhist and Hindu religions, lasted from the ninth to the sixteenth century AD. The collection includes a distinguished group of early bronzes, chief among which is a dignified Maitreya (the Buddhist Messiah) of the tenth century AD; three stone sculptures including a well-composed group of Siva and his consort (twelfth century AD); and a pair of bookcovers painted with the Incarnations of Vishnu in the lively but finical style familiar in Pala illustrated manuscripts (thirteenth century AD).

A small group of early bronzes (eleventh to thirteenth centuries AD) show that southern Tibetan art had already acquired a character of its own with a marked preference for inlay of gold and silver. An early painting, probably of the thirteenth century AD, perfectly preserved on a large wooden book-cover, is the finest Tibetan work of art in the collection. In the fourteenth century AD Tibet felt the impact of her powerful eastern neighbour China, and Indian and Chinese influences begin to appear side by side, most effectively in painting.

By the seventeenth century AD the arts in Nepal and Tibet were content to repeat the old formulas. Craftsmanship however remained of a high order, especially in the elaborate inlays of semi-precious stones on jewellery and musical instruments.

ORISSA *(eighth to sixteenth centuries* AD*)*

The highly original art of Orissa is separately displayed. Lying on the east coast immediately below Bengal and wide open to influences from North India, it remained stylistically an integral part of the Deccan. Also it was left to develop relatively undisturbed by the Muslim Kingdoms until the late sixteenth century AD. The three greatest centres of its art are the temple city of Bhuvanesvar, the present capital of the state, and Puri and Konarak on the coast.

The collection is superlative and covers the whole history of Orissan stone sculpture. Characteristic of the vigour and movement of the early style is an eighth-century AD sandstone panel of Durga killing the Buffalo Demon. Later, in the Jain Mother Goddess holding a child for example, the style becomes smoother but retains, especially in the treatment of the human figure and in decorative carving, a freshness and intimacy absent in the colder, more brilliant conceptions of contemporary North India. A magnificent series of sculptures in black schist illustrate the splendour achieved under the ruling Ganga dynasty in the thirteenth century AD. The huge panel of Siva and Parvati is remarkable not so much for the central pair but for the attendant groups of small flying

7 DURGA KILLING THE BUFFALO DEMON. SANDSTONE. INDIA: ORISSA. 8TH CENT. AD

figures and musicians. From about the fourteenth century AD Orissan art ceases to develop, continuing more or less faithfully to repeat the idiom of its last great period. The results, especially in miniature, are by no means negligible, as is shown by two delightful sixteenth century AD carved ivory panels of lovers.

THE DECCAN (*first to fourteenth centuries* AD)

The art of this vast stylistic province, mainly temples, rock-cut and structural, which have long been controlled archaeological sites, is thinly represented outside India. The collection contains one large group of stone sculptures unique in the West, and many isolated fine things.

In the first two centuries AD the Deccan was ruled by the Satavahana dynasty whose most famous monument was the Buddhist stupa at Amaravati near the east coast. The stupa was destroyed in the last century and the surviving sculptures are now divided between the Madras Museum and the British Museum, which possesses over a hundred large fragments. The delicate condition of these beautiful reliefs makes it necessary to preserve them in an air-conditioned vault where they may be seen on application. Their style, related to that of Sanchi, is reflected in a contemporary bronze female figure. The Deccan was not unified again until the Western Calukya dynasty (about AD 550–753), from which period comes an important male head found on the island of Elephanta in Bombay Harbour, the site of one of the greatest cave-temples in India. The related Eastern Calukya dynasty (seventh to eleventh centuries AD) is represented by a unique group of Buddhist bronzes from Buddhapad which cover in date the whole span of the dynasty's existence. From the Rashtrakuta dynasty (AD 753–973), responsible for the greatest of all Indian rock-cut temples, the Kailasanatha at Elura, comes a single stone figure of Vishnu. There is, however, a fine seated Jain figure from early in the succeeding dynasty of the Late Western Calukyas (late tenth to twelfth centuries AD), and a very important bronze group of Siva and Parvati of unusual size and quality. The minor dynasties of the southern Deccan contribute much to the collection: the western Gangas of Mysore (eighth to tenth centuries AD), with three famous bronzes of a seated Jain figure, a Sarasvati and a Siva; the Nolumbas (ninth to tenth centuries AD) with a small group of stone sculpture of distinctive quality; and the Hoysalas (twelfth to thirteenth centuries AD) with three female dancers which once adorned the pillar-capitals of their ornate temples and a splendid figure of Siva in his terrible form. In the early fourteenth century AD most of the Deccan was invaded and settled by the Muslim rulers of North India. The arrival of the Portuguese at Goa in the sixteenth century was responsible for much ivory and wood carving with Christian subjects. A provincial form of Iberian baroque, it is represented by several examples of the seventeenth and eighteenth centuries AD.

8 SARASVATI, GODDESS OF WISDOM. BRONZE.
INDIA: DECCAN. 10TH CENT. AD

9 GARUDA. GRANITE. SOUTH INDIA. PALLAVA: *c.* AD 700

Little is known of the history of South India and nothing of its art until the end of the sixth century AD. Then the important powers were the Pallavas who ruled the coastal plain from above Madras to the sacred River Kaveri, the Pandyas in the far south and the Ceras in Kerala. The Pallavas (about AD 600–900) were responsible for a remarkable series of rock-cut and structural temples mainly concentrated at their capital Kanchipuram and chief port Mamallapuram, both near Madras. Their temple architecture, though wholly original, represents a development parallel with that of the Deccan. Their sculpture, like their cave-temples, was worked in the hardest stone, gneiss and granite, and consequently needed the strong Indian sun to bring alive the slow and subtle movement from plane to plane. An excellent small group of pieces is exhibited: it includes one great masterpiece of about AD 700, a taut and imperious figure of Garuda, a being half bird, half man, on whom Vishnu usually rides. A slightly later panel of a female dancer with attendants is unfortunately carved in a weathered sandstone.

Just before AD 900 the Pallavas were superseded by the Colas, hitherto a modest kingdom on the River Kaveri, who from their famous capital of Tanjavur remained, with one brief interval, the paramount power in South India until the thirteenth century AD. The Early Cola style (about AD 880–1014) is one of the finest manifestations of the Indian plastic genius. The whole period is admirably covered by five outstanding pieces, chief among which are the Siva bursting from the Linga and the noble Siva as Teacher exhibited in Oriental Gallery II. Equally impressive with their handling of hard stone was their fluid modelling in bronze of images designed to be worshipped in the temple and also to be carried before the people in ceremonial processions. A svelte and elegant figure of Nataraja (Siva as Lord of the Dance) is probably the earliest example in bronze of this popular type of image (about AD 900). Also of importance is a group of Vishnu and his two consorts of about AD 1000. The finest bronze in the collection and one of the greatest outside India is, however, the seated Siva of about AD 950. Though the collection contains no early example of the art of the Pandyas, little of which has survived outside rock-cut temples, there are three good Cera bronzes (tenth century AD) and an impressive large male dancer in wood (thirteenth century AD). A bronze seated Vishnu from Kongunadu, the border region between the Colas and the Ceras, shows that the great dynasties had no monopoly of master craftsmen. The South Indian style in temple architecture and sculpture, virtually untouched by Muslim invasion, survived into the sixteenth century AD. Several examples of this later achievement are exhibited. Bronze-casting and the minor arts retained some quality as late as the last century.

10 SIVA VISHAPAHARANA. BRONZE. SOUTH INDIA. COLA: *c.* AD 950

SRI LANKA (*ninth to seventeenth centuries* AD)

The island of Sri Lanka (formerly Ceylon) at the
southern tip of India has strong historical connections
with North India from which both its language and
dominant religion, Buddhism, are derived. The influences, however, which helped to direct her artistic
development came from the eastern Deccan (Amaravati) and South India. There are two main periods in
the art of the island. The earlier, when the capital was
at Anuradhapura, came to an end when the militant
Cola empire occupied the northern provinces in the
early eleventh century AD. The capital was moved
southwards to Polunnaruwa which gives its name to
the second period. Both sites are rich in Buddhist
monuments and sculpture. From the earlier period
the collection has very little stone sculpture but a
notable group of Buddhist bronzes including a number of small masterpieces of the ninth to tenth centuries AD. The flowering of the Polunnaruwa period
occupied the twelfth and thirteenth centuries AD. Here
the collection contains one of the greatest works of
art from the island, indeed, from South Asia: an almost
life-size gilt-bronze figure of the Buddhist goddess
Tara. During the European domination of the coastal
region, beginning with the Portuguese in the sixteenth
century AD and followed by the Dutch and English,
the islanders distinguished themselves in the minor
arts. A major example of their work is the large ivory
casket of about AD 1600, exuberantly carved with
dancers, birds and animals.

BURMA (*eleventh to nineteenth centuries* AD)

During the first millennium AD Indian forms of society,
religion and art were carried to Burma, as to all the
countries of South-east Asia, by sea-going traders and
colonists. The golden age of Burma came in the
eleventh century AD when the Kingdom of Pagan
(AD 1044–1287) established itself on the River Irra-
waddy as the major political and artistic centre, drawing so heavily on the Buddhist style of neighbouring
Eastern India as almost to submerge its own individuality. This dependence is evident in architecture,
painting, stone sculpture, of which two delicate small
examples are exhibited, and bronze-casting, of which
the finest example outside Burma, a seated Buddha, is
in the collection. More characteristically Burmese are
the glazed terracotta plaques used to decorate brick
temples. Carved in relief they resume a tradition
popular in early Indian art of illustrating the previous
and last existences of the Buddha. After the Pagan
period Buddhist art in Burma quickly sank to a
provincial level. Images continued to be made, often
in wood with the addition of gilt lacquer and coloured
mirror glass. Most of this work is repetitive, though
occasionally something of genuine sensitivity is produced as is shown by a nineteenth century AD wooden
figure of a kneeling monk lacquered black and gilt.

11 THE BODHISATTVA TARA. GILT-BRONZE. SRI LANKA.
12TH CENT. AD

12 THE BUDDHA. BRONZE. BURMA. 12TH CENT. AD

THAILAND (*seventh to sixteenth centuries* AD)

The earliest kingdom in Thailand was that of a Mon people from lower Burma who settled in the valley of the River Menam. This kingdom and its art are known as Dvaravati (seventh to eleventh centuries AD) after the name of the capital. Indian missionary activity had already introduced Hindu art and ritual along with the prevailing Buddhism. Though the prestige of the Sarnath school of the Gupta period is evident, it did not overwhelm the Dvaravati artist: his distinctive style is represented by a powerful stone Buddha head and an attractive version in stucco. In the eleventh century AD southern Thailand became a province of the great Khmer empire of Cambodia. The heritage of the Khmer style appears in stone sculptures from Lopburi and in a group of bronze Buddha heads of a type named after the small principality of U-T'ong (thirteenth to fourteenth centuries AD).

In the thirteenth century AD the ancestors of the modern Thai entered the country from Yünnan and founded the first national dynasties with capitals at Chiengmai and then further south at Ayuthia (fourteenth to eighteenth centuries AD) near the modern Bangkok. A Thai style, inspired by the Buddhist art of Burma and Sri Lanka, was quickly evolved. Its several regional manners are well represented, especially in bronze. An example of the walking Buddha in the round illustrates an original Thai contribution to the history of the Buddha image. By the sixteenth century AD the style retains little more than its competent modelling and rather mannered charm. Alone of the countries of South and South-east Asia Thailand, in the fourteenth and fifteenth centuries AD, made a notable contribution to the art of ceramics. A group of pieces shows the fair range of their work, with a marked preference for a green glaze imitating the famous Chinese celadon.

CAMBODIA (*eighth to thirteenth centuries* AD)

Of the civilizations of South-east Asia stimulated into growth by India, that of the Khmers of Cambodia is the most original. Unfortunately this great art, which served both the Hindu and Buddhist religions, is poorly represented. From the early period comes one exquisite female stone head of the eighth century AD. At the end of the ninth century AD the capital was established at Angkor, which still remains the greatest complex of temple architecture in South-east Asia. A male stone torso of about AD 1000 shows the purity of line of the early Angkor style, while a small collection of bronzes (eleventh to twelfth centuries AD) include both Buddhist and Hindu subjects. From the end of the period (twelfth to thirteenth centuries AD) come a three-headed stone Bodhisattva with the characteristic inward expression of the style and the upper part of a crowned Buddha sheltered by a serpent, a subject of early Buddhist legend popular in South-east Asia. By the end of the thirteenth century AD the colossal building schemes seem to have exhausted the genius of the Khmer people.

INDONESIA (*eighth to fourteenth centuries* AD)

In Java by the eighth century AD Indian culture had created the setting for a civilization second only to that of the Khmers. It developed in two main periods. From about AD 750 to 950 the Sailendra dynasty covered the central Javanese plateau with Buddhist and Hindu temples. Though by no means derivative, the style of architecture and sculpture suggests contacts with South rather than North India. The largest and best known monument is the vast stupa of Borobudur. A typical Buddha head from that site, a serenely beautiful seated male figure and a magnificent male torso in the round, illustrate this great achievement in stone. The rich collection of Buddhist bronzes is no less distinguished, though here the debt to Eastern India is clear. Also of this period is the famous hoard of Buddhist images in gold and silver found at Sambas in West Borneo. After AD 950 the political centre moved to eastern Java where the arts continued to flourish until late in the fourteenth century AD. Craftsmanship was excellent and the stone sculpture was always accomplished, sometimes powerful; but the period is chiefly remarkable for the steady emergence of a native taste which, in architectural ornament and even in narrative reliefs, slowly reduced the highly plastic Indian forms to a flat linear pattern, decorative rather than expressive.

13 THE DIKPALAKA NAIRRITA. VOLCANIC STONE. JAVA. 9TH–10TH CENT. AD

[130]

INDIAN COINS

In Oriental Gallery I groups of coins are exhibited to illustrate the high achievement attained by the mints of South Asia, the lands of Islam and China.

Bactria
The Greek presence in Bactria (Afghanistan) and north-western India, due initially to the eastern conquests made by Alexander the Great, was consolidated by his successors in Bactria between about 250 and 50 BC. Though important for its interaction with Indian civilization this isolated enclave of Greek influence remains scantily attested by the archaeological record. Unique among the surviving objects are the coins, of splendid Hellenistic style, from which something of the lost history can be recovered. On these coins appear vigorous and forceful portraits – that of Demetrius whose character as a great conqueror and indeed successor of Alexander is proclaimed by the elephant skin headgear which he wears; Eukratides seen in a crested helmet, or Archebius seen in a shoulder length view brandishing a spear. The more normal portrait style where the king is simply bareheaded with a simple diadem is exemplified by Menander who, great conqueror though he too was, seems to have had some association with Buddhism in whose literature he is commemorated. A notable feature of the later coins is that they bear the inscription with the king's name and titles in Greek on the obverse and the same translated into an Indian language written in the Kharosthi script, on the reverse – a practice nowhere paralleled in the Hellenistic world and a sign of some amalgamation between the Greek and Indian cultures.

The Kushans
The tribe known from Chinese sources as the Yueh-Chih, and in India as the Kushans, originated in Central Asia and some time in the first century BC moved southwards to occupy the territories of the Indo-Greeks and their Saka successors in Bactria and north-west India. During the first and second centuries AD their empire included all of present-day Afghanistan and India eastwards as far as Benares. Their coinage, in gold and copper, is an essential source for the names and chronology of the rulers. Vima Kadphises, the first of the line to mint gold, issued some splendid double staters showing him armed with a club and seated on mountains, symbolizing his conquests on both sides of the Hindu Kush range. Kanishka, celebrated by Buddhist texts, is portrayed standing and sacrificing at a fire-altar. The coins also show the wide range of deities worshipped by the Kushans: some are Hellenistic (Helios, Hephaistos), others Iranian (Mithra, Nana) or Indian (Siva, Buddha).

The Guptas
The decline of the Kushans coincided with the rise to power in the east of the Guptas, originally lords of a little principality in Bihar or Uttar Pradesh. The first paramount ruler, Chandra Gupta I (AD 319–350), may have issued their earliest gold coins, showing the full-length figures of the king and his queen facing each other. His successors, who extended their domains as far west as Kashmir, have bequeathed us a magnificent series in gold showing the king in various poses: standing bow in hand, playing the lyre, riding a horse, and hunting the lion or the rhinoceros. Samudra Gupta (AD 350–370) commemorates his revival of the Vedic horse-sacrifice by the type of a horse before an altar. The reverse of the coins takes up the popular Kushan type of a seated goddess, now depicted as Lakshmi on a lotus or Durga on a lion. The legends are in Sanskrit, using the Brahmi script.

14 DEMETRIUS. TETRADRACHM

15 ARCHEBIUS. TETRADRACHM

16 VIMA KADPHISES. GOLD COIN

17 SAMUDRA GUPTA. GOLD COIN

18 SAMUDRA GUPTA. GOLD COIN

THE LANDS OF ISLAM

The Islamic collections are exhibited in the west end of Oriental Gallery I. The lands of Islam represented in the exhibition are, in modern political terms, Egypt, Syria, Lebanon, Turkey, Iraq, Iran, Afghanistan, the Soviet Republics of Central Asia, Pakistan and India. The visitor is recommended to follow the arrangement in a clockwise direction.

The religion of Islam was founded by the Prophet Muhammad, who was born at Mecca in western Arabia about AD 570. His flight (Arabic, *hijra*) to Medina in AD 622 marks the beginning of the Islamic era. His revelations from God in the Arabic language were eventually written down to form the Quran. Its central ideas are the Unity and Omnipotence of God (Arabic, *Allah*) and the Day of Judgment when the righteous will be rewarded with the blessings of Paradise and the unrighteous subjected to the torments of Hell. Man's duty is submission to the Divine Will (Arabic, *islam*); and the righteous man is he who submits (Arabic, *muslim*). Those countries in which the Islamic religion came to prevail constituted the *Dar al-Islam*, 'the World of Islam'. Its peoples, governed by Muslim rulers, worshipped in the Arabic language and were subject to Islamic law which regulated each and every aspect of their lives. However much they differed in race and language, Islam gave them a common purpose and way of life so that in the course of centuries a distinctive Islamic culture was created.

The Muslim patron demanded from his artists superlative craftsmanship and design in the objects of everyday use, and it is in the forms and decoration of pottery, glass and inlaid metalwork that Islam excelled. The purely Arab contribution was a script whose remarkable dignity and flexibility was exploited in all forms of art. The Islamic theologians officially condemned the representation of living creatures in art. Partly because of this condemnation (which, however, was often disregarded), the Muslim artist was mainly preoccupied with decoration. The most typical motif which he developed was the arabesque, a continuous stem with leaves at regular intervals and convoluted in an infinite variety of forms.

In the first bay on the left are three examples of Arabic writing; a stone sarcophagus of AD 991, a gravestone of AD 858 and a building dedication of AD 1084, all inscribed in the Kufic script, reserved in the early centuries of Islam for the Quran and for monumental inscriptions.

Pre-Islamic and early Islamic period

On his death in AD 632, the Prophet was succeeded as leader of the Islamic community by the Caliph (Arabic, *khalifa*, 'successor'). Under the first four caliphs who were elected by the community and the caliphs of the Umayyad dynasty (AD 661–749) the Arabs conquered Egypt, Syria, north Africa, Spain, Mesopotamia, Persia, Transoxiana and Sind. The Umayyad caliphs ruled this great empire from Damascus in Syria. Having little artistic tradition of their own, the Arab conquerors employed their subject builders and craftsmen who continued to work in their accustomed style, either the Greco-Roman tradition of Syria or the Sassanian tradition of Persia. The turquoise glazed vase of the Umayyad period from Mesopotamia follows the style and technique of the green glazed amphora of the late Parthian period (second to third centuries AD); and the fine silver-gilt dish decorated in relief follows the conventions of Sassanian Persia.

The Umayyads were succeeded by the Abbasid caliphs (AD 749–1258) who created Baghdad in Mesopotamia as their seat of government. Abbasid power and artistic patronage was greatest in the ninth century AD. The high-fired stonewares of China were imported to Mesopotamia and imitated by native potters who simulated the white glaze of the Chinese original by applying an opaque white tin glaze to the surface of their pottery vessels. The small dish with foliate rim is a close copy of a T'ang original. The potters also decorated the plain tin glaze in cobalt and green as on the fine vase with loop handles. Their greatest technical achievement was painting in a metallic lustre on the tin glaze; some examples combine two or more shades of lustre. The fragments of lustred tiles and frescoed wall decoration were found at Samarra which replaced Baghdad as the capital from AD 836 to 892.

19 EWER. BRASS ENGRAVED AND INLAID WITH COPPER, SILVER AND GOLD. NORTH MESOPOTAMIA: MOSUL. AD 1232–3

20 PILGRIM FLASK. GLASS GILDED AND ENAMELLED. SYRIA. AD 1250–60

PERSIA (*ninth to tenth centuries* AD)

In the ninth and tenth centuries AD Persian dynasties independent of the Caliph in Baghdad were established, such as that of the Samanids in eastern Persia and Transoxiana (AD 874–999). Their pottery, painted in coloured slip under a transparent lead glaze, is among the most attractive of Islamic wares. The finest are painted with Kufic inscriptions, others with stylized flowers, birds or human figures and, in one example, with 'eyes' possibly inspired by the tail feathers of the peacock. The shallow bowl with incised designs under a glaze stained with yellow, brown, aubergine and green splashes is another ware produced by the Samanid potters as well as by those of Mesopotamia.

Early Islamic glass

In Persia, Mesopotamia, Syria and Egypt the Muslims inherited an ancient tradition of glass-making. The most prized glasses were those carved in relief such as the magnificent beaker carved in relief with an eagle flanked by a lion and a griffon. A small bowl from Mesopotamia is a rare example of mosaic glass, an ancient technique revived by the glass-makers of Mesopotamia in the ninth century AD. There are also examples of glass vessels in which the decoration was obtained by blowing the molten glass into a mould.

EGYPT (*ninth to twelfth centuries* AD)

After the conquest, Egypt was ruled by governors in the name of the Caliph; but from the ninth century AD, by independent sovereigns. In AD 969 the country was conquered by the Fatimids, heterodox Muslims claiming descent from the Prophet and styling themselves Caliph. Their capital, the city of Qahira (Cairo), was founded in the same year. The treasures of the caliphs' palaces were described by contemporaries who singled out for praise the rock crystal carvings. The small cylindrical bottle carved with an Arabic benediction in Kufic script found its way to Europe where it was mounted in silver as a reliquary. In Fatimid Egypt lustre decoration was applied to glass as well as pottery, such as the two glass bowls painted in a brown metallic lustre.

PERSIA (*eleventh to thirteenth centuries* AD)

In the eleventh century AD Persia was invaded by the Seljuq Turks, nomads from Central Asia, who established their rule over the greater part of Persia, Mesopotamia, Syria and Asia Minor. The Seljuq rulers were zealous Muslims. Under their patronage a particular style of art and architecture developed and was continued under their successors, the Atabegs in Persia, Mesopotamia and Syria, and the Seljuq Sultans of Rum in Asia Minor. In the twelfth century AD the Persian potters developed a pottery clay which allowed more refined handling. At first they used the technique of decorating in slip under a colourless glaze. At the end of the century they discovered the technique of underglaze painting. Examples of pottery painted in underglaze black and blue come from

21 ASTROLABE. BRASS ENGRAVED AND INLAID WITH COPPER AND SILVER. MADE IN CAIRO BY 'ABD AL-KARIM. AD 1235–6

22 DISH. POTTERY. TURKEY: IZNIK. AD 1540–50

Kashan, an important pottery and tile-making centre from the thirteenth century AD onwards. A greater range of colours was made possible by applying enamels to the glazed surface of the vessel in a second firing. Examples of this ware are painted with scenes of the court and the hunt, as well as fabulous creatures such as the human-headed bird and quadruped. Lustre painted wares were produced both at Kashan and at Rayy near Teheran.

In the twelfth century AD the city of Herat was famous for its inlaid bronze and brass vessels. Outstanding examples of this metalwork are a splendid ewer with fluted sides inlaid in silver with the signs of the zodiac and a beautiful covered bowl decorated with astrological symbols.

MESOPOTAMIA (thirteenth century AD)

In the first quarter of the thirteenth century AD Persia was devastated by Mongol invaders. Many of the metalworkers of Herat found asylum at the court of the Atabek Badr al-din Lu'lu' at Mosul in northern Mesopotamia (AD 1218–59). The inlaid metalwork of the Mosul craftsmen is without equal in the Islamic world. The most important piece is the ewer with inlays of copper, silver and gold made at Mosul in AD 1232 by the Mosul artist Shuja' ibn Man'a. Other pieces by artists of Mosul origin are the unique prognostication instrument made by Muhammad ibn Khutlukh in AD 1241 and a celestial globe engraved with the figures of the constellations, the work of a Mosul astronomer, Muhammad ibn Hilal, who completed it in AD 1274.

SYRIA AND EGYPT (twelfth to thirteenth centuries AD)

The Fatimids were succeeded in Egypt by the Ayyubids (AD 1169–1250) who added Syria to their domains. In Syria, the glass-makers had already learned to gild glass. The fragmentary flask with gilded decoration was made for the predecessor of the Ayyubids in Syria, the Atabek Imad al-din Zangi. In the thirteenth century AD enamelled decoration was combined with gilding. A superb example is the pilgrim flask painted with horsemen and musicians on the sides and arabesques on the front. At Raqqa on the Euphrates lustre and underglaze painted wares were being produced at the end of the twelfth and beginning of the thirteenth century AD. The lustre wares have a distinctive chocolate brown lustre tone. The large storage jar decorated with a Kufic inscription in relief and painted in dark blue and turquoise is of exceptional quality. The Syrian potters also practised the earlier technique of incising designs in white slip under a transparent glaze stained with colours: such as the beautiful rendering of a mounted archer drawing his bow, on a bowl found near Aleppo.

The brass astrolabe with silver and copper inlays was made in Cairo by a Cairene artist 'Abd al-Karim in AD 1235–36. This superb instrument is the earliest known piece of inlaid metalwork produced in Egypt. The astrolabe was used for establishing the position of the observer in relation to the fixed stars, for telling the time and for measuring heights and distances.

PERSIA (fourteenth century AD)

By the middle of the thirteenth century AD Persia and Mesopotamia were joined with Central Asia and China under the rule of the Mongol Great Khan. Political union was accompanied by trading relations between west and east Asia and this led to an exchange of ideas which enriched the arts of Persia. Under the Mongol dynasty of the Ilkhans (AD 1245–1349) there was renewed activity in pottery and metalwork. Techniques remained the same but the style of decoration changed. Flowers and leaves were rendered more naturalistically and certain Chinese motifs were introduced, such as the lotus and phoenix, as in the wares made at Sultanabad in western Persia.

SYRIA AND EGYPT (fourteenth & fifteenth centuries AD)

In AD 1250 the Ayyubids were succeeded by the Mamluks (AD 1250–1517). Inscriptions containing royal titles and executed in a large cursive script known as *thulth* are a prominent feature of Mamluk inlaid metalwork: such as on the great brass cistern made for the Mamluk Sultan Muhammad ibn Qala'un (AD 1293–1340). The Mamluks granted heraldic devices to high officers of state as badges of office. The fine mirror bears an inscription in the name of the wife of a high officer whose blazon, a writing box, indicates that he was probably a chancery official.

The finest gilded and enamelled glass was produced in Syria. The six mosque lamps were all made for the Sultan or his officers as gifts to religious buildings.

PERSIA (fifteenth to seventeenth centuries AD)

The invasion of Persia by Timur, known in the West as Tamerlane, at the end of the fourteenth century AD, was only a temporary setback to Persian civilization thanks to his successors who were enlightened patrons of the arts. The three vessels of dark green jade may have been made at Samarqand, the seat of Timur's grandson, Ulugh Beg (AD 1409–47), who was an enthusiastic collector of jade carvings. Of these, the vase subsequently passed to Jahangir, Mughal emperor of India (AD 1605–28) and a descendant of Timur, who recorded his ownership in an engraved inscription. The form of this vase is related to the brass lidded jugs inlaid in gold and silver which were probably made at Herat.

With the collapse of the Timurid empire at the close of the fifteenth century AD Persia came under the rule of the Safavids (AD 1502–1736). Safavid art was a development of Timurid art. The brass jugs of the early sixteenth century AD are close in form and style to those of the fifteenth century AD. The armourers and swordsmiths of the Safavid period were famous. The superb helmet and armpiece of steel, carved and inlaid with gold, bear dedicatory inscriptions to the greatest of the Safavid dynasty, Shah Abbas I (AD 1588–1629). Two sabres, one signed by a swordsmith of Isfahan, are notable examples of the pattern-welded steel blade. The great astrolabe made in AD 1712 for the last of the Safavid rulers, Shah Sultan Husain

(AD 1694–1722), is a superb example of the high quality achieved by the Safavid instrument makers.

Persian pottery of the seventeenth century AD compares in quality with that of the earlier periods. The large bowl decorated in underglaze blue and black with phoenixes and flying cranes is inspired by the Chinese style. The turbaned head of a youth painted on a large dish is a typical invention of contemporary Safavid painting. The vase decorated in white slip on a soft grey ground, and the base of a *kalyan* (tobacco pipe) painted in polychrome, are examples of other wares.

The political turmoil after the fall of the Safavids was ended by the Qajar dynasty (AD 1795–1924) which brought about a regeneration of Persia in the nineteenth century. In the portrait of two Persian youths painted in oils on canvas, the painter was employing a technique and style borrowed from Europe.

TURKEY *(sixteenth to eighteenth centuries AD)*

In the sixteenth century AD Turkey was the centre of a powerful empire under the rule of the Ottoman sultans. The pointed steel helmet and breastplate are reminders of Turkey's military prowess at this time. The finely patterned steel sabre blade was made for Sultan Sulayman the Magnificent (AD 1520–66).

The Museum has an unrivalled collection of the Turkish pottery produced at Iznik in Asia Minor. The large bowl with blue and white decoration in Chinese taste on the outside and with arabesques on the inside is one the earliest products. The dish
22 painted in two shades of blue, aubergine and green shows the greater colour range achieved in the second quarter of the sixteenth century AD. The mosque lamp was made at the order of Sulayman the Magnificent in AD 1549 for the Dome of the Rock at Jerusalem. In the second half of the sixteenth century AD the characteristic colour scheme consists of tomato red, sea green, turquoise, cobalt blue and, more rarely, coral pink.

MUGHAL INDIA *(sixteenth to eighteenth centuries AD)*

The Mughal empire was founded by Babur (AD 1526–30), a descendant of Timur, and by the seventeenth century AD included North India and the greater part of the Deccan. Unlike the other Islamic countries, the majority of its people were not Muslim, but thanks to the wisdom of its rulers Mughal society was a fusion of Muslim and Hindu culture.

The emperor Jahangir (AD 1605–28) is known to have patronized jade carvers. To this period belongs the magnificent terrapin or tortoise carved from a great block of jade, sea green with greyish striations. The beautiful jade vessel carved in the form of a split gourd bears a dedication to Jahangir's son, the emperor Shah Jahan (AD 1628–58). Besides jade, other hardstones were carved, such as the finely sculpted tiger-head of banded agate. Mughal weapons of the sixteenth to eighteenth centuries AD include fine daggers with blades of pattern welded steel and handles of jade and rock crystal.

ISLAMIC COINS

When, in the early seventh century AD, the bedouin followers of Muhammad broke from the Arabian desert to spread the religion of Islam through the countries of the Near and Middle East, they were virtually ignorant of coinage and of its uses in a settled urban society. Their first emissions, therefore, were perforce modelled on those of the conquered Sassanian and Byzantine territories, even showing (in Syria) the standing figure of the Byzantine emperor and (in Persia) the portrait of the Sassanian king. Religious formulae in Kufic, an early form of the Arabic script, were added by degrees to the type, and
23 in the reign of 'Abd al-Malik (AD 685–705) the warlike figure of the Caliph in bedouin attire made its appearance on gold and copper coins. Further developments in iconography were halted by the same Caliph's great coinage reform in 696, which banished figure designs in obedience to the taboo on the representation of living beings. The gold *dinars* and silver *dirhams* henceforth normally carry inscriptions only, giving the Muslim profession of faith, the name of the caliph
24 (after *c.* AD 800), the mint and the date. Later independent dynasties, such as the Samanids and the Buyids in Persia, added the name of the ruling amir.

23 'ABD AL-MALIK.
DINAR

24 'ABD AL-MALIK. INSCRIPTION.
DINAR

25 SALADIN. BRONZE COIN

26 JAHANGIR. GOLD MOHUR

[135]

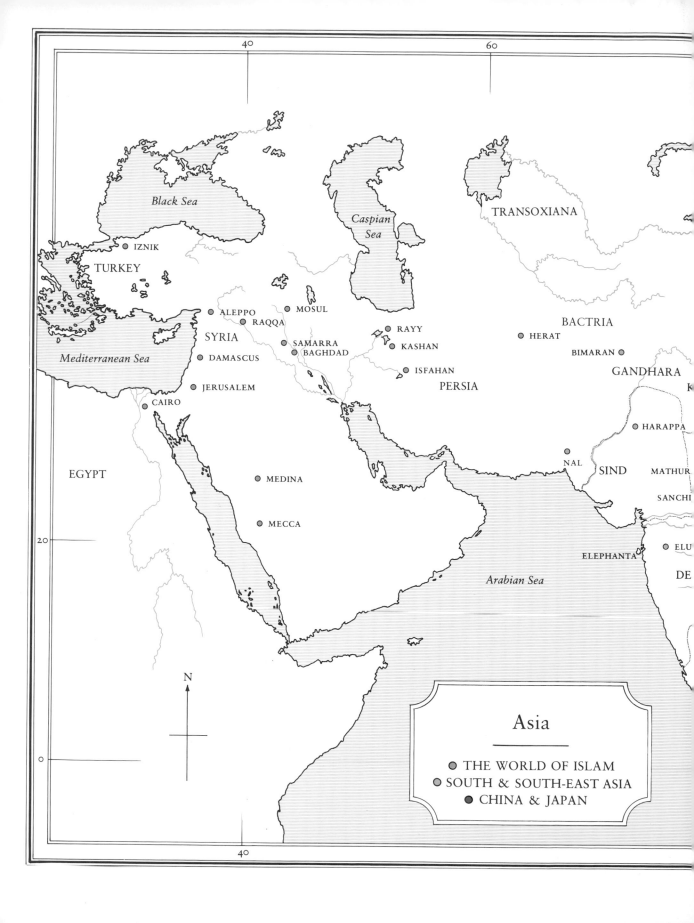

40

60

Black Sea

Caspian Sea

TRANSOXIANA

● IZNIK

TURKEY

● ALEPPO   ● MOSUL
● RAQQA   ● RAYY   BACTRIA
SYRIA   SAMARRA   ● KASHAN   ● HERAT
● BAGHDAD   BIMARAN ●
Mediterranean Sea   ● DAMASCUS   GANDHARA
● ISFAHAN
● JERUSALEM   PERSIA   K

● CAIRO

HARAPPA ●

NAL ●   SIND   MATHUR

EGYPT   SANCHI

● MEDINA   ● ELU

ELEPHANTA   DE

● MECCA   *Arabian Sea*

20

N

0

Asia

● THE WORLD OF ISLAM
● SOUTH & SOUTH-EAST ASIA
● CHINA & JAPAN

40

The coins of the twelfth-century successors to the Seljuqs break with the convention by their revival of ancient coin types (e.g. of the Seleucids) and astrological motifs. A squatting figure of Islamic type is
25 introduced, for instance on a Mesopotamian copper issue of Saladin. Generally speaking, however, decoration is confined to the script, which is exemplified at its best on the gold coins of the Berber dynasties of north Africa. The coins of the Mongols and their successors in Persia exhibit a variety of ornate borders and cartouches, while those of the Mamluks of Egypt include devices borrowed from European heraldry, such as the fleur-de-lis. The Ottoman sultans issued large silver piastres and sumptuous gold medallions showing their *tughra* or monogram. In India Islamic coinage, begun under the sultans of Delhi, culminated with the Mughal Emperors, who attracted Persian artists and die-cutters to their court. Most impressive
26 are the gold *mohurs* of Jahangir (AD 1605–25) carrying his portrait and that of his father Akbar, and a zodiacal series issued by the same emperor at Agra.

CHINESE COINS

The origins of money in China are by no means clear. Archaeological and literary remains provide no definite evidence. Early money objects that have survived point to beginnings in the late Shang and early Chou dynasties, when a two-fold system of barter and exchange of precious materials fulfilled all trade requirements. During the second half of the Chou dynasty these trade patterns developed into a coinage system. From among objects used in barter, spades and knives, being universally useful and of convenient size, became stylized and static units of exchange and were coined for trade by various states and cities. From among precious materials, cowries and jade rings were most acceptable, and copper substitutes for these were coined towards the end of the Chou
27 dynasty and because of their convenience superseded the use of spade and knife coins in trade.

By the end of the Chou dynasty only round copper coins with a central hole were in use. After its collapse, the Ch'in dynasty unified China and also exercised a policy of monetary unification. In 221 BC the Ch'in Emperor forbade the use of all other coins save his own, the *pan liang* – a half-ounce square-holed round cast copper coin. This coin was too large for convenient use and its size was reduced both officially and by forgers. In 118 BC a new size was fixed at five *ch'u*, i.e. 5/24th of an ounce. Coins of this size, and their multiples, in copper and brass continued to be cast and used until the beginning of the Republic. From the T'ang dynasty the normal practice was to inscribe the coins with the name of the dynasty or the era in which they were issued with the characters *t'ung pao* or *yüan pao*, i.e. current money.

Although the only officially made coins were the cast copper or brass cash, from the T'ang dynasty on the majority of commercial and fiscal payments were made in silver, either in the form of ingots or, after the middle of the Ming dynasty, in the form of silver coins imported from abroad.

27 EARLY KNIFE OF CH'IN (HALF ACTUAL SIZE), COPPER CASH OF T'ANG DYNASTY. MIDDLE SPADE COIN FROM AN I

The collection from Central Asia occupies the centre of *Oriental Gallery I* directly opposite the entrance and between the collections from South Asia and China.

In the first millennium AD a great trade route across Asia, the famous Silk Road, connected the Mediterranean world with South Asia and China. Its easternmost section ran through Chinese Central Asia, the modern province of Sinkiang. In this largely desert region a string of oases stretched north and south of the basin of the river Tarim, joining at Kashgar in the west and at Tunhuang in the east. These oases developed into townships prosperous enough to foster a culture which survived the menace of nomad hordes and the pressure of the powers whose luxury goods they interchanged.

Central Asian art, which flourished from about the third to the tenth centuries AD, was a remarkable combination of stylistic elements drawn from India, Persia and China. In the wake of the caravans came Buddhist missionaries from North India, bringing with them not only the religion but also the artistic tradition of Gandhara and later of Kashmir. This is most evident in the monasteries and stupas, some cut into the soft loess cliffs, which followed Indian example both in architecture and in the wall paintings and terracotta and stucco figures with which they were decorated. Stone was scarce and domestic building and furniture were mainly of wood: a fine series of decorated pieces is displayed. Painting in tempera on wood was also practised: one example shows a three-headed Siva in a version of the Kashmir style of the early eighth century AD. Central Asia was not merely receptive: it exercised a profound influence on the Buddhist art of North China in the fourth to sixth centuries AD. By the eighth century the western part of the region (Kashgar) was overtaken by the advance of Islam, while by the tenth century AD the eastern part had become virtually a province of Chinese art.

The Chinese collections are exhibited in the east arm of Oriental Gallery I. The visitor is recommended to follow the arrangement in an anti-clockwise direction. Chinese paintings are not included in this display and have therefore been omitted from this guide. However, temporary exhibitions of paintings from the collection are displayed in Oriental Gallery II from time to time. The most important painting in the Department, the handscroll 'The Admonitions of the Instructress to the Court Ladies' attributed to Ku K'ai-chih (*c.* AD 344–406) but probably a copy of the T'ang dynasty, is permanently exhibited there.

China, the dominating country in eastern Asia, has had a long and confusing political history. In the early period, before the Han dynasty (206 BC–AD 220) unified the area which we now call China, only the northern half of this vast land was occupied by peoples with a distinctly Chinese culture. At many periods during the succeeding centuries China was divided, and parts if not all of the country were often under the rule of foreign peoples. However, China has repeatedly absorbed the invading peoples with their alien artistic and religious influences. Moreover, she exerted a powerful influence over her nearest neighbours Japan, Korea and Vietnam. It is the Chinese language, which because it is written in ideographic characters whose meaning is totally unrelated to local variations in pronunciation and can therefore be understood throughout the whole country, that has provided one of the most important instruments in creating this strong cultural tradition. The government of the country through a complex bureaucracy recruited exclusively from the literate class reinforced the importance of this written language as a unifying force.

The Neolithic period (c. 5000–1600 BC)
The study of Chinese art and archaeology has been completely transformed during the last twenty years by the evidence that the Chinese have brought together from extensive excavations. In no area is this more true than in the discovery and understanding of the complexity of neolithic culture which, originating in the fertile area of the middle reaches of the Yellow river rapidly stimulated other settlements in central and southern China. The diversity of such cultures is represented in the Museum by the different stone axe types. The Museum is particularly fortunate in having acquired an amphora used for carrying water, excavated from a large dwelling site at Pan-p'o in Shensi province. This is a key site in the development of the Neolithic culture known as the Central Yang-shao culture on the Yellow River and its tributary the Wei. It is from a later and westerly extension of this same culture in the province of Kansu that the main group of exhibited burial urns and jars, with elaborate spiral and criss-cross decoration in red and black, come.

Shang dynasty (c. 1600–1027 BC)
Although the casting of bronze was developed at a comparatively late date in China (*c.* 1500 BC) the great bronze ritual vessels, made during the rule of the first

dynasty, the Shang, are among the most astonishing products of any Bronze Age in the world. The vessels were cast directly from constructions of small moulds of tempered clay in which the complicated designs were incised. The earliest of such vessels, which were used for holding wine and food in sacrifice, were small and thin-walled, but during the last centuries of the dynasty, when the capital was established at An-yang in Honan province, the vessels were much heavier and were cast with elaborately attached legs, handles and masks. The most striking vessel is a container known 28 as a *tsun*, supported by the foreparts of two rams with curling horns which is remarkable for the realistic treatment of the two beasts. But much of the decoration on Shang bronzes, both vessels and smaller bronzes such as weapons and fittings, is more mysterious. The most important element is always a mask known as the *t'ao-t'ieh*, in which the circular eye, rounded horns, and upper jaw are visible among a complex of spirals, as on the square food container known as a *fang-yi*. These ritual vessels have been excavated from the large shaft tombs in which the rulers and high dignitaries of the Shang were buried, often accompanied by sacrificial victims executed by such an axe as the example with a face pierced in the blade.

The bronze vessels are the most prominent remains of a complex society which was centred on a few major cities in north China. The bands of infantry armed with halberds, the swift chariots with elaborate decoration and an advanced system of writing inscribed on oracle bones were other products of this powerful and sophisticated state. Less spectacular but equally remarkable are carvings in jade, a rock-forming mineral so hard that it has to be worn away by abrasives such as quartz sand. The smooth surface of the large flat ceremonial blades should be contrasted with the vitality of the small realistic carving of animal amulets, buffalo, birds and tigers.

Western Chou period (1027–770 BC)

Although the Shang dynasty was ignominiously defeated by the Chou, a group of peoples from a western region of north China, the material civilization and the manufacture of bronzes and jades survived and flourished. Indeed, bronze vessels were adapted to the more complicated political relationships of a semi-feudal type which were created as the Chou kings took power over a number of petty monarchs. The long inscription on the Hsing-hou *kuei*, a round four-handled vessel, records the exchange of gifts which reinforced the relationship between the ruler and his dependants. It also illustrates the change from the angular shapes of bronzes of the Shang period to the smoother shapes of the Chou. Among the new designs introduced by the Chou the bird with long decorative tail is the most important, and is seen both on bronzes and on jade.

Eastern Chou period (770–221 BC)

In the eighth century BC the semi-feudal control of the Chou dynasty crumbled as the lesser states took control of different regions of China and vied with each

28 RITUAL VESSEL: TSUN. BRONZE. CHINA. SHANG DYNASTY: 12TH–11TH CENT. BC

other for supremacy. The inscription around the lids of an important pair of bronze wine vessels, or *hu*, records, an interstate meeting which attempted to resolve such persistent conflicts with an alliance. These vessels, of the fifth century BC, decorated with a complex interlace of dragons, are excellent examples of the high level of casting achieved at this date. Inlay in gold and silver superseded this as on a similar wine vessel or *hu*, but is best seen on three remarkable weapons: a spearhead, a halberd, and the newest weapon in the Chinese armoury of the period, the short sword. As in bronze, the levels of artistry and craftsmanship in jade, seen most clearly in four linked plaques worked without a joint from a single small pebble, reached a peak which was never surpassed.

It was in this period that the spread southwards of Chinese culture met with the independent, and in some respects un-Chinese, kingdoms of Ch'u in Hunan province and of Pa and Shu in Szechuan province. What was to become one of China's most distinctive crafts, lacquer painting, originated in these parts of China. Lacquer is the sap of the tree *Rhus verniciflua* which coloured red or black formed a brilliant waterproof coating over a wood or hemp base. In these areas of China vessels were often made in lacquer in preference to bronze. Lacquer was also used to decorate the strange wooden figures with antlers and tongues that represented the spirits whom the peoples of this area believed they had to placate with the help of shamans.

Two groups of bronzes illustrate other aspects of the great differences between the separate states and regions of China before China was unified under the succeeding Ch'in dynasty. A comprehensive group of openwork harness plaques and finials such as an upstanding elk, made by the nomads inhabiting the Ordos region in north-west China, show animals in combat with an emphasis on silhouette and realistic outline quite alien from the fantastic dragons of the ritual bronzes. Similar objects, but treated with more attention to the modelling of form and surface texture, are seen on the weapons and drums from Yunnan province in the extreme south-west of China. A drum converted into a cowrie container and decorated with a frog illustrates a special interest in water creatures in this region which was dominated by a great lake.

Han dynasty (206 BC–AD 220)

The unification of China in the Han dynasty owed its success to the autocratic will of the first emperor of the preceding short-lived Ch'in dynasty (221–206 BC) who not only conquered the other states but unified the script, the weights and measures and the currency. A *pan-liang* or half ounce coin of Ch'in on display (a coin with a square hole) became the only legal currency.

China came to be controlled by an organized bureaucracy rather than by the military will of powerful families. In parallel with these administrative and social changes the rituals which had dictated the casting of elaborate sets of bronze vessels were replaced by different beliefs. A pall, a covering for a coffin, made of glass plaques originally joined to-

29 WINE VESSEL: HU. BRONZE. CHINA. EASTERN CHOU PERIOD: 5TH CENT. BC

30 MODEL OF A WATCHTOWER. EARTHENWARE. CHINA. HAN DYNASTY: 1ST–2ND CENT. AD

gether by metal fastenings represents the new fashion. It is a cheap substitute for jade plaques, which when made up as a suit, were believed to have the power to preserve the body. This was one of the new beliefs which formed part of the religion that came to be called Taoism, a religion which laid great stress on the attainment of an almost physical immortality, both through the control of the mind and by means of magical processes. Associated with this were the magical properties of mirrors, particularly those decorated with symbols similar to the Roman letters TLV or ornamented with the animals of the Four Directions. These animals which consisted of the green dragon of the east, the red bird of the south, the white tiger of the west, and the snake and tortoise of the north were also made as models in bronze. The decoration on a lacquer toilet box in almost perfect condition which is composed of animals and figures wandering in the upper air among clouds, is a delightful illustration of the Taoist search for immortality.

A lacquer wine cup with an inscription dated AD 4 displayed next to this box records another aspect of Chinese life: the organization of craftsmanship. The inscription names a dozen people responsible for the different stages of its manufacture. This complicated and rigid division of labour was a feature of Chinese crafts from an early period in the Bronze Age.

During the Han dynasty the shaft tombs characteristic of the earlier dynasties were replaced by more elaborate multi-chambered tombs. Sometimes these tombs were lined with hollow clay bricks which simulated the interiors of a building with walls, pillars and lintels, and among them were such highly decorated sections as the brick in the form of a gateway. These bricks were stamped with repeated designs some of which, as in this one, are important records of aspects of daily life, including as they do buildings and chariots. The way of life of the Han period is also clearly recorded in the objects made for burial in tombs, the *ming-ch'i*. During the dynasty substitutes in earthenware for real objects in precious materials came to be used for burial. Those on display include figures of men playing a game, farm buildings and a fish pond. The most important model in this group is 30 a watchtower reproducing a multi-storeyed wooden structure with tiled roofs, typical of the architecture of the period.

Three Kingdoms, Northern & Southern dynasties (AD 220–589)

The disintegration of the Han dynasty in the third century AD made way for a number of minor dynasties which, in the north, were followed by rulers of non-Chinese origin. This political turmoil was itself a stimulus to the spread of Buddhism, which was probably introduced into China at the end of the Han period. Two stone sculptures, a stele of the Eastern Wei dated AD 535 and a standing Bodhisattva of the northern Ch'i dynasty (AD 550–577), represent the important stages in the development of sculpture styles in China. A group of small gilt-bronze images, made to be placed on altars, one dated AD 471 and one dated AD 530, illustrate variations of the complicated

drapery in low relief seen on the stele. In the late sixth century AD this was replaced by a more solid rendering of form, seen both in the standing Bodhisattva in stone and in one in gilt-bronze.

This important transitional period also saw the development of the large-scale manufacture of high-fired ceramics, stonewares with a felspathic glaze which, being of feldspar and therefore related into the composition of the clay of the body, fuses with it when it is fired. The most important group were the Yüeh wares from the southern provinces of Kiangsu and Chekiang. These were made as plain vessels or ewers such as the one with a chicken-head spout, or in a more highly decorated form as waterpots in the shape of lions and toads. The high level of these ceramics was founded on a long tradition of stonewares in the Chou and Han dynasties.

Sui & T'ang dynasties (AD 581–618 & AD 618–906)

In AD 581 China was reunified under a single native dynasty, the Sui, who, as part of their consolidation of the empire, gave Buddhism the status of a state religion. The magnificent nineteen-foot figure of the Buddha Amitabha, dated AD 585, is the Museum's finest piece of Chinese sculpture. It is shown on the north staircase.

The T'ang dynasty, famous for the magnificence of its court and the cosmopolitan nature of its capital, succeeded the Sui. The fine tomb figures of horses and 31 camels are a memorial to the animals which played an essential part in the trade along the Silk Route, a trade which brought to Ch'ang-an, the capital, the luxuries of 'Arab' horses, perfumes, fruits and foreign dancers in exchange for silk. But if musicians graced the court, great bands of soldiers were needed to patrol the immense frontier of the empire which the T'ang ruled far out into Central Asia. Silver vessels, of which the Museum has an excellent group, are another example of the luxuries of this period and of the importance of the contacts across Central Asia to the lands of the Iranian west. A stem-cup decorated with scenes of huntsmen and trees, and a lobed bowl with a gilt design of birds and foliage show clear influences of the designs and shapes of silver of the Sassanians (p. 242 below) and their eastern neighbours.

Amid the brilliant life of the court and capital Buddhism by turns flourished and was persecuted. The finest Buddhist figure of the T'ang period is a small gilt-bronze figure of a Bodhisattva, exquisite in detail but with a rather opulent form, which is characteristic not only of such miniature figures but also of the great stone sculptures of the period.

The Museum has an excellent group of ceramics of the T'ang period, including a varied and fully representative group of earthenware vessels made to be buried in tombs, and decorated, as are the tomb figures, with coloured lead glazes. These should be contrasted with the great achievements of this period in high-fired ceramics, white wares, black wares splashed with grey and blue, and the green-glazed 32 Yüeh wares. A ewer with an exquisitely carved phoenix head and decorated with a flowering peony scroll is the most important vessel in the group. It

[143]

marks the transition to the delicate ceramics of the succeeding fifty years, known as the Five Dynasties (AD 907–960). A box in the form of a lotus bud is a typical example of the use of shapes and designs of flowers at this time.

Northern Sung dynasty (AD 960–1126)
& Southern Sung dynasty (AD 1127–79)
The two parts of the Sung dynasty are thus named by the location of their capitals, that of the Northern Sung being at K'ai-feng, while that of the Southern Sung, forced to flee before the conquest of the Jürched tribes, at Hang-chou. In the Museum this period is best represented by a striking array of porcelains and stonewares, However, these alone present only one side of a period which saw great achievements in painting and sculpture. A seated Bodhisattva in wood

displayed in Oriental Gallery II is a fine example of Sung dynasty sculpture. Alongside it is one of the most popular exhibits in the Department, the Lohan from the I-chou caves in Hopei province in lead-glazed ceramic. This was made under the Liao dynasty (AD 907–1025), a dynasty founded by the nomadic Khitan tribe who occupied part of north China after the fall of the T'ang dynasty. Another important aspect of the arts of the Sung period is the self-conscious revival of ancient styles, particularly in bronze and jade. These were based upon serious study of ancient pieces which were discussed and even illustrated in books and catalogues. Two cases of bronzes and jades illustrate this re-working of ancient themes. Among them is a splendid inlaid lamp in Han dynasty style.

31 CAMEL. GLAZED EARTHENWARE. CHINA. T'ANG DYNASTY: EARLY 8TH CENT. AD

The ceramics of the Sung cover a great diversity of taste and technique. Boldly decorated stonewares, which are given the general name of Tz'u-chou wares, are among the largest and most colourful. They include lively subjects such as the dancing bear painted in black on white slip on a pillow, and a vase decorated with peony scrolls in black under a green glaze. Some of the simple white and black vessels, such as a tall flask, belong to this same stoneware tradition and were probably used as simple containers, often for wine, as indeed was a massive Tz'u-chou flask. However, the finely decorated black tea-bowls and, particularly, the delicately carved Ting white semi-porcelains, among which is an exquisite ewer with carved lotus petals, were highly prized by officials and the court. Each region of China, in fact, produced ceramics of a different type, but it was those with bluish or green glazes in particular which came to be requisitioned for imperial use. Most important of all these is a small group of the precious Ju ware. Only three dozen examples survive anywhere in the world. Rather more common is the official or Kuan ware made for the court at Hang-chou. The thick crackled glaze on the slender-necked flask shows the subtle depths which experienced potters could achieve. The celadons made in north China and in the south in Chekiang province at the Lung-chüan kilns illustrate the bold carving and the intricate moulding of the northern celadons and their contrast with the subtle shapes and colours of the southern ones. The skills of the Sung potters culminated in the porcelains with a pale bluish glaze known as *ying-ch'ing* or *ch'ing-pai* glaze. Such ceramics were carved and pared down to extreme thinness and among them the flower-like grace of the earlier ceramics, as in the basin exhibited, is combined with more intricate constructions such as in the wine ewer which was placed in this basin. These porcelains laid the foundation for the great expansion of ceramics of this type under the Yüan dynasty.

Yüan dynasty (AD 1280–1368)
By AD 1280 the foreign kingdoms of north China and the native dynasty of the Southern Sung were both destroyed by the eastern branch of the nomad Mongols, who for a brief period controlled an Asian empire reaching from the Mediterranean to the China Sea. Kubilai Khan, the founder of the Yüan dynasty, established his capital at Peking; its magnificence attracted merchants and craftsmen from Asia and Europe. Fostered by easy intercourse and trade with the Near East, new techniques and styles were introduced which permanently affected the development of the decorative arts in China.

In ceramics certain wares of the Sung dynasty, Tz'u-chou, *ying-ch'ing* and celadon, continued to be made, but the famous underglaze blue painted porcelain, made at the great ceramic metropolis of Ching-te Chen in Kiangsi Province, quickly superseded all other types in popularity both in China and in the markets of South-east Asia, the Near East and eventually Europe. The success and beauty of this new porcelain were due to a combination of china-clay and china-stone which produced a hard semi-opaque

32 PHOENIX-HEADED EWER. STONEWARE. CHINA. T'ANG DYNASTY: 10TH CENT. AD

33 PILLOW. STONEWARE. CHINA. SUNG DYNASTY: 12TH CENT. AD

34 EWER AND BASIN. PORCELAIN. CHINA. SUNG DYNASTY: 12TH CENT. AD

35 JAR. PORCELAIN. CHINA. YÜAN DYNASTY:
c. AD 1350

36 VASE. PORCELAIN. CHINA. MING DYNASTY:
AD 1426–35

body which fused completely with its transparent glaze of china-stone. Under the glaze elaborate designs were painted in a perfectly controlled cobalt blue and, less successfully, in copper red. All the Yüan wares, even the rare underglaze copper red, are well represented, but the collections are particularly rich in the noble vases and large dishes decorated in underglaze blue with flowered scrolls enclosing a wide repertoire of design: striding dragons, peacocks and fish in water-weed ponds, landscape and figure subjects. Sometimes crowded and careless and quite alien to the taste of the Sung dynasty, the general effect of the style is rich and full of life.

Equally original was the Yüan treatment of lacquer. Hitherto lacquer had been used as a beautiful monochrome surface on vessels of simple shape, or as a ground for painting in liquid lacquer, or for inlay in mother of pearl and gold and silver foil. To this surface embellishment, which was not abandoned, was now added a technique in which a sufficient thickness of lacquer was built up so as to allow it to be deeply carved like ivory or jade. This involved the slow and laborious application of up to two hundred coats of lacquer on the wooden core of the vessel, each to be carefully dried and polished before the application of the next. Little carved lacquer, which was to become China's greatest contribution to the art, has survived from the Yüan period, but two handsome round dishes, one black, the other red, illustrate the new achievement. Both are carved down to a buff ground with birds in flight against lotus and other water plants.

A third technique, accepted by the Chinese themselves as of western origin, was that of cloisonné enamel in which bronze vessels were decorated with deep opaque enamels of various colours prevented from running when fired by bronze wires or cloisons soldered to the vessel and outlining the design. Mastery of this technique seems only to have been achieved in the following dynasty and no certain pieces survive from the Yüan, who introduced it.

Ming dynasty (AD 1368–1644)

In AD 1368 the Yüan dynasty was overthrown by the first of the Ming emperors, Hung-wu (AD 1368–98), and the whole of China was, for the first time since the T'ang, ruled by a native dynasty. The capital was first at Nanking but was removed to Peking by Yunglo (AD 1403–24) where it remained. The innovations of the Yüan, especially the underglaze blue painted porcelain and cloisonné enamel, were at first coolly regarded. They survived the change of dynasty however, and under imperial patronage the robust vitality of the Yüan was soon refined and disciplined, both in design and technique, so as to become acceptable to orthodox Chinese taste.

The collections cover all aspects of the Ming achievement in ceramics. The finest period of underglaze blue painted porcelain is undoubtedly that up to the reign of Cheng-te (AD 1506–21). In Chinese eyes the two classical reigns were those of Hsüan-te (AD 1426–35) and Ch'eng-hua (AD 1465–87). Both reigns are superbly represented. Typical of the Hsüan-te style is the vase painted with birds on a branch of flowering prunus, with its taut shape, vibrant blue darkening almost to black when heavily applied, discrete placing of the design and sensitive drawing. Most famous of the Ch'eng-hua types are the so-called 'palace bowls', delicately pencilled with flowering or fruiting scrolls: five are displayed. Nor should the merits of the later reigns be overlooked. Much of it was made for export but the light, fresh touch is often more appealing than the official wares. The porcelain of the troubled period at the end of the Ming dynasty (from AD 1600) painted in a silvery blue is particularly attractive. The difficult copper red was most effectively used as a monochrome in the reign of Hsüan-te, while a rare series of plain white pieces dating from the early reigns is also displayed. Once pictorial designs became acceptable to official taste, the advantages of painting in low-fired enamels in a wide range of colour over the glaze were soon appreciated. Surviving examples are rare however until the reign of Ch'eng-hua, when the enamels were used on small pieces in association with a pale underglaze blue. A jar decorated with dragons and melons is the finest example of this rather finical style in the collections. Enamels were used more boldly and to greater decorative effect in the sixteenth century AD, especially during the reign of Wan-li (AD 1573–1619). In a third technique, which makes perhaps the bravest show of all Ming ceramics, the design was painted in glazes harder than enamels but not requiring the full heat of the kiln. The glazes were kept from running by incised lines or raised clay cloisons. A fine series of these brilliant wares, in aubergine, green and yellow on a dark blue or turquoise ground, is exhibited next to the cloisonné enamel which they so much resemble.

The finest cloisonné enamels were produced during the fifteenth century AD. Perhaps the greatest piece to have survived is the large covered vase decorated with dragons and bearing the reign-mark of Hsüan-te. Associated with it is a group of four pieces of outstanding quality, with the design on a glowing turquoise ground. By the end of the century the enamels were handled with extraordinary virtuosity: the palette was enlarged and the colours allowed to shade

37 softly into each other. A unique example is the lovely box whose cover is decorated with two parrots on a fruiting peach branch. Excellent work was done throughout the remainder of the dynasty: the large salver decorated with dragons is an imperial piece and bears the reign-mark of Wan-li.

The great period of Chinese carved lacquer also covers the fifteenth century AD. The difficult technique was now completely mastered. The closely knit and beautifully controlled designs, in red carved down to a yellow ground, include landscape (a large dish and covered box), flowers (a box with tree peonies and a vase with the flowers of the four seasons), and dragons and phoenixes (a large plaque). The second half of the century is represented by two small, round, covered boxes, one decorated with a rare design of narcissus, the other with two lions holding the tassels of a brocade ball, and by a large covered box, shallowly carved and giving a more pictorial effect, which shows a cavalcade of horsemen approaching an inn. In the

sixteenth century AD polychrome carved lacquer became popular. Two techniques were employed: in the more elaborate, up to seven bands of colour were built up and then exposed to the design by carving, as on a dish dated AD 1592; in the other, the design was carved in the ground colour and then inlaid with various plastic lacquers, the design being outlined with gilt, as on a six-sided dish with the reign-mark of Chia-ching (AD 1522–66). In one Yüan technique the design was incised with the needle and gilt. The rare and beautiful small foliated box with phoenixes dates from the early fifteenth century AD. This technique was introduced to the Ryukyu Islands, between China and Japan, where in the fifteenth century AD was produced one of the finest pieces known, a large cylindrical box with peacocks in flight among peony scrolls, gold on black. The continuing use of painted and mother-of-pearl-inlaid lacquer is also well illustrated.

An excellent group of gilt bronzes dating from the early reigns of the Ming dynasty demonstrates the popularity of Tibetan Buddhism at this period and the strong influence of its style. A powerful head of a Guardian shows the ability of the early Ming bronze-caster to work on a large scale.

Ch'ing dynasty (AD 1644–1912)
In AD 1644 China was again conquered by a foreign power from the north, the Manchus, who established the Ch'ing dynasty. The pacification of the country caused little cultural disturbance, and, unlike the Yüan, the three great emperors of the Ch'ing, K'ang-hsi (AD 1662–1722), Yung-cheng (AD 1723–35) and Ch'ien-lung (AD 1736–95), favoured conservatism in the arts and respect for the past.

The main strength of the collections here is in ceramics. Ching-te Chen enjoyed the generous patronage of the imperial court and was managed by exceptionally able directors. Distinguished by perfect finish and command of material, the techniques do not differ basically from those employed by the Ming potter. The best underglaze blue porcelain of the K'ang-hsi period is wholly admirable, the colour a deep, pure sapphire, brushed on in graded washes. Though its popularity declined after K'ang-hsi, beautiful and often deceptive imitations of classical early Ming types both in underglaze blue and red were made in the reign of Yung-cheng. As in the Ming dynasty porcelain was also decorated in overglaze enamels but with a wider palette, shades of green, a cleaner yellow and a violet blue. Sometimes over-

38 crowded, this so-called green family (*famille verte*) is especially impressive when the white ground is allowed to display the brilliant colour and the strong and fluent drawing. The enamels were also used directly on the unglazed body which produced a particularly soft and melting effect. This technique was used not only for small delicate pieces and figures but also for the large sumptuous vases with black, green or yellow grounds. The Ch'ing monochromes include all the Ming types, superb imitations of the old imperial Sung glazes and many novelties. Especially famous were the *lang yao* red varying from cherry red to ox-blood; 'peach bloom', a pinkish red flecked with

37 BOX. CLOISONNÉ ENAMEL. CHINA. MING DYNASTY:
LATE 15TH CENT. AD

38 DISH. PORCELAIN. CHINA. CH'ING
DYNASTY: EARLY 18TH CENT. AD

green and russet; mirror black; powder blue; pale lavender; and 'apple green', produced by coating a white crackled glaze with translucent enamel.

In the third decade of the eighteenth century AD the *famille verte* enamels were displayed by the opaque enamels of the so-called *famille rose*, in which rose-pinks, derived from gold, predominate. The colours are seen at their best in the Yung-cheng porcelain, where the white surface is embellished in the Chinese taste with a single spray of flowers or fruit or a bird on a branch. The heavily decorated and crowded plates and table services wete destined for the foreign market, as were the quantities of Ching-te Chen porcelain decorated with coats of arms and European subjects. Though the bulk of Ch'ing porcelain was made at Ching-te Chen, there were many provincial factories, two of which are especially important. From Te-hua in Fukien province comes perhaps the most beautiful white porcelain ever made, thick and lustrous with a deep, soft-looking glaze. Rarely decorated it was used for small cups and jugs and for figures and groups, especially Buddhist. European subjects and shapes are not uncommon. The figures are frequently small masterpieces of modelling. At Yi-hsing in Kiangsu Province was made a fine stoneware, usually red but sometimes buff or grey. The small red tea-pots came to Europe as early as the seventeenth century AD, where their perfect shape and warm colour were copied.

Cloisonné enamels were popular under the Ch'ing and made in enormous quantity at the imperial work-shops. Technically superb, their smooth perfection rarely approaches the aesthetic quality even of the later Ming pieces. More interesting are the so-called Cantonese enamels in which the metal surface is coated by an opaque tin glaze on which the design is painted in enamels. This European technique was introduced in the reign of Yung-cheng together with the *famille rose* enamels with which most pieces are decorated. A fair series of pieces both in Chinese taste and for the European market is exhibited.

The collections of Ch'ing lacquer are fully representative. Most of the Ming types continued to be produced. The craftsmanship of the carved red lacquer is expertly meticulous and the quality generally good, if somewhat monotonous on the elaborate pieces. A fine plain piece is a fluted round covered box in the shape of a chrysanthemum with a gilt poem of Ch'ien-lung and dated AD 1777. An exceptionally good example of inlaid lacquer is the large octagonal tray decorated with formal designs, cranes and phoenixes and with the reign-mark of Ch'ien-lung. Tinted mother-of-pearl inlay was also used in association with gold and silver foil: this work, usually on small objects, is of unusual refinement.

Jade and other hard stones also appealed to the Ch'ing, usually in fantastic forms designed to display the skill of the carver. A more restrained piece is the handsome white jade hat-stand carved with dragons in clouds and on its wooden base a gilt inscription indicating that it was for the use of Ch'ien-lung himself. There is also a good display of Ch'ing glass, remarkable for the excellence of its colour and simple dignity of form.

The Korean collections are exhibited in Oriental Gallery I.

Korea, geographically a peninsular off Manchuria, has been greatly influenced and often dominated by China to whom she owed Buddhism and most of the elements of her culture. The Koreans, however, are one of the most creative peoples of Asia and an effortless grace and vitality are apparent in their earliest work.

Three Kingdoms period (fourth century AD to AD 668)
The main evidence for this period, when the peninsula was divided between the three warlike states of Koguryo, Paekche and Silla, is a high-fired pottery of great technical excellence. One of the few groups of these wares outside Korea is exhibited: it includes an expressively modelled duck.

Great Silla period (AD 668–918)
The Silla Dynasty unified the country in the seventh century AD. Buddhism, introduced in the fourth century, provided the basis for a cultured society centred on the capital Kyongju. A rare group of four small gilt-bronze figures of the Buddha Amitabha is typical of the Korean's intimate and gentle handling of religious themes. His skill in metalwork, famous even in China, can also be seen in the gilt-bronze lotus pin, which must have adorned a large image.

Koryo dynasty (AD 918–1392)
The ceramics of the Koryo Dynasty are perhaps the finest expression of Korean art. The most celebrated were the stonewares with a celadon glaze of un-equalled warmth and depth. In a fine group the tall, high-shouldered vase is perhaps the most beautiful. The use of delicately incised designs under the glaze is seen at its most effective in the bowl decorated with ducks and waves. A unique bowl decorated in under-glaze copper-red may pre-date the Chinese use of this difficult technique. A certain Korean innovation is the use of white and black clay slip inlaid into engraved designs under the glaze. A fine example of this popular technique is the *kundika* or ritual drinking vessel displayed next to the bronze which inspired the shape. Inlay dominated the taste of the later Koryo. It can be seen in the form of a landscape, silver inlaid on bronze, on the impressive stand for a Buddhist image and, as mother of pearl and silver wire inlaid in lacquer, on the great box for sutras (Buddhist sacred texts) which is the finest piece in the collection.

Yi dynasty (AD 1392–1910)
Chinese domination, the suppression of Buddhism and, in the late sixteenth century AD, Japanese invasions, impoverished the country, and Korea became the 'Hermit Kingdom', deliberately isolated from contact with the outside world. Though refinement was lost, the instinctive taste of the Korean craftsman remained no less evident in the rough and austere ceramics with their careless decoration in blue or iron-brown under the glaze, and in the boldly designed flower scrolls in mother of pearl on two lacquer boxes.

39 SUTRA BOX. LACQUER INLAID WITH MOTHER-OF-PEARL
AND SILVER WIRE. KOREA. KORYO DYNASTY: 13TH CENT. AD

41 SEATED FIGURE OF THE BODHISATTVA MIROKU
(MAITREYA). GILT-BRONZE. JAPAN. EARLY BUDDHIST
PERIOD: 7TH CENT. AD

40 HANIWA IN THE FORM OF A WOMAN. RED POTTERY.
JAPAN. 5TH–6TH CENT. AD

JAPAN

The Japanese collections are exhibited in Oriental Gallery III. The visitor is recommended to follow the arrangement in a clockwise direction.

The Japanese islands are separated from the Asian mainland by over 100 miles of rough and dangerous water. Though Japan received most of her culture from China often by way of Korea, her semi-isolation enabled her native taste swiftly to assert itself. Eager to adopt new ideas, the Japanese have a strong sense of tradition so that the history of their art is one of ever-increasing complexity and variety. The unstable nature of the land and lack of good building stone encouraged the Japanese preference for light, easily renewable architecture and sculpture in wood, and the exercise of a superb natural craftsmanship on objects small and portable.

Prehistory (7000 BC–AD 552)

Until the introduction of Buddhism and with it the art of writing in the sixth century AD, the islands formed part of a culture, nomadic in origin, which included Manchuria, Eastern Siberia and Korea. The influence of China is often strong but rarely overwhelming.

Jomon period (7000–300 BC)

A distinct hunting, gathering and fishing way of life had developed by 7000 BC. It is called Jomon ('rope-patterns') after the low-fired and hand-made pottery which was sometimes impressed with patterns made by twisted rope. Before the first millennium BC the shapes, of which a wide-necked beaker is a fine example, are clean and elegant and a wide repertory of incised, stamped and applied patterns was employed. An impressive series of fragments illustrate the style, together with other objects from the middens left all round the coasts by the Jomon gatherers of shell-fish.

Yayoi period (300 BC–AD 250)

About 300 BC a wave of immigrants introduced rice-culture, the potter's wheel and the use of bronze. The origins of the Shinto religion ('the way of the gods') seem to lie in this more settled society. Shinto recognizes gods in hills, trees and waterfalls, in crafts and skills such as sword-making, in all the Japanese dead, and in the idea of Japan itself. It gives a feeling of unity to the Japanese nation and its activities, including the artistic. Even now the traditional wooden Shinto architecture is very like the building of the Yayoi period. The collection is small but impressive. Outstanding are the three large bronze bells called *dotaku*, obviously the products of an advanced metal culture: their purpose remains a mystery. A large jar with pointed base and incised decoration of a rice-sheaf, is perhaps the finest piece of Yayoi pottery outside Japan.

Great Tombs period (AD 250–552)

About AD 250 a warlike iron-using people from Korea conquered most of southern Japan and by the fifth century AD had established a recognizable political state. The period is named after the many great barrows left by the emperors and nobles. The collection of grave-goods exhibited is the best outside Japan. It includes a splendid pottery coffin, a large group of the high-fired and beautifully potted stoneware, and iron and bronze implements and weapons. The jar with a group of figures in a boat modelled round the neck gives some idea of the everyday life of the period, as does a remarkable *haniwa* (clay figure placed outside the tombs as a form of protection) whose mask-like face is symbolic of the subservience of the retainers to their great lords.

Early Buddhist period (AD 552–710)

The official date for the introduction of Buddhism from Korea is AD 552. With it came the art of writing in characters and the highly evolved civilization and art of the mainland. The period is marked by the change from large tomb-burials to Buddhist cremation and by the emergence of the Buddhist temple as the cultural centre of the community. For such a temple, possibly the great Horyuji itself near Nara, was made the only sculpture of this period outside Japan, a gilt-bronze Bodhisattva which to the simple strength of the Korean model adds a withdrawn, less human quality typically Japanese.

Nara period (AD 710–94)

With the first settled capital at Nara, royal as well as priestly patrons encouraged the development of the arts. Direct Chinese influences were added to those of Korea. A rare example of the wooden sculpture of this short period, both vigorous and refined, is the expressive wooden mask of a youth, used in the semi-religious *gigaku* dances performed in Buddhist temples.

Heian period (AD 794–1185)

In AD 794 the capital was moved to Heian, the modern city of Kyoto, which remained the centre of courtly and ecclesiastical life for most of Japan's history. In the Heian period, largely peaceful and isolated from mainland influence, Japanese art developed its own mature taste, whose main characteristics are a softness of feeling verging on sentimentality, an impeccable sense of design and proportion dominated by a dislike of the symmetrical, and a deep love of nature and the changing seasons. All these can be seen in the beautiful document box inlaid with grasshoppers and crickets in mother-of-pearl on black lacquer, and made in the twelfth century AD. By this time the Japanese lacquerer had surpassed his Chinese and Korean masters, and lacquer became a basic material for temple furnishings, domestic utensils, furniture and personal ornaments. A small group of wood sculpture includes a figure of the Goddess of Happiness (Kichishoten), and a colossal head of the Buddha Amida exhibited in Oriental Gallery II.

Kamakura period (AD 1185–1392)

In AD 1185 the first Shogun (military dictator) Yoritomo moved his government to the provincial town of Kamakura, leaving a powerless court at Heian. The long dominance of a metropolitan court culture was broken, and a new sense of involvement in the real world inspired the artist and craftsman. The art of wood sculpture displayed an almost brutal power which is one of Japan's great artistic contributions to the world. Perhaps the finest sculpture in the collection is the thirteenth-century AD seated figure of the saint Binzuru, a vivid portrait of an austere personality.

42 GIGAKU MASK OF A YOUNG MAN. WOOD, GESSO AND TRACES OF PAINT. JAPAN. NARA PERIOD: 8TH CENT. AD

[151]

Ashikaga period (AD 1392–1573)

The period is named after the ruling family of Shoguns, who re-established their capital at Heian. The traditional forms of Buddhism were replaced by Zen imported from Korea and China. With its insistence on contemplation and intuitive thought and action Zen Buddhism profoundly influenced all the arts, especially swordsmanship and sword-making and the tea ceremony, itself Zen in origin. Among the sword-blades exhibited the best and the earliest date from this period. Their cold beauty appealed to the native aesthetic sense, and their forging and use demanded a deeply serious response, nourished by both Zen and Shinto. This combination of qualities, which has led many Japanese to value the sword above all their artistic achievements, should be understood in front of such a blade as that made by Kanemoto in the fifteenth century AD. The sober pottery favoured for the tea ceremony is well represented, the earliest pieces being also of this period.

Momoyama period (AD 1573–1614)

In the middle of the sixteenth century AD the general Oda Nobunaga began to unify the country after a century of civil war. This new period of national self-confidence and of secular values in the arts was symbolized by the great Momoyama Castle at Osaka. The brilliant screen-paintings on gold backgrounds designed for such castles set a new style for Japan. The arrival of European traders and missionaries introduced Japan for the first time to the West. Japanese lacquer was soon appreciated by the foreigner. Two fine examples of this export lacquer are a round covered box with a Christian monogram and a chest of European shape, both decorated in gold lacquer and mother-of-pearl. A very rare feather jacket worn over armour illustrates the flamboyant taste of the period, enlivened by contacts not only with Europe but much of Asia.

Edo period (AD 1614–1867)

Tokugawa Ieyasu finally unified Japan at the beginning of the seventeenth century AD and established a military government at the city of Edo, which, far from the court at Kyoto, grew into the modern Tokyo. Under the stable government which lasted until the middle of the nineteenth century AD an urban, largely middle-class culture developed. Also, after her brief flirtation with the outside world, Japan imposed upon herself an almost complete isolation. The result was that the artist tended to concentrate his talent for the miniature on the objects of everyday Japanese life: *netsuke* (the retaining toggles for purses hung from the sash) in boxwood and ivory; sword-furniture, on which an unrivalled repertoire of metal techniques was employed; tea ceremony pottery of a sophisticated rusticity; and *inro* (seal-cases) on which was lavished every technique of the lacquerer. Collections of all these, including many minor masterpieces, are exhibited. An important innovation of the period was the making of porcelain which the Japanese did not attempt until about AD 1600. By AD 1660 the great ceramic-making town of Arita was providing the Dutch East India Company with porcelain decorated in underglaze blue and enamels. Often made to order with European shapes, the decoration is sometimes coarse and crowded but Japanese taste usually imposes a quieter manner. This is particularly evident on the beautiful porcelain in the so-called Kakiemon style, where the unerring placing of the brilliant enamels on the fine white body was much admired and copied by the early European porcelain factories. A fine example is the figure of a young man of fashion which reached England before AD 1688. Of all these wares and of the equally beautiful Nabeshima style the collections are outstanding. Another important feature of the period is the development in the seventeenth century AD of an art-and-craft movement begun by the calligrapher Koetsu. A designer in the modern sense, he provided drawings and specifications for pottery and lacquer. The writer's box decorated on its curved lid with maple leaves fallen on the famous Uji bridge over waves in silver and gold is an outstanding example of his individual style and of Japanese lacquer at its best.

44 FIGURE OF A YOUNG MAN. PORCELAIN. JAPAN. EDO PERIOD: 17TH CENT. AD

43 DOCUMENT BOX DECORATED WITH INSECTS. LACQUER INLAID WITH MOTHER-OF-PEARL. JAPAN. HEIAN PERIOD: 12TH CENT. AD

Prehistoric & Romano-British antiquities

Upper levels

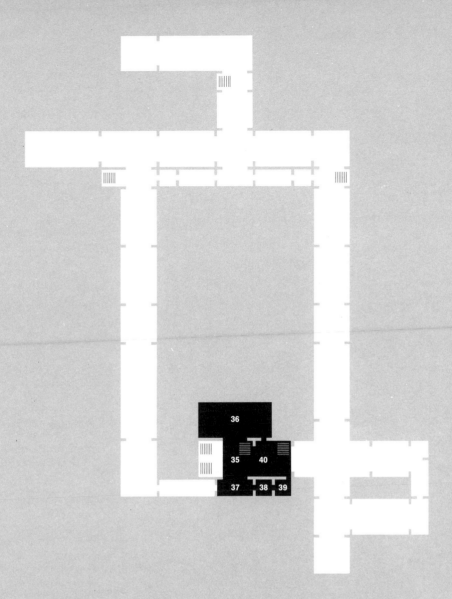

35 Prehistory and Roman Britain
36 Man before metals
37/38/39 Later prehistory of Europe
40 Roman Britain

The Department of Prehistoric and Romano-British Antiquities was formed in 1969 when the former Department of British and Medieval Antiquities was divided. Its collections represent virtually the whole span of human history from man's earliest appearance – more than two million years ago – up to the Christian era. Geographically the collections cover the whole of the Old World for the earlier periods (Palaeolithic and Mesolithic), Europe in the later Prehistoric periods (Neolithic, Bronze and Iron Ages) and Britain when a province of the Roman Empire. Prehistoric remains from the Americas, Australasia and Oceania, and Neolithic and Iron Age material from Africa (except Egypt) are housed in the Museum of Mankind in Burlington Gardens. Material from the post-Palaeolithic prehistoric period in Egypt, the Middle East and the Far East can be seen in the Egyptian, Western Asiatic and Oriental Departments, antiquities of the Greek Bronze Age and Italian Iron Age in the Greek and Roman Department.

The scientific study of prehistory is of recent origin, indeed the word was only coined in the nineteenth century when man's great antiquity was for the first time recognized. Prehistory is concerned with the pre-literate period of man's past which must be reconstructed by archaeologists without the help of written records. It is a subject with popular appeal as it seeks to satisfy a common human curiosity about origins and beginnings, to answer questions about human evolution, early man's environment and life-style and, as far as possible, behaviour. The collections also illustrate the work of the archaeologist, for all the information we have about early man is inferred entirely from material remains, whether casually collected or scientifically excavated.

The Prehistoric section of the Department aims to stimulate the visitor to reconstruct for himself, often from sparse cultural remains, a valid picture of the life of prehistoric man. The Department is consequently as concerned with the mundane day-to-day aspects of the prehistoric past as with man's early artistic achievements, and while masterpieces of prehistoric and Romano-British art and craftsmanship are displayed, an attempt has also been made to provide material for ecological and environmental studies. The Department is fortunate in possessing some notable former private collections particularly the Morel collection of Celtic Art objects from France, purchased in 1901, the collection of early Bronze Age antiquities made by the nineteenth century antiquary, Canon Greenwell, and the Sturge, Christy and Lartet collections of Old Stone Age artefacts.

1 STONE HAND-AXE FROM OLDUVAI GORGE, TANZANIA

The Quaternary collection, spanning the Palaeolithic and Mesolithic periods (or Old and Middle Stone Ages – from two and a half million years to about five thousand years ago) is one of the finest of its kind in the world. It is unparalleled for its British Palaeolithic material and is particularly rich in artefacts from France, Africa (Kenya, Tanzania and South Africa especially), the Near East (notably the Levantine coast) and the Far East. The most remarkable feature of this period is the vast time-span it encompasses – over two million years. The exhibits in the 'Man before Metals' display aim to illustrate the very slow and gradual technological progress made by early man over this long period, and his first attempts at artistic creation.

1 The true significance of much archaeological material can only be fully appreciated if recovered with the background information that only modern scientifically based excavation can provide. The series of stone artefacts from the famous Palaeolithic site of Olduvai Gorge in Tanzania illustrates this point. Here the excavating team was able to prove for the first time, by dating a part of the lowest bed in the stratified sequence in which human remains and artefacts have been found, that man's history extended over almost two million years. From the unique dated sequence of stone artefacts recovered the evolution of stone tool technology can be observed in the context of the geological sequence – simple choppers and chopping tools first appearing in Bed I; the first true hand-axes in a later part of the sequence.

2 If these tools prove the antiquity of man, the Solutrean blade from the Volgu hoard and the Magdalenian sculptures from Bruniquel exemplify the technical and artistic achievements of man by the Upper Palaeolithic period. The Solutrean hunters whose cultural remains are confined to Spain and France around 18,000 BC are acknowledged to be the finest of Palaeolithic flintworkers – particularly noted for their finely flaked laurel and willow-leaf blades. The example shown here is a beautiful laurel-leaf blade found at Volgu near Châlon-sur-Saône, France, in 1874. Probably a projectile head, it is mottled greyish-brown in colour with very fine bifacial pressure flaking and has been retouched, possibly to straighten the curve produced by the initial flaking.

The successors of the Solutrean people in this part of Europe were the Magdalenians – with their specialized economy geared to fishing and hunting cold-climate animals. They are noted especially for their use of bone and antler but their best known achievements are in the realm of art. Their drawings and paintings, both on rock surfaces and miniature art, flowered between about 17,000 and 11,000 BC but very suddenly died out. The magnificent paintings in the caves and rock-shelters of south-west France, Spain and the Pyrenees are famous, but the Magdalenians' decoration of artefacts is less well known although some of their most delicate work was done in this medium. The Museum contains three outstanding examples of their miniature art. The most remark-

2 FLINT BLADE FROM VOLGU, FRANCE

3 REINDEER SCULPTURE IN MAMMOTH TUSK FROM BRUNIQUEL, FRANCE

4 SCULPTURE OF A MAMMOTH IN REINDEER ANTLER FROM BRUNIQUEL, FRANCE

3 able is the point made from mammoth tusk carved in the form of two reindeer with antlers and ears swept back and heads extended, apparently swimming. This was found in the Montastruc rock-shelter at Bruniquel, near Montauban in south-west France, along 4 with a mammoth carved in reindeer antler. The trunk of the mammoth extends to the forefeet, and the tusks, carved along the length of the antler for convenience, are distorted. It is possible that this carving formed part of the handle of a spear-thrower, a type of artefact much used by the Magdalenians. Objects that were functional were frequently decorated, perhaps as part of a belief in sympathetic magic, one interpretation offered of cave art. A further piece of engraved bone comes from the Trou des Forges cave, also at Bruniquel. This is a rib bone carved with five life-like horses' heads, three on one side and two on the other.

In the areas vacated by the Magdalenians a culture is detectable around 10,000 BC – the Azilian, named after the type-site of Mas d'Azil in France. The art of the Magdalenians had died out but these people made their own crude artistic representations on pebbles. Various signs were painted on the pebbles in red ochre in geometric and anthropomorphic shapes – lines, dots, curves, etc. They are curious objects whose purpose is unknown, but use in games or notation systems has been suggested. Their charm is perhaps attributable to the contrast they present with the artistic achievements of their Magdalenian predecessors.

5 ANTLER FRONTLET HEAD-DRESS FROM STAR CARR, NORTH YORKSHIRE

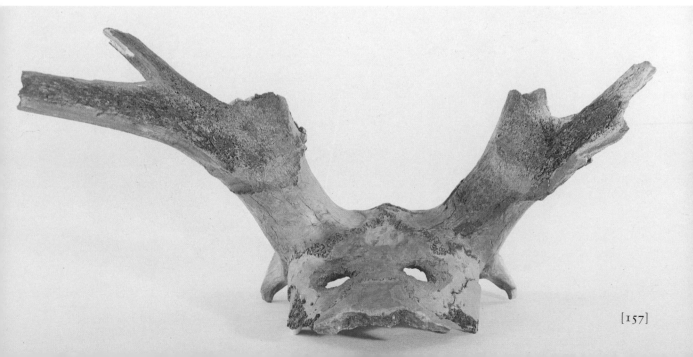

6 SEATED FIGURINE IN CLAY FROM VINČA, YUGOSLAVIA

The succeeding period, the Mesolithic, was marked in northern Europe by climatic change, the spread of forests and significant changes in the animal population. One of the seasonal settlements of the Maglemosan people was discovered at Star Carr, near Scarborough in Yorkshire, and the Department has a representative collection of the material recovered. This includes organic substances such as birch bark, wood and antler preserved by the water-logged conditions, along with numerous microliths – tiny pieces of flint which served as the tips and barbs of arrows. Prominent in the display, and almost unparalleled in prehistory, are the worked antler frontlet headdresses found at the site. Made from the skull and antlers of red deer, the antlers have been pared down and there are perforations made through the skull. Ethnographic parallels suggest their use in ritual dances or as hunting decoys.

In the Near East in the period immediately preceding the first Neolithic communities, a Mesolithic culture, the Natufian, appeared in that part of the Levantine coast formerly known as Palestine. The Natufians were a semi-sedentary people whose sickle blades and querns indicate the intensive collection of wild wheat supplementary to their basic hunting and fishing economy. The Natufians were skilled sculptors in stone and bone, producing both animal and human figures. The erotic figurine exhibited, carved in calcite, was found at a typical Natufian rock-shelter dwelling site at Ain Sakhri in the Judaean desert. It dates from the Early Natufian period, about 10,000 BC.

Material of the Neolithic period (or New Stone Age) forms the second part of the 'Man before Metals' display. This section aims to demonstrate the changes in food production brought about by agriculture and the rearing of domestic animals, with the resulting establishment of settled communities with a cultural environment encouraging to technological innovation.

7 FIGURINE IN CALCITE FROM AIN SAKHRI, JORDAN

8 CHALK FIGURE FROM GRIME'S GRAVES, NORFOLK

Here, therefore, emphasis is placed on the environmental questions with which much modern archaeology is concerned and many of the exhibits illustrate technical or economic achievements.

Stone technology progressed during the Neolithic period as increasing numbers of stone implements were needed – axes and adzes for clearing the virgin forests and for house construction, digging sticks for planting, sickles for reaping, and querns to grind the grain. But pottery was the major technological innovation of the period. Its chief uses were for cooking and storage but these were supplemented by an appreciation of the artistic potential of such a malleable material.

A valuable insight into the total range of domestic objects in use during the Neolithic was revealed by a remarkable series of Swiss lake-side settlements discovered during the nineteenth century. Waterlogged conditions ensured a high level of organic preservation and items that would normally have decayed, such as artefacts of wood and leather, and textiles, have survived. These, along with the grains and seeds of cultivated plants, and nuts and fruits collected in the woodlands, have provided the basis for an informed reconstruction of the prehistoric economy. The hafted axe of polished stone is a typical product of the Neolithic of this area. The axe blade was mounted in a sleeve of deer antler to absorb some of the impact of use, reducing the likelihood of the haft being split.

The aesthetic, and perhaps spiritual, aspirations of Neolithic society are reflected in the figurines of the period. The practices and beliefs possibly associated with these pieces are not known and cannot be accurately deduced, but the figures on display give some idea of the range of expression in this aspect of the peasant farmers' art. There is the monumental stone figure from the Greek island of Karpathos in the Dodecanese, and a seated pottery figure from Vinča in Yugoslavia, fired red, with hands on hips, pierced shoulders, elbows and ears, and a strange triangular-shaped head. By contrast, the chalk figure from the Grime's Graves flint mines in Norfolk is a crude piece of craftsmanship.

By 2000 BC Europe could show a rich and varied culture pattern with a high level of economic adaptation to differing environments, and increasing technological sophistication. In Eastern Europe a new era had already dawned with the discovery of metallurgy, which had implications far beyond those of the simple superiority of copper and bronze tools over those of stone. As the components of bronze – particularly copper and tin – are found only in certain areas of Europe, trade became a marked feature of the Bronze Age, bringing prosperity to those who controlled the sources and dispersal routes. With trade came the exchange of other materials, in particular exotica such as gold and amber used for personal ornament. Most of our evidence for the Bronze Age comes from graves and hoards of metalwork. From the graves comes a wide range of pottery, weapons and ornaments illustrating the fine craftsmanship of the period in media as diverse as gold, amber and jet; hoards enable us to study the widening range of tools and weapons in use and to gain some insight into the technological achievements of the age.

The first metalworkers in western Europe are characterized by a well-defined pottery type. Known as Beakers, these pots are outstanding for their consistent symmetry and elaborate decoration, usually created in toothed comb stamp or cord impression. The decoration concentrates on integrated schemes using repeated geometric motifs. The example shown here comes from Barnack in Cambridgeshire.

The Folkton Drums, displayed in this gallery, are dealt with below, p. 162.

9 BEAKER FROM BARNACK, CAMBRIDGESHIRE

In the succeeding Early Bronze Age period the individual drinking vessel was on rare occasions made of materials other than pottery. These vessels in amber, shale or gold illustrate the interplay of personal prestige and specialized craftsmanship characteristic

10 of the period. The Rillaton gold cup, placed on permanent loan by King Edward VIII, comes from a burial in the Rillaton Barrow in Cornwall and is one of only three such found in temperate Europe. It is of sheet gold ribbed for both reinforcement and decoration and has a remarkable ribbon-like handle secured by rivets with lozenge-shaped washers.

West European craftsmen showed an early interest in the decorative possibilities of sheet gold. In Ireland, Beaker ceramic motifs were transferred to crescent-shaped neck ornaments or *lunulae*. The zoned geo-

11 metric designs, such as those seen on the *lunula* from Mangerton, Co. Kerry, often achieved a fine degree of intricate detail. Elsewhere this crescent form for necklaces was reproduced by strings of beads maintaining the desired shape through being held by com-

12 plex, bored spacer plates in amber and jet. The necklace from Melfort, Strathclyde, is a typical example of a jet necklace in crescent shape and a characteristic find in Scotland from this period. The acme of sheet goldwork in the West European Bronze Age tradition, dating to about 1200 BC, is the great gold cape found in a grave at Mold in Clwyd. Made from a continuous piece of metal, beaten out over a block to obtain the shape, its surface is decorated in *repoussé* (hammered into relief from the reverse side) with bosses and ribs in a pattern that may imitate the folds of cloth. The cape was presumably for ceremonial use, since the wearer cannot move his arms once the cape is in place.

The Roman mosaic pavement and window grille from Hinton St Mary, the Basse-Yutz flagons and Celtic fire-dog, also displayed in the central saloon, are discussed below, pp. 166–7, 175, 181, 182.

10 GOLD CUP FROM RILLATON, CORNWALL

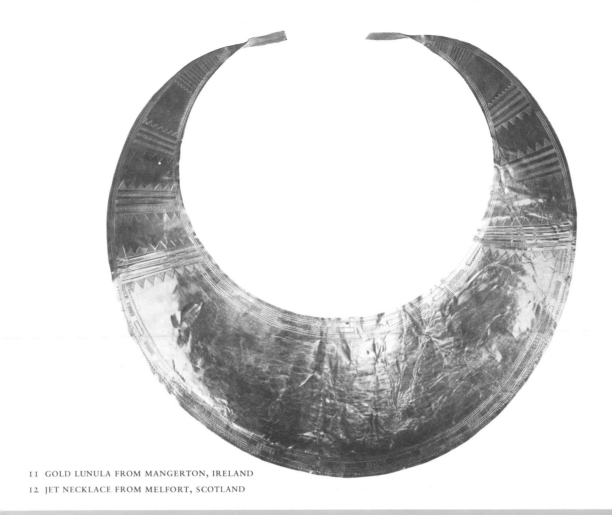

11 GOLD LUNULA FROM MANGERTON, IRELAND
12 JET NECKLACE FROM MELFORT, SCOTLAND

The Folkton Drums hint at artistic achievement in other materials. These three chalk cylinders were found in a child's grave in North Yorkshire and are elaborately carved with circle and star motifs and other geometric designs. The faces carved on the 'Drums' are, however, their most striking feature, with eyebrows, nose and eyes clearly indicated and on one a lozenge-shaped mouth. The treatment of the chalk recalls wood carving and suggests that wooden pieces of this kind existed but have failed to survive.

It is clear from the hoards of the Bronze Age that an increasing range of specialized weapons and tools was made, with a high point of achievement reached towards the end of the period from about 1200 BC. The daggers, halberds and spears of the earlier period were later supplemented or replaced by more substantial weapons, first by the rapier then by the heavy, leaf-shaped, cut-and-thrust sword. Parade gear in sheet bronze appears alongside the new weaponry. Particularly outstanding are the large decorated shields of Yetholm type such as the shield from Aberystwyth, Dyfed, decorated with twenty rows of bosses alternating with a similar number of ribs. This competence in sheet bronzework was also extended to the manufacture of large riveted buckets and cauldrons and a variety of trumpets and horns.

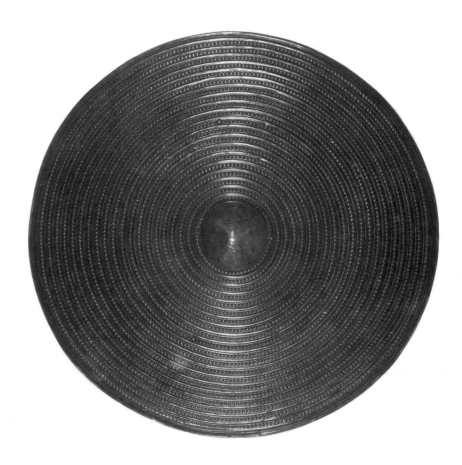

13 BRONZE SHIELD FROM ABERYSTWYTH, WALES

14 CHALK 'DRUMS' FROM FOLKTON, YORKSHIRE

Bronze and Iron Age pottery tends to be over-shadowed by the metalwork of these periods, but much fine pottery was made especially in the Hallstatt period (encompassing the late Bronze and early Iron Ages in Europe). In the seventh and sixth centuries BC the people of the Alb Salem group of south-west Germany were making magnificent pottery. One fine
15 example is the massive dish from Tailfingen in Württemberg. It is red fired, differentially blackened with graphite and incised with bold patterns of geometric decoration in triangular shapes enclosing dots and parallel line hatching. Rather different are the later Iron Age (La Tène period) pots (in Room 39) which often imitated the shapes of metal vessels and the curvilinear patterns of contemporary metalwork. Probably influenced by contact with the Classical world, later Iron Age pottery imitated the shapes of flagons and ewers and the earlier geometric styles give
16 way to more free-flowing decoration. An example from this period is the elegant painted urn from Prunay in the Marne region of France, dating from about 300 BC. With a reddish-buff surface painted with exuberant swirling scroll patterns in a brown pigment, the Prunay urn is one of the most beautiful objects from prehistoric Europe in the Museum.

15 DISH FROM TAILFINGEN, GERMANY

16 URN FROM PRUNAY, FRANCE

Any consideration of Iron Age Europe is bound to be dominated by the Celts whose art represents perhaps the high point of achievement in the prehistory of Europe. Though classical authors and archaeology provide us with confused and often contradictory information about their origins and movements, we know from their material culture that the Celts' approach to art was eclectic. They absorbed influences from the classical world, from the Persians and Scythians and from Bronze Age traditions of Central and Eastern Europe. Using these, they evolved a series of styles which constituted a new synthesis of abstract design that continued to develop from the fifth century BC through to the Middle Ages.

17b   The British Museum is fortunate to possess two outstanding examples of early Celtic (or La Tène) art – the elegant bronze beaked flagons from Basse-Yutz on the Moselle in France, known as the Lorraine flagons (displayed in the central saloon). The vessels, dating from about 400 BC, are inlaid at the foot and throat with coral which has now faded to white, contrasting with the present patina of the bronze. The Celts were fond of coloured decoration and used coral and red enamel to enliven their metalwork. Various influences are detectable in these pieces in which the craftsman has achieved a mature artistic synthesis from disparate elements. The handle comprises a strange elongated creature, possibly a dog or wolf, with no hind legs but prominent head, ears and forelegs, showing Persian or possibly Scythian influence. The base of the handle shows the animal's body spreading out into a masked face with drooping moustache – a favourite Celtic motif derived from Etruscan prototypes – with coral settings for eyes and

17a   beard. There are more fabulous beasts on either side of the neck and a small duck appears to be swimming unconcerned down the wine stream – perhaps a lingering remnant of the old Hallstatt tradition in which the duck motif figured prominently. The flagon is a masterly adaptation of an Etruscan design and well illustrates Celtic contact with the classical world, the source of wine and other luxury goods on which Celtic society, vividly described by the classical authors, depended.

17a DETAIL FROM BASSE-YUTZ FLAGON

17b BRONZE FLAGON FROM BASSE-YUTZ, FRANCE

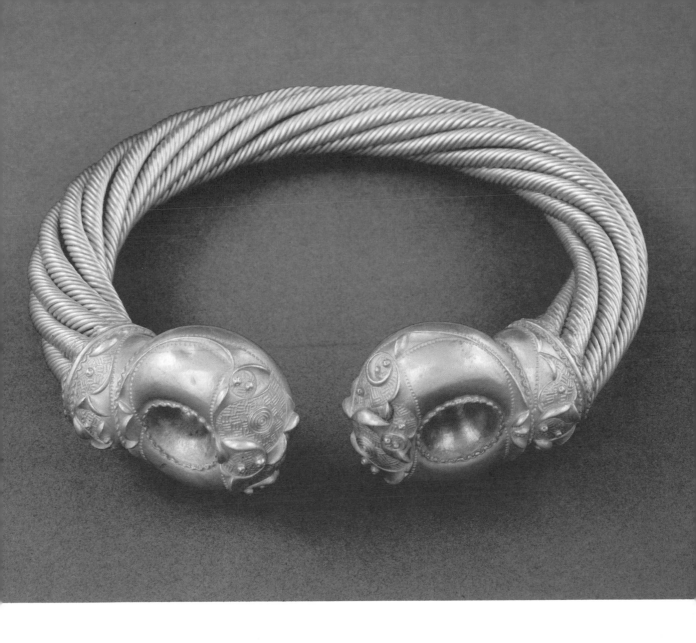

18a ELECTRUM TORC, AND DETAIL OF A TERMINAL, FROM SNETTISHAM, NORFOLK

18b SECOND ELECTRUM TORC (RIGHT) AND GOLD BRACELET FROM SNETTISHAM (ACTUAL SIZE)

18c DETAIL OF ORNAMENT ON THE SNETTISHAM BRACELET

One mysterious artefact associated with the Celts is the torc, an ornamented metal neck ring properly made of twisted strands of metal – hence the name. Torcs were probably worn only on special occasions and were frequently too fragile or unwieldy to allow regular use. Classical writers claimed they were worn by Celtic warriors in battle, perhaps as talismen, but archaeological evidence, especially from the La Tène graves of north-east France, suggests they were worn by women. The problem remains unresolved. Two torcs from different periods illustrate the variety of approach to decoration. The bronze torc from Courtisols in the Marne *département* of France comes from a grave of the third century BC and is a typical example of the 'plastic' style of Celtic art. This was applied particularly to ornaments and chariot-fittings to give a three-dimensional effect, and is heavier and more fluid than earlier work. The Courtisols torc, part of the Morel collection of La Tène grave material, features staring faces below the terminals, reminiscent of the faces on the Basse-Yutz flagons. Other faces appear inverted below the terminals and scroll patterns link the two ends.

A later torc, from Snettisham in Norfolk, is very different in style and more impressive in effect. It is dated to around 50 BC by a coin, a quarter-stater of the Atrebates tribe, concealed in one of its terminals. Made from electrum, a gold/silver alloy, it is composed of several strands of metal wire twisted together, whose ends are inserted into hollow ring terminals. This torc was linked by a fragment of another to a fine gold bracelet; together they constituted one of several hoards from Snettisham that may have been the treasury of a paramount chieftain. The incomplete torc was used to round up the weight of the bracelet and complete torc to exactly twenty-five Celtic ounces. This and the association of these objects with the gold coin indicate a change in the value-system as torcs came to be valued as much for their dead weight as for their aesthetic appeal and the prestige conveyed by ownership. A distinctive 'Snettisham' style has been deduced from the decoration on the complete torc and bracelet which comprises a pattern of curved ridges enclosing incised hatched areas and small spherical bosses. The style is seen on other British metalwork of the period.

19 BRONZE TORC FROM COURTISOLS, FRANCE (ACTUAL SIZE)

Indeed one of the most interesting aspects of Celtic art was the development of 'Insular' styles in the British Isles from the third century BC. Britain was at this time a receiving area for influences as well as people from the Continent. Thus as a result of trading and interchange, especially with Gaul, the products of Gaulish and Rhenish craftsmen, latterly under the influence of Rome, and of Rome direct, penetrated these recesses of the Celtic world. One of the most appealing manifestations of an insular style is mirror decoration. This developed in southern Britain in the later first century BC and continued until the Claudian invasion in the first century AD. Bronze mirrors were made in circular and non-circular shapes and their backs were vehicles for refined curvilinear ornamentation whose style appears to be unique. The mirror from Desborough, Northamptonshire, carries a symmetrical pattern of swirling leaf-like curves with negative and positive areas of chased matt hatching between. The Museum also displays the Holcombe and Saint Keverne mirrors, the latter incised with an asymmetrical pattern. A typical Celtic jest can be seen on the Holcombe mirror. When held with the handle upwards, as may have been the intention with the larger mirrors, a small cat's face can be seen at the point where the handle joins the body of the mirror.

Insular artists were, however, also producing fine warrior equipment which in some cases may have been intended only for parade purposes, as many items are too fragile to have stood up to combat. Outstanding and well-known examples of this equipment are the Witham shield and Waterloo helmet. Both were found in rivers, the Witham and the Thames respectively, and many of these objects may have been votive deposits flung into rivers to appease the gods.

20 BRONZE MIRROR FROM DESBOROUGH, NORTHAMPTONSHIRE

21 The Witham shield is a typical Celtic long shield but with a bronze facing, whereas functional battle shields were generally made entirely of wood or leather. It comprises a plain bronze sheet, originally backed with leather and was once ornamented in the centre with a rather stylized boar figure, probably modelled in relief. This was later removed or became dislodged and can now only be detected by the corrosion marks and pattern of nail holes. A midrib was later added with circular terminals and moulded central boss decorated with coral studs. Horse-mask motifs can be seen on the midrib next to the terminals. The central boss was intended to give protection to the hand-hold behind the shield, implying that the shield was designed at least to be carried, if not actually to be used, in battle.

The helmet was an equally vital part of the Celtic warrior's battle equipment. The two-horned bronze 22 example dredged out of the Thames near Waterloo Bridge is unique in that it is the only surviving Celtic horned helmet, though classical writers described them, and they feature in sculptural representations of Celtic warriors. It is likely that they were normally made of organic materials and consequently have not survived. The Waterloo helmet is decorated with five round studs, cross-scored to take red enamel, with a *repoussé* design of thin ridges and bosses on front and back. It has a somewhat similar style of ornamentation to that on the Snettisham torc. The scored and enamelled studs are characteristic of late La Tène art in Europe.

There is both historical and archaeological evidence for the presence in southern Britain of various distinctive Celtic tribes during the first century BC. Archaeologically an Aylesford culture can be identi-

21 BRONZE SHIELD FROM THE RIVER WITHAM, LINCOLNSHIRE

22 BRONZE HELMET FROM THE RIVER THAMES, LONDON

fied, characterized by a group of distinctive material remains first discovered at the type-site in Kent. Here, in 1886, a grave was unearthed containing cremated bones and a set of bronze brooches enclosed in the remnants of a bronze-bound wooden bucket. A pattern of similar burials in the same area was later established – always featuring a cremation, the burial rite thought to be associated with the Belgae, distinctive pottery including pedestal urns and corrugated beakers, wine amphorae and bronzes. The bucket at Aylesford was about ten inches high, and had been constructed of wooden staves held together by three horizontal bronze strips whose decoration, and that of the bucket handle, is the main point of interest. The upper band features stylized horses recalling those on contemporary coinage, although their floral-style heads and the faces on the bucket handle hark back to earlier styles. The heads at the bases of the hooped handle have broad foreheads, low cheeks and slanting eyes. Above the brow is a ridge, probably representing a cap, surmounted by a plume.

Further burials found at Welwyn and Welwyn Garden City in Hertfordshire have yielded some remarkable items. From one of the Welwyn cremation 23 burial sites, discovered early in this century, two iron firedogs were unearthed. These are perhaps the most typical possessions of a Celtic chief and most evocative of the feasting tradition and the importance of the hearth as the central focus of society. The firedogs 24 have the traditional ox-headed terminals and were designed to be placed around an open fire. One example is displayed in the central saloon and amply illustrates the importance of the blacksmith's craft, emphasizing his vital role in the economy of the pre-Roman Iron Age.

24 DETAIL OF FIREDOG   23 IRON FIREDOG FROM A GRAVE AT WELWYN, HERTFORDSHIRE

In 1965 a further burial was found at Welwyn Garden City, in which the body had probably been wrapped in a bearskin before cremation. Along with a group of amphorae and an imported Roman silver cup, the grave-goods included a set of glass gaming pieces. Whereas firedogs are familiar features of the Celtic chieftain's household, the glass gaming counters are unique in Britain but may be imports from Gaul. There are 24 domed and slightly pointed glass pieces, six each in blue, light green, white and yellow, decorated with 'eyes' or glass rods sunk into the pieces and forming interlocked curves. Since amber and glass bead and bracelet fragments, possibly used as dice, were also found, the pieces probably belong to a board game – perhaps a race game like backgammon – requiring four players.

25

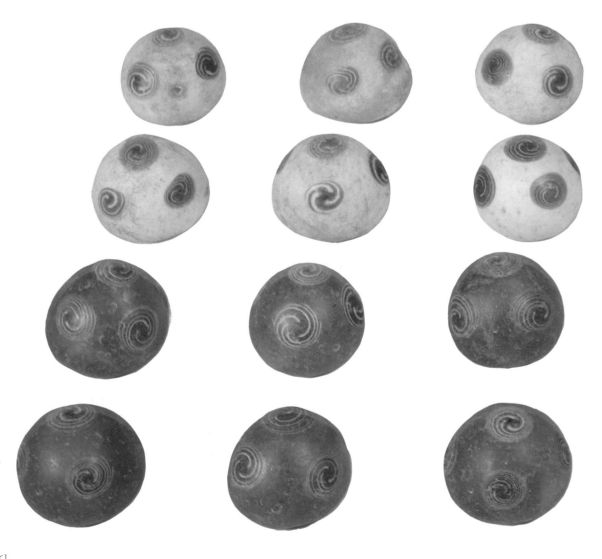

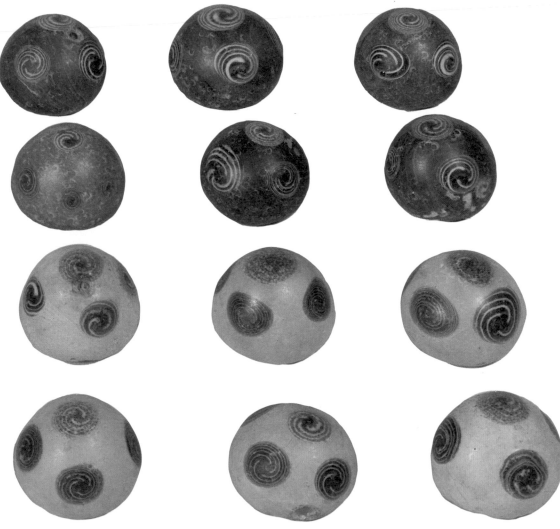

25 GLASS GAMING PIECES FROM A GRAVE AT WELWYN GARDEN CITY, HERTFORDSHIRE

The incorporation of Britain into the Roman Empire as a result of the Claudian invasion in AD 43 did not lead to the suppression of native art and technology. But the influence of the conqueror was, in many areas, irresistible, effecting changes not only in administration, economy and religion but also in art style, artefact types and modes of production. After the initial military conquest, the imperial policy was to involve the population, at least the élite, in a Roman style of self-government by encouraging a taste for education and luxury goods – articles in the classical style hitherto either unknown in Britain or limited to a small privileged group. The increase in demand for everyday household goods was met by changes in production methods, and workshops sprang up to provide local copies of imported wares. Naturalistic classical styles of art tended to replace, though not entirely, native Celtic traditions. Most important, new art media were introduced to the province by the Romans, particularly mosaics and mural paintings.

Rarely do history and archaeology exactly coincide, which makes one item in the Roman Britain collection outstanding – the tomb of Classicianus. Tacitus tells us that Classicianus was the procurator (financial head) of the province after the rebellion of Boudicca in AD 60–61 and was responsible for checking the retaliatory policy of the general who had put down the rebellion. The discovery of Classicianus' tomb, therefore, though found in fragments and reconstructed, is of great interest to archaeologists and historians alike. It had been broken up and some stones had been re-used in the foundations of the city wall in Roman London. But clearly, as the reconstruction shows, it had once been a large and imposing monument.

The Mildenhall Treasure is perhaps the most impressive item in the Romano-British collections. It comprises 34 superb pieces of silver tableware which were ploughed up during the Second World War at Mildenhall in Suffolk and acquired by the British Museum as Treasure Trove in 1946. The pieces were buried about the middle of the fourth century AD, perhaps to prevent them falling into the hands of barbarian invaders. They were certainly imports, probably from Gaul or the Mediterranean area. The Treasure consists of dishes, cups, bowls, spoons and 26 ladles, the most magnificent item being the great dish. This is decorated in relief with Bacchanalian figures on the outer frieze, nereids (sea nymphs) on the backs of sea monsters on the inner frieze and a dominating figure, possibly Neptune, in the centre of the dish. In contrast to these pagan scenes, three of the spoons bear evidence of Christianity – with the ☧ (Chi-Rho monogram), the early Christian symbol comprising the first two letters of Christ's name in Greek, inscribed between the Greek letters Alpha and Omega. Two other spoons bear inscriptions of names and wishes for good health and may have been christening gifts.

26 GREAT SILVER DISH FROM THE TREASURE FOUND AT MILDENHALL, SUFFOLK

27 SECTION OF WALL-PLASTER FROM LULLINGSTONE ROMAN VILLA, KENT

The presence and impact of Christianity is also illustrated by two other objects from Roman Britain – the Lullingstone wall plaster and the Hinton St Mary mosaic pavement. Thousands of fragments of wall plaster were collected in 1949 at the Lullingstone Roman villa in Kent where in antiquity the plaster had shattered when falling to the floor and was further confused by falling through to the basement. A painstaking reconstruction programme has been carried on at the Museum and two restored parts are on display. One shows a painted Chi-Rho monogram and the 27 other a frieze of six figures whose outstretched arms may indicate an attitude of prayer.

The mosaic pavement which is laid out in full at the head of the main stairs was found at Hinton St Mary in Dorset in 1963, where it had covered two rooms of a villa. Most private villas and the more important civic buildings in Roman Britain had mosaic floors. The central feature of the pavement in the larger of 28 the two rooms is a man's head with the Chi-Rho monogram behind it. This is the earliest known representation of Christ executed in mosaic on a floor from the Roman Empire. In each corner of the larger floor the head and shoulders of a human figure appear which might be representations of the four evangelists. The part of the mosaic that was in the smaller room

28 SECTION OF PAVEMENT FROM HINTON ST MARY ROMAN VILLA, DORSET

29 SAMIAN BOWL FROM GREAT ST HELEN'S LONDON

portrays Bellerophon, mounted on his horse Pegasus, killing the Chimaera, and hunting scenes showing hounds with jewelled collars chasing stags.

Passing from the magnificent and rare to the comparatively humble and common, we should now turn to the type of artefact which would have been owned by most households; Samian pottery, for example, frequently occurs among the archaeological remains of Roman Britain. It was widely used throughout the Empire and appears to have been the most durable tableware. It is a glossy red mass-produced pottery, often made with moulded or barbotine (piped like icing on a cake) decoration. Details of ornamentation or a potter's name stamped on the pots normally enable its place of manufacture to be determined. In fact most Samian ware was made in Gaul, but there were a few local imitations. The example illustrated 29 here is a typical decorated bowl, complete with potter's stamp, made in the late first century AD in southern Gaul, and found in London. The decoration, which is moulded, shows flowers and birds in a scroll pattern.

Glass is a substance that became much more widely used in Britain in the Roman period, particularly in the household for windows and many kinds of vessels. The latter were often elegant in shape and of fine coloured or translucent glass. Most of the glass in Britain came from industries established in northern Gaul and the Rhineland in the first century AD. A fine 30 example is a flagon, pale bluish-green in colour, found in a grave at Bayford in Kent, dating to the late second or third century. Fragments of window glass are often found, but whole windowpanes have rarely been recovered. The Roman collection, however, does include the first such pane (from Garden Hill, Hartfield, Sussex) discovered on a Romano-British site. The Museum possesses an iron window grille, a rare object, recovered from a room in the Hinton St Mary villa. It is composed of eight flat iron bars arranged at right angles with iron cross-pieces securing the joins.

30 GLASS FLAGON FROM BAYFORD, KENT

31 BRONZE HELMET FROM RIBCHESTER, LANCASHIRE

Sculpture in Roman Britain features a classical naturalism which is well illustrated by the official statues introduced by the Romans. The bronze statue of the Emperor Nero from Barking Hall in Suffolk is a fine example of imperial grandeur combined with classical form. It shows the Emperor striking a stylized pose, with a tunic and breastplate inlaid with copper, silver and niello (a black substance of metal alloys). The colossal bronze head of the Emperor Hadrian (displayed in the gallery), which was found in the Thames at London Bridge, and an arm found elsewhere in London, are all that remains of a massive official statue of the Emperor which may originally have been sited in central London. It was possibly made to commemorate Hadrian's visit to Britain in AD 122 and its dismemberment may have been the work of raiders in late Roman times.

One item which evokes the new militarism of the conqueror, while harking back to the Celtic warrior tradition, is the famous helmet from Ribchester in Lancashire. Made in the late first or early second century AD, it is a cavalry parade helmet of bronze with a vizor-mask and a crown embossed with fighting scenes. The helmet is too fragile and elaborate to have been worn in active combat and was probably used only for cavalry exercises, introduced by Celtic auxiliaries in the Roman Army. It makes an interesting comparison with the Celtic Waterloo helmet, itself a ceremonial object.

Indeed, the older artistic traditions were not entirely superseded during the Roman occupation. A final, interesting note to the Romano-British collections is contributed by a small ornament found at Icklingham in Suffolk which appears to combine the two artistic traditions. It is a bronze mount in the form of a triskele, or three-legged figure, of three *peltae* (a type of Greek shield and a motif popular with the Romans) but the design is executed in typical Celtic 'trumpet' style. This is a survival which perhaps aptly links the prehistoric past with the Dark Ages which succeeded the collapse of Roman rule in Britain.

32 BRONZE STATUE OF THE EMPEROR NERO
FROM BARKING HALL, SUFFOLK

33 BRONZE ORNAMENT FROM ICKLINGHAM, SUFFOLK
(ACTUAL SIZE)

Prints & Drawings

67 Prints & drawings

The Department of Prints and Drawings, which houses the national collection of Western graphic art, has no permanent display: not only is the collection itself too large and too varied, but drawings and prints are easily damaged by excessive exposure to light. Temporary exhibitions on particular themes or drawn from particular sections of the collection are mounted two or three times a year, but the bulk of the collection is stored in solander boxes and portfolios and can be consulted in the Students' Room by anyone holding a valid student's ticket. A few prints and drawings that are too large to be stored in this way are on permanent exhibition: Michelangelo's *Epifania* (which measures about $8 \times 5\frac{1}{2}$ ft and is the only known complete cartoon by him, using the word in its technical sense of an immediately preliminary drawing on the same scale as the intended painting), and Raphael's cartoon for the *Madonna with the Tower* in the National Gallery, in the alcove immediately opposite the entrance to the exhibition gallery; Dürer's enormous woodcut of the *Triumph of Maximilian* on the landing outside; and in the entrance vestibule of the Students' Room the finest known complete impression of the first state, dated 1500, of Jacopo de'Barbari's bird's-eye view of Venice.

The collection of drawings, though relatively small by comparison with some of the great Continental accumulations such as those in Paris and Florence, is one of the best balanced and most representative in the world, for in it most of the greatest masters of the major schools are well, and in many cases superbly, represented. Its foundations were laid in the eighteenth century by the bequest of Sir Hans Sloane (whose collections constituted the nucleus of the whole Museum) in 1753. This was followed by the bequests of William Fawkener in 1769, the Revd C. M. Cracherode in 1799 and Richard Payne Knight in 1824. On the nucleus thus formed the collection has been built up over the last 150 years by a systematic policy of acquisition. Other important accessions include the purchase in 1836 of the John Sheepshanks Collection of some 800 Netherlandish drawings, mostly of the seventeenth century, and 41 volumes of Netherlandish etchings and engravings; the purchase in 1895 of the Malcolm Collection of about 900 drawings of all schools, many of them of the finest quality; the purchase in 1902 of the James Reeve Collection of about 500 English drawings and watercolours, mostly of the Norwich School; the transference on indefinite loan from the National Gallery in 1931 of the drawings, numbering nearly 20,000, from the Turner Bequest; the anonymous gift in 1946 of the Phillipps-Fenwick Collection of more than 1,500 drawings, mostly Italian, the largest remaining fragment of the great collection formed at the beginning of the nineteenth century by Sir Thomas Lawrence; and the bequest by César Mange de Hauke in 1968 of sixteen important French nineteenth century drawings.

In the Italian section, the Early and High Renaissance are particularly well represented. Among outstanding drawings of the fifteenth century in Florence is *The Prisoner before a Judge* by Antonio Pollaiuolo, a drawing that exemplifies the Florentine tradition that conceived the fundamental language of artistic expression in terms of the nude figure in action. This tradition was continued in the vigorous black chalk nude studies by Pollaiuolo's younger contemporary and pupil Luca Signorelli, and was carried to its fullest pitch of expression by Michelangelo. The complementary aspect of Florentine art is the linear graceful

1 style represented by Sandro Botticelli, whose drawing of *Abundance* or *Autumn* is one of the most beautiful Renaissance drawings that has come down to us, analogous in spirit to the artist's painting of *Primavera* (Florence, Uffizi). Andrea Verrocchio is represented by one drawing, the magnificent head of a woman. The emphasis on the complexity of the *coiffure* anticipates the work of his pupil Leonardo da Vinci, 21 of whose drawings are in the collection. They vary in type, the most remarkable perhaps being the Verrocchiesque *Ideal Head of a Warrior* in metalpoint.

In north Italy during the *quattrocento*, the chief artistic centres were Venice, Padua and Verona. Nine drawings are kept under the name of Giovanni Bellini, the greatest Venetian artist of the period, but some of these are possibly by his brother-in-law, the Paduan Andrea Mantegna. Drawings by Mantegna are very rare, and the group in the Museum, which numbers at least six and possibly as many as nine, is unrivalled both in quantity and quality. It includes the carefully

2 finished, coloured, *Mars, Venus and Diana* – a drawing as beautiful in its own way as the Botticelli *Abundance*. By Giovanni Bellini's elder brother, Gentile, who visited Constantinople in about 1470, we have the drawings of a *Turkish Lady* and a *Janissary*; and by their father, Jacopo Bellini, the so-called 'sketchbook' of some 100 leaves, with black chalk drawings of a great variety of subject, religious, allegorical, mythological, architectural, etc. (The companion volume is in the Louvre.)

The collection includes a few fine examples of drawings by Andrea del Sarto and Fra Bartolomeo, the chief protagonists of the High Renaissance style in Florence; but in the early sixteenth century the artistic initiative had begun to shift from Florence to Rome, where the Florentine-trained Michelangelo executed many of his greatest works, and the Umbrian Raphael all of his. Both artists are magnificently represented in the Museum, Raphael by 39 drawings, Michel-

3 angelo by more than 80. Raphael's include an early self-portrait, done at the age of sixteen or seventeen, and studies for some of his greatest works – the *Parnassus* and the *Disputa* in the Vatican, the *Sibyls* in S. Maria della Pace, Rome, and the Vatican *Transfiguration* – and also the cartoon for the *Madonna of the Tower* (National Gallery), on permanent display

4 in the exhibition gallery. The group of Michelangelo drawings, the largest outside Italy, illustrates almost every phase of his long career: especially noteworthy

1 SANDRO BOTTICELLI 1444–1510. 'Abundance' or 'Autumn'

2 ANDREA MANTEGNA 1431–1506. Mars, Venus (?) and Diana

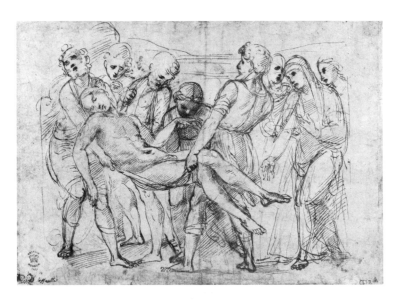

3 RAPHAEL 1483–1520. Study for the *Borghese Entombment*

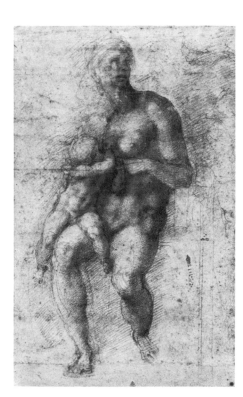

4 MICHELANGELO 1475–1564. The Virgin and Child

are the study for a figure in the early cartoon of the *Bathers*, the sketch of the first, discarded scheme for the decoration of the Sistine Ceiling, the series of designs for the tombs in the Medici Chapel in S. Lorenzo in Florence, and the group of very late *Crucifixion* drawings. His only surviving complete cartoon, the large-scale *'Epifania'*, is also on permanent display in the exhibition gallery.

Michelangelo, essentially a solitary genius, had no pupils, but there are five drawings by his most important follower, Sebastiano del Piombo (the drawings by Michelangelo also include four that he made to assist Sebastiano with his paintings of the *Flagellation* and the *Raising of Lazarus*). Raphael, in contrast, headed a flourishing school, and the Museum possesses a very good representative collection of drawings by his pupils and/or associates Giulio Romano, Perino del Vaga, Baldassare Peruzzi and Polidoro da Caravaggio. Towards the end of his life Raphael was developing in the direction of the graceful, decorative style which is usually called 'Mannerism', and after his premature death in 1520 the tendency was carried further by his younger associates. The same development away from the ideals of the High Renaissance was formulated independently in Florence by Rosso and Pontormo. It was continued there by Bronzino, Francesco Salviati and Vasari, and in Rome by Daniele da Volterra, Taddeo and Federico Zuccaro, Pellegrino Tibaldi and Raffaellino da Reggio; there are drawings by all these artists in the collection and it has been the Museum's especial policy in recent years to build up the representation of this phase of Italian art.

5 PIETRO DA CORTONA 1596–1669. Jason and the Golden Fleece: Allegory of the Arms of the Borghese Family

Although Rome was the most important theatre for the evolution of the High Renaissance style, Parma and Venice contributed their own local variants. There are 17 drawings by the Parmese Correggio; his more prolific compatriot and follower Parmigianino, whose work belongs with Mannerism, is represented by nearly 100. Only one certain drawing by the greatest Venetian painter of the sixteenth century, Titian, is in the collection – a small study in black chalk for an Apostle in the altarpiece of the *Assumption* in S. Maria dei Frari, Venice; but his younger contemporaries Jacopo Tintoretto and Paolo Veronese are well represented, and there is an important group of about 90 composition sketches in oil on paper by the younger Tintoretto, Domenico.

The beginning of the seventeenth century in Italy is marked by a naturalistic reaction. No drawings by Michelangelo da Caravaggio, the exponent of a highly realistic style, are known; but Annibale Carracci, whose idealized naturalism was of seminal influence upon the development both of the Classical and of the Baroque style of the 1620s, returned to the High Renaissance example of Raphael and Michelangelo in making numerous preparatory studies for his paintings. The Museum possesses a large group of his drawings, some 24 in all, which include, besides several landscape drawings in pen and ink, the cartoon of a helmsman for the fresco, *Ulysses and the Sirens*, in the *camerino* of the Palazzo Farnese in Rome. Annibale's brother Agostino, and their cousin Lodovico, are also well represented. Annibale's Bolognese followers, Guido Reni, Albano, Domenichino and Lanfranco adhered to their master's working method, and were

accomplished draughtsmen; there are many drawings by them in the Museum, and no fewer than 57 by the prolific Guercino, also a Bolognese, who was a pupil of Ludovico Carracci.

As the influence of the followers of Caravaggio and Annibale Carracci waned, the true Baroque style developed in Rome. This is typified in the grandiose decorative works of Pietro da Cortona, 16 drawings by whom are in the Museum; his pupils Ferri, Romanelli and Baldi are also represented. Bernini, who was primarily a sculptor and architect, was another brilliant protagonist of the Baroque. The collection includes two self-portraits by him, in youth and in age. Towards the end of the seventeenth century Roman painting came to be dominated by Maratta's high Baroque classicism. The essentially academic basis of his art is shown by the fact that most of the 17 drawings by him in the collection are studies from the model.

In the eighteenth century, it was above all in Venice that the great tradition of Italian painting continued, with Giovanni Battista Tiepolo, whose lively rococo figure style parallels contemporary developments in France, and the two great view-painters, Francesco Guardi and Antonio Canaletto. Both of them specialized in townscapes, especially of Venice, but the collection also includes a number of Canaletto's views in England. Another chiefly topographical draughtsman who is well represented in the collection is Giovanni Battista Piranesi, who though also a Venetian by birth spent his working life mainly in Rome – the city which is the subject of most of his etchings and drawings.

6 GIOVANNI BATTISTA TIEPOLO 1696–1770. Entrance to a Farm-Yard

7 CANALETTO 1697–1768. A view from the Artist's House in Venice

In Germany the art of the Renaissance flowered briefly but intensely, and it is fortunate that the Department's representation of this School is mainly concentrated in that period. The collection of drawings by the greatest of all German artists, Albrecht Dürer, is the largest in the world and one of the most representative, and is particularly strong in watercolour landscapes and portrait drawings. The other great German artist of the early sixteenth century, Hans Holbein the younger, best known as a portrait draughtsman, is unevenly represented by a large group of designs for jewellery and metalwork, but by only two portrait drawings, both of ladies, one traditionally identified as Sir Thomas More's daughter, Margaret Roper, the other as Queen Anne Boleyn.

Our collection of the rest of the German School (with which may be linked the Swiss) from the fifteenth century to the end of the seventeenth is small but choice. Outstanding among drawings by the followers of Dürer in Nuremberg are those of Hans von Kulmbach and Hans Schaufelein, while those by Hans Holbein the Elder and Hans Burgkmair at Augsburg illustrate the rise of the Renaissance in southern Germany. Among the seventeenth-century drawings may be particularly noted the group of technically

8 ALBRECHT DÜRER 1471–1528. A House in a Lake ('Weierhaus')

9 ALBRECHT DÜRER 1471–1528. A Windisch Peasant Woman

highly accomplished landscapes in bodycolour that are traditionally attributed to Adam Elsheimer.

The collection of drawings of the Netherlandish school (which, after the breakup, in the later sixteenth century, of the Low Countries into the Protestant North and the Catholic South is subdivided into 'Dutch' and 'Flemish') goes back to the beginning of the fifteenth century, with a group of portraits in silverpoint by or attributed to Jan van Eyck and Rogier van der Weyden. Subsequent developments can be studied in detail here, and include fine examples from all the important artistic countries, Bruges, Ghent and Antwerp, as well as the only known brush drawing by Hieronymus Bosch, the *Entombment*.

The two most important treasures of the sixteenth century are the unrivalled group of twelve drawings by the precocious genius, Lucas van Leiden, and the group of landscape drawings, together with the only known drawing of an allegorical subject, *The Calumny of Apelles*, by Pieter Bruegel the Elder. The leading draughtsmen of the next generation, Hendrick Goltzius and Jacob de Gheyn II, are well represented, together with many of their lesser contemporaries.

10 ROGIER VAN DER WEYDEN 1397/1400–1464.
 A Young Woman

11 LUCAS VAN LEIDEN 1494–1533.
 Study for a *Virgin and Child*

12 PIETER BRUEGEL THE ELDER *c.* 1530–1569. Landscape

From the beginning of the seventeenth century in the Catholic South (Flanders) the artistic world was dominated by Peter Paul Rubens. All periods of his career and most aspects of his interests can be studied here. There are five studies after the model (of which perhaps the most impressive, both in the skill displayed and in the feeling expressed, is that of *Christ on the Cross*) and preparatory studies for parts of compositions, for instance, the large sheet of Dancers for the painting of the *Flemish Kermesse* in the Louvre. Rubens closely studied the work of his predecessors and the collection is rich in copies after Michelangelo, Raphael and others. His antiquarian and collecting interests are reflected in sketches after the Antique, and by the numerous drawings by earlier masters that he improved by retouching. A small but important group of landscapes includes his famous *Trees at Sunset*, while among the portraits is one of his most outstanding, that of his first wife, *Isabella Brant*. His

13 PETER PAUL RUBENS 1577–1640. Dancing Peasants

14 PETER PAUL RUBENS 1575–1640.
Isabella Brant, the Artist's First Wife

15 ANTHONIE VAN DYCK 1599–1641. Landscape

designs for title-pages and preparatory drawings for engravings after his paintings are also well represented.

While the collection of drawings by Rubens is less comprehensive than the Louvre's, that of those by his brilliant assistant, Anthonie van Dyck, is without rival, even apart from the 'Italian Sketchbook' acquired from Chatsworth in 1957. There is a good representation of his early pen studies, which sometimes are not easy to distinguish from those of Rubens. After his return from Italy in 1627 he was principally interested in portraiture. There are four preparatory drawings in the Department for engravings in his *Iconography*, executed in black chalk on white paper with the occasional use of brown wash, which admirably illustrate his portrait style before he settled in England in 1632. For the portraits he painted in this country he made studies in a technique of black chalk on blue paper, perhaps inspired by the sixteenth-century Venetian School. The Museum's collection of drawings of this type is without parallel and includes many studies for famous paintings, such as the various versions of *Charles I on Horseback*. Most of his charming landscape drawings, of which the Museum has an impressive group, seem to date from his second English period.

The only other Flemish artist of that period who was of any real importance is Jacob Jordaens. His spirited, down-to-earth nature, while akin to Rubens's in its vitality, lacks the latter's intellectual refinement. He was essentially a decorative artist, and this aspect is given full scope in his tapestry designs (see, for instance, *The Falconer*). The work of most of Rubens's assistants is of interest chiefly as a reflection of his influence. Frans Snyders, who specialized in animal and still-life subjects; Jan Brueghel, the landscape and still-life painter; and Adriaen Brouwer, the greatest master of peasant *genre*, are notable exceptions, by whom there are fine examples in the collection.

16 JACOB JORDAENS 1593–1678. *The Falconer.* Design for a Tapestry

Although the collection of Rembrandt drawings is relatively small it is, apart from landscape drawings, one of the most representative. It is particularly rich in drawings made in connection with etchings. As a draughtsman, Rembrandt was extraordinarily original and versatile. His use of a kind of pen and ink short-hand to capture the mood of the moment makes the study of his drawings one of continuous fascination. The freedom which his disregard of conventional technique gave him made possible in his maturity the brilliant economy of brushwork in the *Sleeping Girl*, and the virtuosity with the reed pen in *A Girl seated* (both possibly studies of Hendrickje Stoffels). He differs from Rubens in that his greatest achievements as a draughtsman are the complete composition studies of religious and secular subjects, mostly made not with a painting in mind but for their own sake, in which his chief preoccupation was to explore the dramatic possibilities of the subject. He often returned to the same theme after many years with ever-deepening insight.

In addition to those undeniably by Rembrandt, there is a large collection of drawings by pupils, some of whom aped his style so well that it is often not easy to distinguish their drawings from the Master's; but his most important followers or associates, such as Jan Lievens and Gerard Dou, have quite distinctive styles.

The particular specialities of the rest of the seventeenth-century Dutch school are also represented: landscape by fine examples of Jan van Goyen, Jacob van Ruisdael, Anthonie Waterloo and Aelbert Cuyp; marine painting by Renier Zeeman and Ludolf van Backhuisen; and *genre* by Adriaen van Ostade.

Towards the end of the seventeenth century in both the Dutch and Flemish schools we find an increasing use of watercolour and a growing dependence on French culture. These tendencies became even more evident in the eighteenth century. Dutch art of this period is well represented, but after the glories of the previous century its effect is inevitably one of anti-climax. Subsequent developments are hardly illustrated, except by the magnificent pen and ink landscape by Vincent van Gogh which was part of the César de Hauke Bequest in 1968.

17 REMBRANDT 1606–1669. The Good Samaritan

The representation of French masters in the collection is very uneven: many of the most eminent masters are inadequately represented while two of the greatest, Claude and Watteau, can be seen here more completely as draughtsmen than anywhere else.

Portrait drawing reached a high level of excellence in the early sixteenth century at the court of Francis I, in the work of Jean and François Clouet, and there is a large group of drawings of the Clouets and their successors bequeathed in 1910 by Mr G. Salting which provides a primary source for the study of this school. In the tradition of manuscript illumination, are the fifty watercolours by the sixteenth-century Huguenot artist, Jacques Le Moyne de Morgues. His surviving work consists almost entirely of plant drawings and miniatures of great refinement and surprising naturalism. The collection is also rich in sixteenth-century architectural and ornamental drawings of which the 122 vellum sheets of French châteaux by Jacques Androuet Ducerceau are the most notable.

The development in Lorraine in the early seventeenth century of a native Mannerist school produced two remarkable draughtsmen and etchers, Jacques Callot and Jacques Bellange. By the former there is a quite large group of drawings of landscape, small figure-compositions, and studies of horses, some of them connected with etchings. Bellange is represented by five drawings, including a remarkable study of a girl in pen and blue wash.

There are only a few authentic drawings by Nicolas Poussin, the greatest and most influential of the French 'classical' masters of the seventeenth century, or by the other artists working in the same tradition, Simon Vouet, Eustache le Sueur, Laurent de la Hyre and Charles le Brun. On the other hand, the collection of some 500 drawings by Claude Lorrain, who like Poussin spent his working life in Rome and who as a landscape painter and draughtsman overshadows all his contemporaries, is the largest in existence. Most of them are sketches of an astonishing freedom and poetry made directly from nature in the Roman campagna; distinct from these, and in their own way no less beautiful, are the 205 drawings in the *Liber Veritatis* which was acquired from the Devonshire Collection at Chatsworth in 1957. These were made by the artist, whose works were extensively forged and imitated even in his own lifetime, as a record of his work and a protection against forgery.

18 CLAUDE LORRAIN 1600–1682. Landscape with Pine Trees

The classicism of Poussin and his followers survived into the eighteenth century, but the emphasis was shifting to the men and manners of the new age. Antoine Watteau was largely instrumental in bringing about this change. The Museum's collection of about 60 drawings by him is the finest and most complete and covers every phase of his brief career from the elongated forms and timid handling of his earliest studies of military subjects to the brilliant portrait and costume drawings of his maturity. By use of the technique *à trois crayons* – a combination of black, red and white chalk – he achieved an unequalled effect of mingled richness and precision. One of the outstanding drawings by him in the collection, and the only one of its kind known, is the design for a fan leaf.

The other leading masters of the eighteenth century, François Boucher and Jean-Honoré Fragonard, the two most characteristic personalities of the *rococo* period, and Hubert Robert and Gabriel de Saint-Aubin, are represented, though less well; while of the Neoclassic movement of the end of the century there is only one interesting group of drawings, by Joseph-Marie Vien, the master of Jacques-Louis David, and a characteristic female nude study by Pierre-Paul Prud'hon from the de Hauke bequest.

The nineteenth century, though still inadequately represented, has been strengthened by the de Hauke Bequest of fifteen important drawings. Eugène Delacroix, leader of the Romantic movement in painting, is represented by interesting drawings in pencil, pen, watercolour and pastel; *Studies of a seated Arab* is a masterpiece of delicate and perceptive portraiture. His pupil Théodore Géricault has some effective drawings to his name, most of them from his English period, notably *The Coal Waggon*. Jean-August-Dominique Ingres, the upholder of a rigid classicism and the outstanding draughtsman of his age, can be studied in a group of preparatory and finished drawings including two remarkable portraits, *Sir John Hay and his Sister* and *M. Charles Hayard and his Daughter*, as well as studies for the *Golden Age* and

19 ANTOINE WATTEAU 1684–1721. Studies of a Young Woman's Head

the *Apotheosis of Homer*. The Barbizon school of landscape is represented by drawings by Théodore Rousseau, Jean-François Millet and Charles-François Daubigny. By Jean-Baptiste-Camille Corot, there is little in the way of landscape, but two excellent portraits in pencil. The few examples of the work of the Impressionists and the artists associated with them, include a nude study by Auguste Renoir; a group of drawings by Edgar Degas, in particular two oil-sketches from the de Hauke bequest; several characteristic examples of the work of Camille Pissarro; two watercolours by Berthe Morisot; and five portraits and figure studies by Toulouse-Lautrec. Cézanne is represented only by two relatively minor works, whereas Georges Seurat, the exponent of Neo-Impressionism, can be studied in six carefully executed drawings, including two studies for *La Grande Jatte*.

Of the major figures and movements of the twentieth century, from the Cubists onwards, there is nothing apart from one drawing by Picasso and two portrait drawings and two nude studies by Henri Matisse.

20 ANTOINE WATTEAU 1684–1721. Design for a Fan Leaf

The main strength of the small collection of Spanish drawings lies in its good representation of some of the major seventeenth-century masters; there are seven drawings by Jusepe Ribera, who though a leading member of the Neapolitan school always insisted on his Spanish nationality; at least 20 by Bartolomé Esteban Murillo, the foremost artist of the school of Cordova; and a few by other masters of the same school including the only drawing generally accepted as being by Francisco Zurbaran, a powerful study in black chalk of the head of a monk.

The greatest master of the Madrid School, Diego Velasquez, is virtually an unknown quantity as a draughtsman; but the black chalk study of a man on a horse, attributed to him when in the collection of Mariette, the great French connoisseur of the eighteenth century, has been accepted by some authorities. Others of the Madrid School who are represented include Vicente Carducho, Antonio Pareda, Juan Carreno and Claudio Coello.

The representation of eighteenth-century masters is by comparison thin and of lower quality: designs for church decoration by Mosen Domingo Saura and Teodoro Ardemans are still in the seventeenth-century Baroque tradition, and there are two interesting and accomplished portraits, one by Luis Paret of Maria Luisa de Borbon, the other of Elizabeth Farnese by Miguel Jacinto Menendez.

By Francisco Goya, one of the greatest Spanish painters and unquestionably the greatest Spanish draughtsman, there are seven drawings. The earliest, *The Garotted Man*, dates from the 1780s and derives in technique, though not in subject-matter or mood, from G. B. Tiepolo. The others include the red chalk 21 sketch of the Duke of Wellington, done from life in 1812 after the Battle of Salamanca, which served as basis for all Goya's painted portraits of him, and a brush drawing of a group of victims of the Inquisition, *For being of Jewish Descent*, which can be dated after 1814. Goya's influence is all-pervading in the small group of drawings by his follower, Eugenio Lucas. Another nineteenth-century artist whose influence was felt within and outside Spain was Mariano Fortuny, by whom the Department possesses eighteen characteristic drawings, mostly in watercolour.

21 FRANCISCO GOYA 1746–1828. The Duke of Wellington

The Department's collection of drawings by British artists, or by artists from abroad who made their careers in England, is inevitably larger than that of any other school. It covers the period from the mid-sixteenth century until the present day and includes, as well as drawings in chalk, black lead, ink, and pencil, a comprehensive representation of the English watercolour school from its origins in the seventeenth-century 'stained drawing'.

English drawings of the sixteenth century have survived in very small numbers, but the Department possesses one rare design in pen and ink by the miniaturist Nicholas Hilliard for the Irish Great Seal of Queen Elizabeth, and the earliest and finest set of ethnographical watercolours in John White's drawings of the Algonquin Indians and the flora and fauna of Sir Walter Raleigh's original colony of Virginia. Of English seventeenth-century draughtsmen the most important are Inigo Jones, a number of architectural drawings by whom are in the collection, including some for Whitehall Palace, and Francis Barlow, whose work as an illustrator is well represented, especially by the designs for the *Aesop's Fables with his Life*, 1666. There are also series of drawings by the York topographer, Francis Place, and by several of the continental artists who worked in England at the period; in particular Wenceslas Hollar, Willem van de Velde the elder, and Sir Peter Lely, 16 of whose studies of figures in the Garter Procession at Windsor are in the collection. There are examples of the portrait studies of Lely's German successor, Sir Godfrey Kneller, and of the Swedish portrait painter Michael Dahl. The tradition of pastel portraiture in England is not particularly well illustrated, but there are drawings in the medium by Edward Lutterell, Edmund Ashfield, John Greenhill and others, as well as a group of plumbago (lead pencil) miniatures by Thomas Forster, David Loggan and Robert White.

In the eighteenth century English artists became self-consciously concerned with founding a national school to vie with those of the Continent. Sir James Thornhill painted grandiose decorative schemes on the model of those by the Italians Verrio and Ricci and the Frenchman Laguerre, and the Department's book of sketches by him for schemes of this sort is one of the most important surviving documents of the English Baroque period. His son-in-law William Hogarth was even more influential in establishing a new status for the artist in England. The Department 22 possesses an extensive group of drawings by him, including the rough and the finished designs for many of the episodes in the series *Industry and Idleness*, in addition to examples of his power as a portrait draughtsman. An underrated contemporary of Hogarth's who was to some extent his follower, was Francis Hayman, also well represented here by a series of illustrations to Smollett's translation of *Don Quixote* (1755).

22 WILLIAM HOGARTH 1697–1764. 'The Idle 'Prentice at play in the Churchyard during Divine Service'

Of the great portrait painters of the later part of the century, Sir Joshua Reynolds did not practise drawing to any great extent, but an unusually large collection of studies by him is in the Department, in addition to two of the notebooks that he used in Italy in 1750, and a self-portrait dated in the same year. Reynolds's great rival Gainsborough can be seen both as portrait draughtsman and as landscape artist, with several full-length figure studies (including some for the unfinished picture of the *Richmond Water-Walk*) and over 80 sketches of trees and plants and imaginary landscape compositions. Downman, Hoppner and Lawrence also figure in the collections, as does Romney, whose romantic figure subjects are well represented by several dramatic wash studies. These, together with Fuseli's Roman sketchbook of the 1770s (one of the principal documents of the early Romantic and Neo-classical movements) and the excellent

representation of Flaxman's work as a draughtsman, form a background to the Blake collection which, apart from the illuminated books, includes the complete series of drawings for Young's *Night Thoughts* and a number of the subjects from the late series of illustrations to Dante.

The humorous figure draughtsmen of this period are also present: there are many good examples of Thomas Rowlandson's lively watercolours, preparatory studies by James Gillray for his savage political cartoons of the Napoleonic War period, and drawings of comic social observation by John Nixon, Henry Bunbury and Nathaniel Dance. These provide a general view of the social background of the period, as do the charming watercolours of Paul and Thomas Sandby and the little ones of rural scenes by Thomas Bewick which he himself engraved on wood as vignettes in his classic *History of British Birds*. There

23 THOMAS GAINSBOROUGH 1727–1788. A Lady standing

is also a very large collection of sketches by George Cruikshank, who continued the tradition of comic and satirical draughtsmanship down to the middle of the nineteenth century.

The Romantic movement manifested itself as much by an interest in nature as by concern for the more passionate aspects of human behaviour. It was above all in landscape that colour came to be seen as an integral expressive part of a finished drawing, and the landscape watercolour is the most important British contribution to European art since the Middle Ages. The mood of Romanticism, already foreshadowed in the first half of the eighteenth century in the drawings of William Taverner and Jonathan Skelton, appears even more obviously in the views which William Pars made in Greece and Switzerland in the 1760s and 1770s, imbued as these are with the enthusiasm for ruins and mountain scenery that was to become wide-

24 WILLIAM BLAKE 1757–1827 'Beatrice on the Car, Dante and Matilda': Illustration to *Purgatorio* xxix

spread in the next generation. All Pars's finest drawings of these subjects are in the Printroom, where his
associates in Rome in the 1780s, Francis Towne and
John 'Warwick' Smith, can also be studied in breadth.
Two other artists of an earlier generation who were
also inspired by Italy, but who did not work in watercolour, were Richard Wilson and Alexander Cozens.
The Department possesses a large number of studies
of landscape and details of landscape by Wilson in his
characteristic medium of black and white chalk on
grey paper, and several of Cozens's ideal 'blot'
25 landscapes in brown wash together with a group of
pen-and-ink sketches made in Rome when he was a
young man. John Robert Cozens, his son and arguably
the finest English watercolourist before the generation
of Turner and Girtin, is represented mainly by the
group of early drawings of Alpine landscape bequeathed by his patron Richard Payne Knight. Both
Wilson and John Robert Cozens exercised a fundamental influence on the early development of J. M. W.
Turner, who lived to become one of the world's
greatest landscape painters and the only British artist
26 who unquestionably takes rank with the very highest.

25 ALEXANDER COZENS *c.* 1700–1786. Mountainous Landscape

26 J. M. W. TURNER 1775–1851. The Church of SS Giovanni e Paolo, Rome, from the Palatine

About 20,000 sheets of studies in pencil and in water-colour, many of them in sketchbooks, which were bequeathed by Turner to the nation, are deposited in the Printroom on indefinite loan; and these, together with the Henderson, Salting and Lloyd Bequests of finished watercolours, give a very complete picture of this greatest, most versatile and most prolific of British painters. The Printroom also possesses an unrivalled collection of watercolours and drawings by his contemporary Thomas Girtin, including five well-preserved sections of the preliminary design in 27 watercolour for the *Panorama of London*, which together constitute the artist's masterpiece.

The collection of drawings by John Constable, though smaller than that in the Victoria and Albert Museum, is well balanced and includes a newly discovered sketchbook of 1819, and a fuller represen-tation of the artist's figure drawings than exists else-where. The acquisition in 1902 of the Reeve collection of watercolours by members of the Norwich School brought to the Department a very large number by John Sell Cotman, among them several of the well-28 known 'Greta' subjects of 1805 and the famous *Dismasted Brig*. Peter de Wint's large view of Lincoln is the most impressive of a small group of watercolours by this artist; David Cox, on the other hand, is represented by a comprehensive collection of works from all periods of his life. The drawings by Richard Parkes Bonington are mostly pencil studies, many of them made in the Louvre, but there are a few water-colours, including the lively *Château de Berri*. Two

27 THOMAS GIRTIN 1775–1802. Westminster from Lambeth: Study for the *Eidometropolis* or *Panorama of London*

28 JOHN SELL COTMAN 1782–1844. Greta Bridge

29 SAMUEL PALMER 1805–1881.
  Landscape with a Cliff-Edge: from the 1824 Sketchbook

30 DANTE GABRIEL ROSSETTI 1828–1882. Hamlet and Ophelia

29 of Samuel Palmer's sketchbooks are in the Department, one dating from his early youth (1819), and of interest chiefly as a document, the other from the period 1824–1825 when he was at his most intensely poetic and idiosyncratic. Palmer's associate Edward Calvert can be seen at his rare best in the tiny, miniature-like *Primitive City* (1824), the only surviving drawing in the same spirit as the early engravings that are now recognized as his best work.

The work of later nineteenth- and twentieth-century artists has not been collected as energetically as has that of their predecessors; for certain aspects of watercolour in England, especially for large, finished works, it is necessary to consult the collections of the Victoria and Albert Museum. Nevertheless, there are good holdings of such artists as Edward Lear, William Muller, and John Frederick Lewis, and a small but representative and well-chosen group of Pre-

30 Raphaelite drawings, including fine ones by Rossetti and Millais, and a substantial quantity by Burne-Jones. The latter include two important sketchbooks, one a volume of pencil studies dating from the 1870s, including designs for the *Days of Creation*, the other containing a series of circular designs in watercolour suggested by the names of flowers and known as the 'Flower Book'. There are also examples of the draughtsmanship of Lord Leighton, Alma-Tadema, and Charles Ricketts – Ricketts's notebook of jewellery designs being a particularly telling record of his delicacy of invention and technical refinement. Many of the great book illustrators of the period figure in the collection: Beardsley, du Maurier, Charles Keene, Kate Greenaway, Edmund Dulac and Beatrix Potter among them – the last represented by the complete set of watercolours illustrating *The Tale of the Flopsy Bunnies*.

In the early years of the twentieth century Continental art once more became, as it was in the seventeenth century, an important influence on English vision, and the mannerisms of Impressionism and Post-Impressionism appeared in the work of men like Roger Fry, Robert Bevan, Charles Ginner and Ambrose McEvoy. This generation was dominated by Walter Sickert, a wide range of whose drawings is in the Department. There are also good representations (including sketchbooks) of Frank Brangwyn, Muirhead Bone, George Clausen and Sir Charles

31 Holmes. Of more recent figures, Henry Moore can be studied in drawings from all periods of his career, and Barbara Hepworth, John Piper, Edward Bawden, John Nash and Elizabeth Frink are also represented. The Department has recently acquired sketchbooks by Edward Ardizzone and Ceri Richards, and drawings by David Hockney; and it is hoped that the acquisition of work by contemporary artists will increase in the coming years.

31 HENRY MOORE b. 1898. Miners at the Coal-face: from the Castleford Sketchbook

The multiplication of visual images began in Europe, in south Germany and Italy, in the first half of the fifteenth century, rather before the earliest dissemination of the written word by printing from moveable type. Prints have been used for many purposes: not only as original works of art and as reproductions of works of art, but also for book illustration, for religious or political propaganda, for the recording of historical events and the appearance of famous people and as patterns for decoration – to name only a few of their innumerable uses. But the most important distinction is between the 'original' print, in which the artist exploits the resources of the medium in order to produce a work of art, and the reproductive print, in which he reproduces a design by another. (An intermediate category, in which the engraver transforms another's idea into something valid as a work of art in terms of engraving, might be termed the 'interpretative' print.) The Department possesses one of the finest and most complete collections of original prints in the world. Over and above these there is a vast mass of prints that are of interest primarily for the information of one kind or another that they convey.

Prints can also be categorized by technique: intaglio prints (engravings, etchings, dry-points) in which the design is incised in a metal plate which after being inked is wiped clean and printed under pressure so that the ink remaining in the incised lines is forced out on to the paper; relief prints (woodcuts, wood-engravings and metal-cuts) in which the white areas are cut away on the block; and surface prints (lithographs) in which the design is drawn in an ink-absorbent medium on an ink-repellent surface. In addition, there are the 'tone processes': stipple and aquatint, which are varieties of etching and always used in conjunction with the etched line, and mezzotint, in which the plate is first roughened so that if inked it would print dead black, and the lighter areas are then burnished down.

The earliest techniques were woodcut and engraving on metal. Relief printing from woodblocks was first used for the decoration of textiles and in the manufacture of playing-cards, and for the crudely executed representations of religious or devotional subjects made as souvenirs for pilgrims. The wider use of the process coincided with the invention of printing, for since text and block can be printed together it was ideally suited to book illustration. The history of woodcut in the fifteenth and sixteenth centuries is thus closely involved with that of the printed book, and the Department possesses, in addition to cuts either issued separately or extracted from books, a considerable collection of books with woodcut illustrations, chiefly German. The culmination comes at the beginning of the sixteenth century with Dürer, to whom about 150 woodcuts are attributed (he did not actually cut them himself, but he so closely supervised the craftsmen who did that they must count as original prints; some of the original woodblocks are in the collection), and with the woodcuts produced in Venice in the circle of Titian, many after his designs. An earlier Venetian masterpiece is the great bird's-eye view of Venice, dated 1500, by Jacopo de' Barbari.

Though the process was still used in the later sixteenth century, it gradually gave way to metal engraving, and the only significant development was the introduction of the 'chiaroscuro' woodcut, printed in colours from two or more blocks in imitation of a wash drawing. Of these the Department has a good collection, from Ugo da Carpi in the early sixteenth century to the English amateur John Skippe at the end of the eighteenth. Otherwise, woodcut came to be used mainly as a cheap method of illustrating chapbooks and broadsides, but towards the end of the eighteenth century, there was a revival of the process when it was discovered that a block of very hard wood, such as box, cut across the grain, could be worked with engraver's tools. The wood-engraving thus differs fundamentally from the woodcut, which is made with a knife on a block of softish wood cut parallel with the grain, and its effect depends largely on the use of white line on black. Wood-engravings are usually small in scale, but some of the most beautiful work ever done on wood was produced in the early nineteenth century by Thomas Bewick, William Blake (in the illustrations to Thornton's *Virgil*) and, under Blake's inspiration, Edward Calvert. (The blocks of Blake's *Virgil* and of Calvert's five wood-engravings are in the Department.) In the middle years of the nineteenth century wood-engraving was much used as a reproductive process for book illustration, and its practitioners displayed astonishing skill in translating the pen and ink drawings made by the artist on the block. The Department owns a large collection of proofs from the workshop of the most famous of these engravers, the Dalziell brothers.

Towards the end of the nineteenth century the revival of fine printing, associated above all with William Morris and Charles Ricketts, brought with it a revival of woodcut illustration that was at first consciously inspired by fifteenth-century northern and Italian examples. The revival continued until well into the following century, mainly on traditional lines; but of particularly original work in this medium should be mentioned the woodcuts of William Nicholson and James Pryde ('The Beggarstaff Brothers') and Paul Nash, and the very effective semi-abstract experiments of C. R. W. Nevinson and Edward Wadsworth.

A process which involved the use of metal plates but which is essentially analogous to woodcut rather than to metal engraving was the method of 'relief etching' invented by William Blake for the production of his illustrated books. The design was drawn with the 'resist' so that the areas to be left white were bitten away, and the plate was printed from in the same way as a woodblock. The Department has a very good collection of Blake's illustrated books.

Printing from engraved metal plates originated, like woodcut, in South Germany and Italy in the early fifteenth century, and developed from the goldsmiths' practice of taking impressions from chased decoration. This origin is reflected in the timid technique of the earliest German engravings and in those Florentine ones classified as the 'Fine Manner'. (Closely related in style to these is the volume of drawings in the Department known as the 'Florentine Picture Chronicle', which seems to have served as a pattern book for the Fine Manner engravers.) Another group of Florentine engravings is classified as the 'Broad Manner', and to that tradition belongs not only the one indisputable masterpiece of the Florentine school, Antonio Pollaiuolo's *Battle of Naked Men*, but also the engravings of the Paduan master, Andrea Mantegna, who had been a pupil of the Florentine sculptor Donatello. The seven plates now accepted as being from Mantegna's hand reproduce the effect of his vigorous style of drawing in pen and ink. As an original creative process line-engraving reached its height in the late fifteenth and early sixteenth centuries with Mantegna, Dürer and the German 'Little Masters' (so called because of the small size of their plates) Altdorfer, Cranach, Beham and the rest, Marcantonio Raimondi in Italy, and Lucas van Leiden in Holland. Dürer and Lucas van Leiden were wholly original engravers, responsible for the design and the execution of their plates. Marcantonio's original plates are of little interest, but those after Raphael, with whom he worked in close collaboration, reveal him as one of the greatest and most influential masters of interpretative engraving. The technique that he evolved for translating Raphael's conceptions into the language of engraving was to have a fundamental influence not only on his immediate followers and imitators, but on much of the reproductive engraving of the later sixteenth and seventeenth centuries. The last major exponent of original engraving, at the beginning of the seventeenth century, was the Dutch mannerist Hendrik Goltzius; technically brilliant though he was, with him virtuosity seems to have become an end in itself. From the early seventeenth century onwards line-engraving was more and more confined to reproduction; and though an ever-increasing degree of technical skill was developed, engraving as a medium of original creative expression gave way to the altogether freer and more rapid process of etching. (The early eighteenth-century English painter and engraver, William Hogarth, might be cited as an exception to this rule; but though his numerous engravings are all after his own designs, their essential character is reproductive rather than original.) In an engraving the line has to be laboriously incised into the metal whereas in etching the plate is coated with an acid-resisting substance, either wax or resin (the 'resist'), through which the design is scratched with an etching needle and then bitten by immersion in acid. The potentialities of the medium for free and direct expression were not all at once recognized. Dürer, for example, experimented with it but the results do not differ fundamentally in treatment from his engravings, and it is broadly true to say that in the sixteenth century the process was mainly used either in combination with line-engraving or as a short cut to achieving the same effect. There are a few exceptions, notably Parmigianino, who has the distinction of being the first 'painter etcher', and from whose hand seventeen etchings are known, characterized by the same graceful elegance as his drawings; but it was not until the first half of the seventeenth century, in Holland, that the process was first properly exploited, by Hercules Seghers and, even more, by Rembrandt. Seghers's landscape etchings, often printed in coloured

32 ink on tinted paper or even cloth, display an extraordinary degree of freedom and fantasy. They are extremely rare, but the Department possesses 24 – a number exceeded only by the considerably larger group in the Amsterdam Printroom. Rembrandt's output was far greater and his range far wider. The 300 or so etchings that are generally accepted as his represent landscapes, portraits, biblical subjects and

33 *genre* scenes. The interest of many of them is greatly enhanced by the fact of there being several 'states' (a term denoting any alteration to a plate). In the vast majority of prints, differences of state, when they exist, are of trivial importance; but Rembrandt's show him developing his ideas as he went along, and by preserving his successive changes of mind they provide a unique insight into the creative process.

Original etching was widely practised in Holland in the seventeenth century by many beside Rembrandt and his followers. The work of all of these artists is very fully represented in the Department, mostly in the Sheepshanks Collection. But in his range of subject-matter and profundity of treatment, as well as in his technical mastery of the medium, Rembrandt stands

32 HERCULES SEGHERS 1589/90–1633/4. Landscape. Etching

alone in his own period and overshadows all but one or two of his successors. It is true that many other leading painters also made etchings – in the later sixteenth century, Federico Barocci and Annibale and Agostino Carracci in Italy and Pieter Bruegel in Holland; in the seventeenth century in Italy, Guido Reni, Salvator Rosa and Claude Lorrain, and in Flanders Van Dyck (who himself etched some of the portraits in his *Iconography*); in the eighteenth century in Venice, Giovanni Battista Tiepolo and the two view-painters Guardi and Canaletto – but these constitute a very much less significant part of their artists' total *oeuvre* than do those of Rembrandt. There were others working in the early seventeenth century for whom etching was the primary means of expression: Jacques Callot, a native of Nancy who worked in Florence, and Stefano della Bella, a Florentine by birth, both of whom etched more than 1,000 plates; and Wenzel Hollar, a native of Bohemia who worked in England, and who produced as many as 2,700. The etchings of all three are of very varied subject-matter and tend to be small in scale. In the eighteenth century the most outstanding original etcher was Giovanni Battista Piranesi, who worked on a large scale and specialized in architectural fantasies and in views, equally touched with fantasy, of ancient and modern Rome.

34

33 REMBRANDT 1606–1669. 'The Three Trees'. Etching

34 GIOVANNI BATTISTA PIRANESI 1720–1778. Plate from the *Carceri d'invenzione*. Etching

Two technical innovations were introduced in the course of the eighteenth century: soft-ground etching, which reproduces the effect of a chalk drawing, and aquatint, by which an area of tone is achieved by biting the plate through a partly porous granular resist. These were mainly used in reproductive engraving, though Gainsborough etched a number of soft-ground landscapes and in many of Goya's etchings aquatint is used to great effect in combination with the etched line. Francisco Goya is the only etcher unquestionably in the same rank as Rembrandt. The series that he produced, *Los Desastres de la Guerra* (which record the atrocities committed during the Napoleonic occupation of Spain), *Los Caprichos* and *Los Proverbios*, are unique in their powerful and unforgettable combination of satirical bitterness, fantastic imagination, brutality and compassion. Goya is an isolated phenomenon. The few other early nineteenth-century artists who made original etchings were mainly inspired by Dutch examples: the Norwich School painter, John Crome, by the seventeenth-century landscape etchers, and Wilkie and Andrew Geddes by Rembrandt. What has been called the 'etching revival' began in the middle of the nineteenth century in France, with the painters of the Barbizon School – Rousseau, Daubigny, Millet and the rest – Charles Meryon (who was exclusively an etcher), and James McNeill Whistler, equally well known as a painter. Many of Whistler's best etchings (e.g. the 'Thames Set' of the 1860s) were produced in England, but his technique owes much to his years in France

and to the example of Meryon. In his artistic aims he differs so completely from Rembrandt and Goya that comparison is hardly possible, but he is certainly their equal in technical mastery. Other nineteenth-century etchers include Seymour Haden, whose landscape etchings are strongly influenced by Whistler, his brother-in-law, and the more isolated figure of Samuel Palmer, best remembered for his early visionary landscape drawings of the 1820s, who etched a few plates that are among the best work of his later years. Of succeeding generations, some of the more distinguished etchers are Muirhead Bone and F. L. Griggs, each in his own different way preoccupied, one realistically and the other fancifully, with architecture; D. Y. Cameron, who etched mainly architecture and landscape; W. R. Sickert, whose etchings represent the same kind of urban *genre* as his paintings; and Augustus John, who in his early years produced a number of brilliant portrait and figure subjects.

Mezzotint, invented in the middle of the seventeenth century, is a tone process, differing essentially from all others in that the artist works from dark to light: the plate is roughened so that if inked it would print an intense black, and the lighter areas of the design are then progressively burnished down. Like the other tone processes it was used almost entirely for reproductive engraving, especially in England, where in the eighteenth century mezzotint engravers attained an extraordinary degree of technical skill in the reproduction of portraits by Reynolds, Gainsborough and their followers. It was little used in original engraving.

35 FRANCISCO GOYA 1746–1828. 'Tras el vicio viene el fornicio'. Etching from the series *Los Proverbios*

Goya experimented with it in one of his greatest and rarest prints, *El Coloso* (of which unfortunately the Department has no impression) and in the early nineteenth century mezzotint on steel was used to great effect by John Martin and by J. M. W. Turner, impressions of whose very rare 'Little Liber Studiorum' are in the Department.

Lithography was invented at the very end of the eighteenth century. It involves the use of a particular kind of limestone that has the property, when wetted, of repelling water. The design is drawn in a greasy ink-absorbent chalk or ink either directly on the stone or on lithographic transfer-paper from which it is transferred to the stone, which is then wetted, inked, and printed from. The essence of print-making as a creative art lies in the skill with which the artist adapts his conception to the technical limitations of the process. This element of conflict hardly exists in lithography which provides an exact facsimile of a free-hand drawing, and the process was in fact mainly used as a cheap and convenient means of reproduction. There were, however, a number of 'artist lithographers' who produced original work in this medium, the most successful being the chalk lithographs which took advantage of the grained surface of the stone to produce a uniquely beautiful texture: Goya (the first major artist to experiment with the process); in

France, Géricault (whose pen lithographs are almost indistinguishable from his drawings), Ingres, Delacroix, Daumier, and the symbolist painter Odilon Redon; in England, above all Whistler and Charles Shannon.

The collection is not confined to original prints. Notable features of the reference collection are: reproductive engravings, classified by designers; reproductions of drawings, including the Gernsheim *Corpus Photographicum* of more than 60,000 photographs (still in progress); portrait engravings, classified by subject; prints illustrating British and foreign history, classified by date; topographical prints and drawings, especially of London (these include the Crace Collection of nearly 6,000 London drawings and prints, the 22 volumes of the Potter collection of material relating to North London, and the 17 portfolios of watercolour views of London made in the 1840s and 1850s by J. W. Archer); satirical prints, both political and personal, especially British from the seventeenth to the early nineteenth century; the 3,000 photographs of the National Photographic Record made by Sir Benjamin Stone *c.* 1900; Lady Charlotte Schreiber's collections of playing cards and fans and fan-leaves; and the Franks and Viner Collections of bookplates.

36 J. A. MCNEILL WHISTLER 1834–1903. Black Lion Wharf. Etching from the *Thames Set*

Western Asiatic antiquities

Main floor

North
entrance

Main
entrance

16 Khorsabad
   and stairs down to Lecture Theatre
17 Assyrian Saloon
18 Stairs down to Assyrian basement
19/20 Nimrud
21 Nineveh
24 Ancient Palestine
26 Assyrian Transept

Upper levels

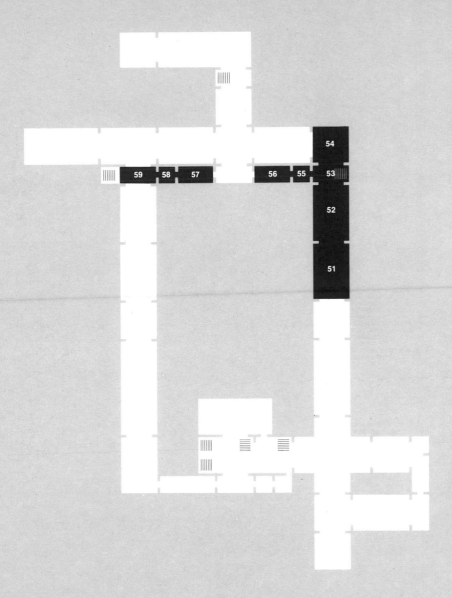

51 Ancient Iran
52 Ancient Anatolia
53 Neo-Hittite landing
54 Babylonian room
55 Western Asiatic prehistory
56 Ancient writing
57 Ancient Syria
58 Nimrud ivories
59 South Arabia

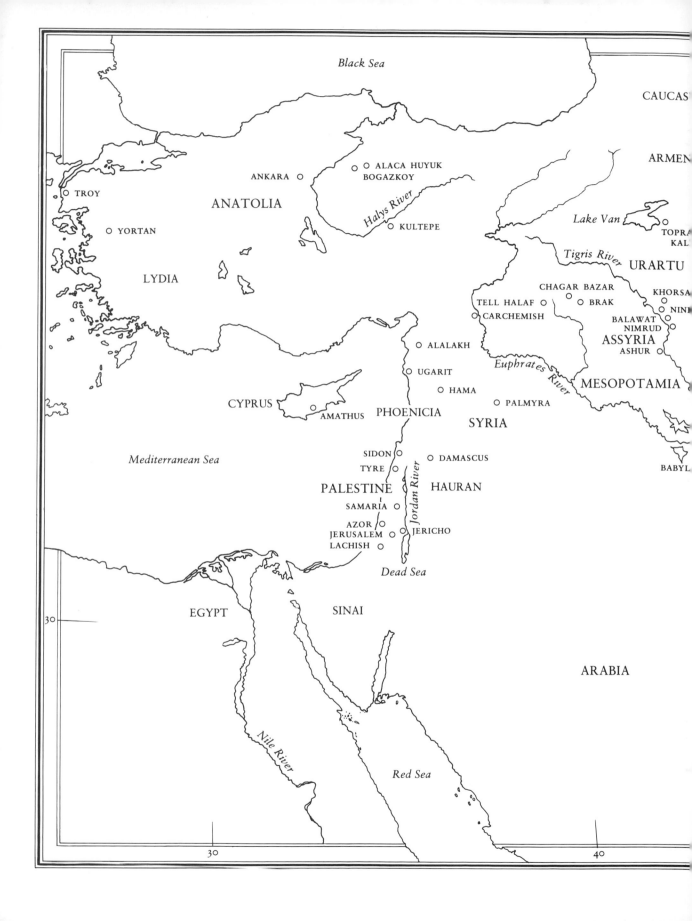

Black Sea

CAUCAS

ARMEN

ANATOLIA

TROY

YORTAN

ANKARA

ALACA HUYUK
BOGAZKOY

Halys River

KULTEPE

Lake Van

TOPRA
KAL

Tigris River

URARTU

LYDIA

CHAGAR BAZAR

TELL HALAF

CARCHEMISH

BRAK

KHORSA

NINI

BALAWAT
NIMRUD

ASSYRIA

ASHUR

ALALAKH

UGARIT

Euphrates River

MESOPOTAMIA

CYPRUS

AMATHUS

PHOENICIA

HAMA

PALMYRA

SYRIA

Mediterranean Sea

SIDON

TYRE

DAMASCUS

Jordan River

HAURAN

PALESTINE

SAMARIA

AZOR

JERUSALEM

LACHISH

JERICHO

Dead Sea

BABYL

EGYPT

SINAI

30

Nile River

Red Sea

ARABIA

30

40

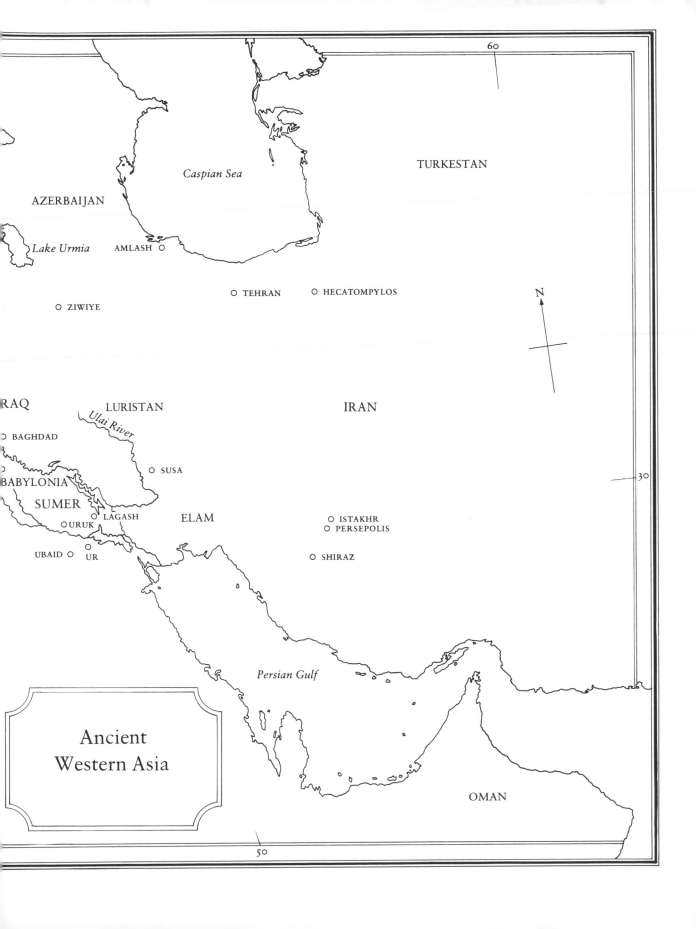

Caspian Sea

TURKESTAN

AZERBAIJAN

Lake Urmia   AMLASH ○

○ TEHRAN   ○ HECATOMPYLOS

N

○ ZIWIYE

RAQ   LURISTAN   IRAN

Ulai River

○ BAGHDAD

○   ○ SUSA

BABYLONIA

SUMER

○ LAGASH   ELAM   ○ ISTAKHR
○URUK   ○ PERSEPOLIS

UBAID ○ ○
      UR   ○ SHIRAZ

30

Persian Gulf

Ancient
Western Asia

OMAN

50

Western Asiatic antiquities

The collections of the Western Asiatic Department include objects from many different areas and civilizations. Their geographical range covers virtually all those lands, east of Egypt and west of Pakistan, where Semitic, Turkish and Indo-European languages are now spoken. It also extends westward to include Phoenician colonies throughout the Mediterranean, while excluding Greek and Roman remains from Western Asia itself. The earliest items in the collections date from about 6000 BC (see the Department of Prehistoric and Romano-British Antiquities for anything earlier still). The latest are from the time of the first Muslim conquests in the seventh century AD (see the Department of Oriental Antiquities for the Islamic world). The arrangement of the items on display is based on modern political geography, but the different regions passed through comparable stages of development; most of them communicated with one another, directly or indirectly, from a very early date. These links continued to grow stronger throughout the historical period. One common theme in the different regions is the development from primitive to imperial levels of political organization, a development which was naturally reflected in the arts.

I ASHURNASIRPAL II, KING OF ASSYRIA

The ground floor galleries

THE ASSYRIAN SCULPTURES

Assyria lies in what is now northern Iraq, in the valley of the river Tigris. The area is divided from Babylonia, the traditional centre of Mesopotamian civilization, by a wide stretch of desert; the people of Assyria spoke their own dialect and developed their own arts and institutions. The land itself is a natural cross-roads, and Assyrians established trading posts as far afield as Anatolia from an early date. The military expeditions of the Neo-Assyrian kings, between the ninth and seventh centuries BC, extended their power from Egypt to the Persian Gulf, and deep into what are now Iran and Turkey. Their exploits were commemorated on carved stone slabs which lined the palace walls in the successive capital cities of Nimrud (ancient Kalhu), Khorsabad (Dur-Sharrukin), and Nineveh. The carvings were intended at the time both to entertain the Assyrians who saw them and to intimidate foreigners. Their value now is partly artistic but also, more obviously, documentary: they offer an extraordinarily detailed picture of the Assyrian world as seen through contemporary eyes. The palaces which contained them were eventually destroyed in 612 BC by a combined army of Iranians and Babylonians.

The slabs in the British Museum were excavated between 1845 and 1855 principally by two men, Layard and Rassam. At that time Great Britain was a valued ally of the Ottoman Empire, and the excavators were allowed to remove the lion's share of what they found. Their discoveries, together with some already made by a Frenchman, Botta, first opened European eyes to the high achievements of Mesopotamian civilization. The collection of sculptures brought back by them to England is still much the finest in the world. The British Museum is the only place where one can see so many sequences of magnificently preserved slabs, re-erected in their original order.

26 THE ASSYRIAN TRANSEPT

The first Assyrian to commission sculptures on a large scale was Ashurnasirpal II (883–859 BC). This king moved his capital from the ancient city of Ashur, where the national god called Ashur had his shrine, and settled at Nimrud, which he rebuilt.

Ashurnasirpal himself is represented by a free-standing statue, found in one of the temples at Nimrud, where its purpose was to remind the god of the king's energetic piety. There is no pretence of naturalism, and the king's features are no portrait but simply an ideal of static dignity. These characteristics persist in most Assyrian art. The same king also appears on a colossal stela which was erected in front of another temple at Nimrud. Here the king is wearing the distinctive Assyrian crown, an ancient equivalent of the fez but with a conical peak on top. His right hand points skyward in a peculiar gesture, as if he had just snapped his fingers; this gesture had a religious significance, and the objects carved above his hand are the symbols of various gods. The cuneiform inscription which covers the surface of the stela, like those which are to be seen on most of his sculptures, gives Ashurnasirpal's titles and describes his achievements in war and peace.

Assyrian obelisks, like Egyptian ones, were probably set up outside temple doors. Only two have ever been found complete, and both are now in the British Museum. The better preserved, the Black Obelisk, made for Shalmaneser III (858–824 BC), shows people from the extreme ends of the Assyrian empire bringing tribute before the king. He himself appears twice, once as a conqueror with bow and arrow, and a second time carrying a cup. The tributaries, and the nature of the tribute, are described in captions above the rows of carving. We see among them elephants, monkeys, and other exotic animals. One group of tribute is provided by Jehu, King of Israel. Another panel, showing a lion attacking a deer in a wood, seems quite irrelevant to the imperial theme, but is an example of something we often find in Assyrian art, the observation of nature and landscape which puts history in context.

The most important points in Assyrian temples and palaces were guarded by huge statues of lions or of supernatural beings which shared the characteristics of several different animals. They were imagined as prowling to and fro on guard, keeping out the evil spirits which brought bad luck and sickness into a house. Each of this pair of protective beasts has the body and claws of a lion, the head of a man, and the wings of an eagle; it was therefore endowed with strength, subtlety and speed. The rope round the waist is one often worn by semi-divine figures in Mesopotamian art. This pair originally stood at one end of Ashurnasirpal's throne-room, facing the throne and guarding the way up to the roof. They have one peculiarity which seldom attracts immediate attention, but which illustrates how the Assyrian sculptors tended to think in two dimensions only. Seen from in front, or from one side, they each have two front legs. Seen from an angle, however, they each have three.

Colossal animals such as these frequently flanked magnificent doorways. A small town near Nimrud, now called Balawat, has produced three pairs of Assyrian doors, of which two are in the British Museum. They were made of wood, decorated at intervals with strips of worked metal. The larger pair dates from the reign of Shalmaneser III (858–824 BC), and a full-scale model of it stands against the wall; the metal strips on the model are electrotype reproductions of the original bronzes, which are in a showcase to the left. The pictures, many of which have cuneiform captions, exemplify the range of subject-matter of Assyrian narrative art. Battles, sieges, captives, tribute-bearers, and occasionally a more elaborate event, are represented in the minutest detail; little is left to the spectator's imagination.

For example, the bottom left-hand band on the gate, as it is arranged here, shows one of Shalmaneser's campaigns in what is now Turkey. The picture is in two registers, the lower of which comes first. It starts at the left-hand edge, with the king in his chariot passing a burning city whose inhabitants are being

2 BLACK OBELISK OF SHALMANESER III

massacred. Then he moves along a river valley, and has to leave his chariot and travel by horse. His entourage next arrives at a cavern which is the source of the river Tigris; there is a sacrifice, and sculptors hastily carve commemorative rock-sculptures (which can still be seen today) on the cliffs of the gorge. This scene occupies the right-hand end of both registers. Further left, in the top row, we see the king returning to his camp, and being met by officials who kneel to congratulate him on his exploit.

Not all the bronzes are so full of circumstantial detail, but each has a story to tell. The second strip up on the right shows the king worshipping on the shores of Lake Van. The strip above this represents the tribute of the kings of Tyre and Sidon, cities on the Mediterranean coast. One of the kings stays sensibly on his island, while his servants cross to the mainland with gifts to buy Assyrian friendship or forgiveness. The strip above shows Shalmaneser in Babylonia, progressing through a landscape of canals and palm-trees; far ahead an Assyrian official supervises the construction of a bridge of boats. Several of the other strips show the consequences of resisting the Assyrian army; the battle is always a one-sided affair, with few or no Assyrian dead, and then the enemy fortresses are stormed and the survivors are escorted into captivity.

19 THE NIMRUD GALLERY

This room is entirely occupied by an imposing series of sculptured slabs from the palace of Ashurnasirpal II (883–859 BC). Several of them show supernatural beings who were regarded, like the colossal winged lions, as protective powers. One example is the winged figure, with a man's body and an eagle's head, who seems to carry a fir-cone in one hand and a bucket in the other. Both cone and bucket were used in some magic ritual of protection.

The king himself appears, in duplicate and guarded by a pair of these spirits, on a slab that was originally placed behind the throne. Between the two kings is a highly stylized symbolic tree, and above is an Assyrian version of the winged sun-disc, familiar on Egyptian and Hittite monuments. In this case there is a god in the disc, and he is most probably not the sun-god but the national god, Ashur, to whom the king was responsible for the welfare of the land, and who also appears hovering above the battlefield in some of the narrative scenes opposite.

The narrative carvings too come from the royal throne-room at Nimrud; each slab originally had a band of inscription between the two registers of carving. There is the same range of royal activities as on the bronze gates of Shalmaneser. An additional

3 ASSYRIANS VISITING THE SOURCE OF THE TIGRIS

subject is the king hunting lions and bulls, at the far left end of the sequence; these left-hand slabs were originally placed close to the royal throne, where the king himself could enjoy them. The remainder show a number of distinct scenes, but the compositions run into each other without a break. In one the Assyrian army is seen crossing a river, probably the Euphrates: the king is ferried, but his men are swimming with the aid of skins which they continue inflating while in the water. Elsewhere we are shown an elaborate military incident. The Assyrian army, attacking a town, have brought up a siege-engine: this is a tower, with archers on top, and a battering-ram protruding from below. One of the enemy has let down a chain and looped it

round the ram, in order to dislodge it; but Assyrians with hooks are holding it down in position. Other enemies have thrown blazing torches at the siege-engine, but a continual shower of water, poured from inside the tower, ensures that its surface will stay damp and not catch fire. Meanwhile more Assyrians are busily undermining the wall by hand.

The stone of all these slabs is a soft gypsum, common in Assyria, and the carving was done when the slabs were already in position. The colour of the stone was originally lighter than it is now, and many details were once picked out in colour. In a few places, especially on the feet of the larger figures, one can still see traces of red and black.

4 EAGLE-HEADED GENIE BEHIND THE KING

Between 800 and 750 BC the power of the Assyrian kings was restricted by military difficulties and lack of political unity. Tiglath-pileser III (744–727 BC), however, again campaigned far and wide, and began to build himself a new palace at Nimrud. We have his picture, and several narrative slabs. One of the finer pieces shows an enemy horseman attempting to ward off his pursuers, and there is another good slab in the Ancient Palestine Room. Most of Tiglath-pileser's sculptures, however, are greatly inferior in workmanship to those of the previous century.

16 THE KHORSABAD ENTRANCE

Sargon (722–705 BC) decided to build himself a new capital city on a fresh site, Khorsabad. His new palace was extensively decorated with carved slabs; these were excavated by a French expedition, and relatively few of them are in London. They do include, however,
6 two magnificent winged bulls from a gateway into the citadel. Each of them weighs about 16 tons. Assyrian methods of moving such large weights are illustrated on two reliefs in the Nineveh Gallery.

Beyond the bulls, against the wall, is a carved slab, originally the sill of a palace doorway. Its elaborate
7 floral design, reminiscent of embroidery, seems to be a straight translation into stone of the kind of patterns that might have been seen on Assyrian carpets. The floors of the palaces were evidently covered with the richest textiles obtainable, and their colours were probably much like those of some modern oriental rugs.

17 THE LACHISH ROOM

When Sargon died in battle, his son Sennacherib (704–681 BC) lost no time in choosing yet another city for his own royal residence. This was Nineveh, already one of the most ancient and important towns in the Assyrian empire, and well positioned on the river Tigris near where the modern town of Mosul has developed. Here Sennacherib built a new palace, decorating it with some two miles of sculptured slabs. When Nineveh fell, in 612 BC, the palace was burnt and many of the sculptures were turned to lime. One series which suffered less than most shows Sennacherib's capture of Lachish in Judah about 701 BC.

On the left we see the Assyrian army, 'like the wolf on the fold', advancing to the attack through mountainous country. There are Assyrian troops in pointed helmets and a host of imperial levies, including some from southern Iran. As they approach the city, the slingers and archers open fire; but the city itself is represented at a slightly later moment in time. Steep ramps have been built against the walls, and Assyrian forces charge up them, headed by siege-engines. The enemy throw missiles of every kind, but cannot prevent the outworks from falling: captives are already being led out of one gate. Further to the right the captives are brought before Sennacherib. Some have their possessions with them, piled in carts ready for the journey into exile; others have been condemned to death. The king watches the proceedings from a sumptuous throne set up outside his tent; his bodyguard and chariot wait behind him. Still further to the right is the Assyrian camp, with priests worshipping and servants making beds and preparing food. This scene closes the series, which originally went all round one small room. The story has been told in what is essentially one composition, but one that steps forward continuously through both space and time, like a moving film rather than a strip-cartoon. By itself any fragment of Assyrian narrative sculpture, for example the captive harpists on another wall, is deprived of its real meaning; it must be understood as part of a much larger unit, such as the Lachish series.

5 BATTLE AROUND A SIEGE-ENGINE

6 COLOSSAL HUMAN-HEADED WINGED BULL

8 LION AND LIONESS IN A GARDEN

7 PAVING-STONE CARVED AS A CARPET

In peace-time the Assyrian kings exercised themselves in the hunting field. The sculptures of Sennacherib include a series of grooms leading horses, which originally lined a sloping passage-way to a postern-gate. His grandson, Ashurbanipal (668–627 BC), had a comparable series of sculptures, and it is clear that both groups showed processions going out to the hunt. The hunt itself was often more of a massacre than a contest. One of the most attractive Assyrian sculptures shows a lion and lioness resting in a garden hung with vines; this idyllic scene, which came from one corridor of Ashurbanipal's new palace at Nineveh, must be contrasted with the sculptures of another corridor nearby, which represented a lion-hunt.

Lions, which survived in Mesopotamia up to this century, were a menace to farmers, and it was part of the Assyrian king's duty to ensure that they were kept under control. The performance of this obligation gradually became a sport. It is probable that lions were bred specifically so that Ashurbanipal could kill them.

In the great lion-hunt scenes, on either side of the Assyrian Saloon, the animals are released one by one from cages into an arena enclosed by ranks of soldiers. The people of Nineveh, spectators, clamber hastily up a safe hill. The king's arms are tested and his chariot harnessed. Then the king rides to and fro in his chariot shooting the lions down, while courtiers on horseback act as beaters or picadors. Some of the lions hurl themselves at the chariot, others are on the point of death. One novel feature of these scenes is the treatment of space: the background is not filled with superfluous detail, and we can concentrate on the main subject. Another feature is the skill and thoughtfulness with which the injured lions are drawn. They compare favourably with the stilted majestical king

and the awkwardly posed spectators, and it has been suggested that this shows the sculptors' sympathy for the lions.

Another method of killing lions was on foot. A small-scale series shows a strip-cartoon of incidents. First a lion is released from his cage; then he springs forward and is hit by an arrow; then he leaps at the king, and is held off by the bodyguard's spear while the king fires another arrow. There is a second version of the same strip-cartoon among the small-scale sculptures on the end-wall; here the king, without his crown on this occasion, finally kills the lion with his own sword.

The bottom register of the sculptures on the end-wall shows other kinds of animal being hunted. Onagers, or wild asses, are pursued by hounds; one mare pauses helplessly to look back at her foal; any that are not shot or pulled down run into an ambush, where they are lassoed. Further left there is a herd of gazelle grazing; one looks nervously over its shoulder as an Assyrian approaches, and the herd will shortly gallop off. At the far left, on their line of escape, we see Ashurbanipal waiting in a pit with bow and arrow, ready to shoot them down.

These pictures were carved when the slabs were already on the walls, as had been done in the ninth century. The sculptors were also assisted by clay models which they could copy; one example, in a wall-case to the right, shows the king killing a lion. The quality of different slabs is variable; there must have been large numbers of masons working under the control of a few masters. Some details were added last of all, and were liable to be forgotten altogether. A series, at the top of the stairs to the Assyrian Basement, has a procession of courtiers carrying hunting equipment; but two slabs have conspicuously rough, unfinished surfaces.

10 WILD ASSES FLEEING FROM HOUNDS

9 LION SHOT BY THE ASSYRIAN KING

The strip-cartoon method of illustration was also suitable for military narrative, and Ashurbanipal's wars with Teumman, King of Elam, in what is now southern Iran, are treated in this way. They face the stairs as one goes down. We have parts of four scenes from an original cycle of ten, and they start with the great battle of Til-Tuba in 653 BC; cuneiform captions explain the details. The series starts in the lower register with an Assyrian charge. The Elamites are already breaking, and abandoning their positions on the mound of Til-Tuba itself. Then we see the fate of

11 Teumman, in a series of dramatic moments, as he first falls out of his chariot and then hurries away, supported by his son; next they turn to fight, but are eventually killed; an Assyrian soldier finds Teumman's crown in a bush; and Teumman's head is carried back to a tent where Assyrians, with Elamite advice, are recording the numbers and identities of the dead. Teumman is recognized, and while the remnants of his army are driven pell-mell into the river Ulai on the right of the picture, the head of the defeated king is carried off triumphantly leftwards, for dispatch home to Assyria.

The next scene, to the right, shows subsequent events in Elam, when the Assyrians install a puppet king in Teumman's place, and the Elamite people welcome him with processions and music.

The upper register, above the installation, shows the events which followed the defeat of Teumman's allies in Babylonia. Several of them are being executed in various ways, while their chiefs (one of whom has Teumman's head hung round his neck) wait their turn to die. Ashurbanipal watches from his chariot on the right. These massacres and tortures had the strictly political aim of deterring future opposition. We also have occasional pictures of an ideal, peaceful world. A slab on the wall to the right shows, in its upper register, a walled town beside a river; overlooking the battlements is a building with human-headed winged bulls, and massive columns supported on lion-bases. This is probably a picture of Sennacherib's palace at Nineveh. Another part of the same picture, to the right, shows the type of public works

12 for which Sennacherib was responsible: a stone aqueduct, on pointed arches, carries irrigation water into an extensive garden, overlooked by a royal stela.

Other people whom Ashurbanipal fought included the Arabs, the Egyptians, and the Babylonians. A series of slabs, on the far, north side of the partition wall of the Assyrian Basement, shows an Arab force on camels being pursued by Assyrians; after the battle the Arab women are killed and their tents are burnt.

11 THE ROUT OF THE ELAMITES

13 AFRICAN PRISONERS OF WAR

The wars in Egypt are represented by one slab on the long side-wall. It shows the capture of a Nubian fortress, and some of the captives have characteristically African features. We do not possess a picture of the capture of Babylon in 648 BC, but we can see Ashurbanipal inspecting the captives and the loot. He himself is drawn on a larger scale than the people around him, an innovation that may have been copied from Egyptian monuments. Some of the men are bringing him the regalia of the Babylonian king, including his crown and private rickshaw. In the row below the Babylonians and Chaldaeans are marching into exile.

Ultimately Ashurbanipal collected no less than four Elamite ex-kings. The capture of one of them is shown in two scenes on a single sculpture; underneath a lioness stalks her prey. These Elamites were kept at court, and there is a picture of two of them being forced to carry food for Ashurbanipal. This is part of a series which culminated with Ashurbanipal himself, reclining beside his queen, out of doors in a garden guarded by soldiers. Musicians play, courtiers pick flowers, and Teumman's head hangs unobtrusively on a nearby tree. Ashurbanipal's couch may well have been made of ivory, overlaid with gold. Large quantities of broken ivory furniture have been found in Assyrian palaces, and some of the plaques resemble those in the sculpture. They are displayed upstairs in the Ivory Room.

The show-cases in the Assyrian Basement mostly contain small articles made in Assyria or under Assyrian influence. One has arms and armour; the Assyrians generally used iron weapons, but their protective armour was sometimes bronze. An iron saw-blade was probably used for cutting slabs of stone, such as those on which the sculptures were carved.

One of the two central cases includes a silver cup with gold foil round its rim. This was buried before the sack of Nimrud, and crushed by the weight of earth above it. It is one of the few Assyrian articles in precious metal to have survived. Weights were often made of bronze: one complete set, in the shape of lions, was found in a palace at Nimrud. A much larger bronze object is the hip-bath from Ur. This had been used as a coffin when it was found, but the delicate incisions on its sides are typically Assyrian in style. The coloured plaques on the wall behind the bath, and the jar beside it, are examples of a technique, the glazing of pottery, which became increasingly important in later periods.

A second staircase leads back to the Khorsabad Entrance.

12 ASSYRIAN GARDEN WITH AN AQUEDUCT

The larger the Assyrian empire grew, the more hostility it aroused. Weakened by invasions and civil wars, it eventually collapsed and was never permitted to revive. Even shortly before the end, however, it appears that sculptors were still conscientiously recording the defeat of nations which were far from defeated. Two long series of campaigns in marshy country, among palm-groves, extend on either side of the door into the Nineveh Gallery from the Assyrian Central Saloon. These scenes were carved in Sennacherib's palace, but they must be dated either to the last years of Ashurbanipal or to the reign of one of his sons. The marsh-dwellers were Chaldaeans, living in southern Mesopotamia, and a Chaldaean founded the Neo-Babylonian Empire which inherited Assyria's position in the Middle East. These sculptures are as full of anecdote and human detail as any Assyrian work: one may observe, in the left-hand series, the natives hiding in clumps of reeds, the Assyrians cooking meat beside a fire, the secretaries with their scrolls and hinged writing-boards, and the officer fastening a bracelet, like a medal, on the wrist of one of his soldiers.

Besides these late carvings, there are others which date from Sennacherib's reign. One group shows a colossal winged bull being roughly shaped in a quarry, and then moved with levers and rollers. Hundreds of foreign captives pull on the ropes; in the background boats loaded with equipment are moving up the Tigris; Sennacherib looks on from his rickshaw, and wild animals lurk in the reeds beside the river.

14 ASHURBANIPAL FEASTING IN A GARDEN

One area of the Middle East that lost its independence to the Assyrian empire, and subsequently became part of the Babylonian successor state, was Palestine. This country, because of its interest to Christians and Jews, has been more thoroughly explored than most of Western Asia, and one room is devoted to it. The Prehistoric Room and the Room of Writing upstairs, and the Lachish Room among the Assyrian sculptures, also contain items from Palestine.

Trade routes between the more sophisticated lands of Egypt and Syria ran through Palestine, which was therefore open to many foreign influences. Case 2 has some remarkable cuneiform letters, found in Egypt but written from Palestine about 1480 BC; they include appeals for help from attacks of the 'Hapiru', and it has sometimes been suggested that these are the Hebrews. A crude golden pendant in Case 3 probably represents one of the fertility goddesses worshipped in Palestine a little before this time.

A complete Palestinian tomb has been reconstructed in this room. The original was cut into solid rock, near the town of Jericho, about 2200–2000 BC. Some three centuries later it was used again, for the burial of a woman. There are also several other skeletons in the tomb and some of them have lost their right hands. One possibility is that these were tomb-robbers who were caught and executed; they may have been left in the grave to act as servants to the owner of the tomb in the next world. The articles in the tomb include pottery jars, beads, and wooden chairs and tables.

Relics of the biblical kingdoms of Judah and Israel are scarce, apart from pottery (Case 5). Among them, in Case 3, are some ivories which were damaged during the Assyrian sack of Samaria about 722 BC; they are indistinguishable in style from others found in Assyria itself (which may be seen in the Ivory Room), and both lots probably derived from Phoenician workshops. This was a time of extensive international communication and exchange of ideas.

In the first century BC Palestine was independent, under Roman protection, and the centre of the expanding Jewish religion. It seems to have been prosperous, and it possessed its own characteristic culture. The British Museum has two elegantly carved ossuaries or stone chests (Case 7), which were designed to contain the bones of the dead; one belonged to the family of a man who had presented a new set of gates to the Temple at Jerusalem. These chests date from about the time of Christ, and this is also, approximately, the period of the Dead Sea scrolls (Case 9).

Subsequently Palestine became a Roman province, but was devastated by a series of rebellions. One can follow the history of this phase through coins (Case 6).

The local coinage minted by the Hasmonean and Herodian dynasties consisted of small copper coins of the 'widow's mite' variety. Only at the time of the great revolt from Rome of the Jews (AD 66–70) did the independent state based on Jerusalem produce a coinage of silver shekels, which are of a striking and impressive character; these bear chalice and flower designs and are dated by each of the five years of independence terminated by the Roman recapture of the city in AD 70. A revival of silver coinage took place subsequently during the second revolt from Rome led by Bar Kochba in AD 133. His coins were frequently stamped on existing Roman money, and the shekels display as their main device the front of the Temple.

From outside the Ancient Palestine Room the staircase leads to the upper galleries of the Department of Western Asiatic Antiquities.

15 FERTILITY GODDESS. PALESTINE

16 OSSUARY. JERUSALEM

17 BAR KOCHBA REVOLT. SHEKEL

55 THE PREHISTORIC ROOM

The first people with whom we have to deal had a way of life comparable with that of the unwesternized tribes which still exist here and there across the world. Displays in the Museum of Mankind indicate the extraordinary richness and variety of surviving primitive cultures, not only in material goods but also in social conventions and imaginative thought. The articles in daily use among them, however, are often made of perishable materials such as wood, textiles, or skin. The same was evidently true of the primitive cultures of ancient Western Asia, and the things which are preserved in the earth for the archaeologist to discover give an unavoidably distorted picture of what life was then like. Nor do we have any written records to fill the gaps. We can nonetheless reconstruct something of the economic basis of prehistoric communities, and see that similar evolutionary pressures led time and again to similar solutions.

The people relied basically on their own local resources, mainly as settled farmers or as migrant herdsmen and hunters. The smallest groups may have contained only a few families, but circumstances sometimes favoured the growth and survival of larger groups, where several thousand people were associated in interdependent units, or in single towns and tribes. Some groups lived in areas with local resources that were more than adequate for their own needs (Case 9): resources like obsidian, a volcanic glass with a fine cutting edge; volcanic lava, which makes excellent grinding stones for grain; natural bitumen, for glueing and water-proofing; metals and metal ores; decorative coloured stones such as lapis lazuli; cowrie shells, and so on. Some of these items were exchanged over hundreds or even thousands of miles, perhaps accompanied by travelling merchants or craftsmen. At the same time there had to be occasional contact and competition between previously unrelated groups of people. Factors such as these ensured that widely separated areas shared, in some respects, a common culture.

Each successive period in a region of Western Asia is now called after the excavation site where adequate remains of that date were first identified. In Mesopotamia, for instance, the most familiar names are those of Hassuna, Halaf, and Ubaid (altogether covering about 6000–3500 BC, though our methods of dating prehistoric remains are open to improvement). Within this period of time, there may have been sudden changes and developments, but we are not entitled to assume that our succession of names represents anything more than gradual evolution, with many overlaps and anomalies. We do, however, have a convenient way of distinguishing one period from another, and that is by their different styles of pottery. The incised wares of Hassuna, for instance, could never be confused with the fine painted wares of Halaf (Case

18 PREHISTORIC BOWL. BAKUN, IRAN

7). There are many more such distinctions, seldom so conspicuous, which can even enable us to date an ancient site by simply glancing at pottery fragments found on its surface. Pottery is therefore an invaluable aid to the archaeologist working in prehistoric contexts, and is correspondingly prominent in this Room.

Most of the prehistoric pottery was made on a slow wheel rotated by hand. Before being fired the smaller vessels were often painted with patterns which are sometimes reminiscent of woodwork or weaving. Pictures of people and animals are relatively scarce, and they are drawn, when they do appear, in a schematic form which exaggerates some physical characteristics and omits others. This attitude to living subjects can also be seen in prehistoric figurines. Some of these, notably two from Chagar Bazar in Syria which seem to show women offering the breast (Case 6), emphasize the importance of fertility beliefs in many primitive farming communities. The nature of the subject is tolerably obvious, but there is no attempt at realism.

Another aspect of prehistoric religion is represented by a plaster head, modelled over a human skull, one of several models of this kind which were found in an early level (6000 BC or earlier) at Jericho in Palestine. This head is clearly naturalistic, and there is evidence to suggest that it represented a dead relative and was preserved in a family shrine.

The manufacture of stone stamp-seals begins even before 6000 BC, but some of the finest date from the late prehistoric period about 3500–2800 BC (Case 8). They were used in much the same way as seals and signatures are today. To prove, for instance, that he was responsible for a delivery of oil, a particular person applied his personal seal to wet clay smeared over the top of the oil-jar; no one could then open it without breaking the seal. This habit of using clay tags as a means of identification was a preliminary step towards the invention of writing. Writing itself developed between about 3500 and 3000 BC, by which time numerous small towns had evolved over much of Western Asia (see the Room of Writing).

Fortifications and religious buildings on a monumental scale were already being built in the prehistoric period. A reconstruction, using original materials, shows part of a half-columned façade from a temple at Uruk in southern Mesopotamia about 2900 BC: geometric patterns were created by pressing coloured cones into wet plaster. The same elaborate kind of mosaic decoration was used as far away as Brak in Syria. Excavations at the Brak temple produced thousands of small amulets or 'eye-idols', probably offerings made to win the god's favour (Case 6). An elegantly stylized human head also comes from this temple. A simpler form of architecture is represented by a terracotta model of a hut (about 3300 BC); this came from Azor in Palestine, and was a receptacle for the bones of the dead.

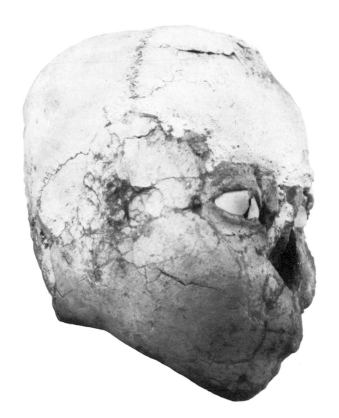

19 NEOLITHIC SKULL. JERICHO

20 CARVED TROUGH. URUK, IRAQ

The Sumerians lived in southern Mesopotamia (Iraq), in the alluvial plain of the Tigris and Euphrates rivers. The origin of the Sumerian language has been disputed, but we may presume that the people who spoke it were mainly descended from the prehistoric inhabitants of the same region. Certainly their civilization was strongly influenced by what had gone before. A gypsum trough, which shows sheep returning to the fold where their lambs are waiting, is the Museum's finest example of Mesopotamian art about 3000 BC. This may have come from Uruk, where a magnificent temple complex continued to flourish in the Early Dynastic period, about 2800–2370 BC.

The inlaid decoration from the façade of a temple at Al-Ubaid, about 2600 BC, included another series of pastoral scenes. Still more imposing, and of great technical interest for the history of metallurgy, are the copper heads and plaques representing lions, cattle, and deer. The columns of this same temple façade were found fallen in a heap, together with the rest of the decoration, but have been restored on reliable evidence. They were originally made of palm-tree trunks coated with bitumen, and their surface was then covered with shaped pieces of pink limestone and mother-of-pearl.

The temples of Sumer owed their great wealth to the theocratic system of government which existed in many Sumerian cities. Everything in a city belonged, theoretically, to the city's gods. The people were servants of the gods, contributing their labour and receiving rations in return. Their cooperation ensured that labour was available for major public works, especially the upkeep of irrigation canals, and specialist craftsmen were supported by their comrades working in the fields. We do not know if this theoretical ideal was ever realized. In practice the priests and controllers of the temple bureaucracies established themselves in power, and spent the surplus wealth of the community not only on the temples but also on themselves. The results of this policy are seen most dramatically in the Royal Tombs of Ur.

The city of Ur lay close to the Euphrates. Archaeologists were first attracted by its 'ziggurrat', a massive brick tower which once had a temple on top, but excavations in the 1920s also uncovered a cemetery which had remained in use for centuries. The excavator, Sir Leonard Woolley, was working on behalf of the British Museum and the University Museum, Philadelphia, and these two institutions were each awarded a quarter of what the expedition found; the other half remained in Baghdad. Even the British Museum's share, however, amply demonstrates the lavish way in which the tombs were furnished, and the extraordinary skill which Woolley brought to the task of excavating them. The finest of the articles on display are thought to have belonged to the ruling family at a time, about 2500 BC, when Ur was the most powerful city in Mesopotamia. Sometimes the dead man or woman had been accompanied to the grave by as many as sixty attendants, who brought with them everything necessary to ensure that their master

21 GOAT AND TREE. UR, IRAQ

continued to live, after death, in the style to which he had been accustomed. Woolley's discovery of these 'death-pits' aroused extensive controversy among scholars at the time, as Mesopotamian literature is singularly devoid of reference to any such macabre ceremonies, although similar kinds of mass burial do seem to have been practised in some other cultures.

We can still see the skulls of a helmeted soldier and of a female attendant wearing a jewelled headband, as they were found crushed in the ground. Some of the finest objects, however, have been restored to their original shapes. The goat with his forelegs resting on a tree – often called the Ram in the Thicket because of a fancied connection with the story of Abraham and Isaac – is one of a pair. The two probably supported a small table on which delicate vessels of gold and silver, or the Sumerian equivalent of a chess-set (Case 9), may once have stood. This highly ornamental goat was made on a simple wooden core; the surface consists of carved stones, shell, and sheet metal, with bitumen as glue. Musical instruments were constructed in the same way: the British Museum has one silver lyre, and another pair of inlaid instruments, a

harp and a lyre, which have been restored in wood. The sounding-boxes of the lyres represent bulls, and a text tells us that the music was imagined as coming out of the animals' mouths.

A lyre of the same kind is shown in a scene on the so-called Standard of Ur, a lectern-shaped box with mosaic panels all round. One of the two main sides shows people bringing gifts and tribute; the lyre-player is entertaining the king and his high officials at a banquet in the top row. The other side shows a different aspect of Sumerian civilization, with chariots charging, and warriors bringing captives into the royal presence. The chariots are pulled not by horses but by a kind of ass native to Mesopotamia; one of these animals is represented on an electrum rein-ring, also found in a royal grave. The rein-ring was part of the harness attached to a queen's ox-drawn sledge. Jewellery, such as the queen's attendants wore, and numerous other articles, are shown in the centre of the room and in Cases 9–11. It is worth noting that all the metals used, together with the carnelian and lapis lazuli, must have been imported.

22 LYRE-PLAYER. UR, IRAQ

24 WILD ASS ON REIN-RING. UR, IRAQ

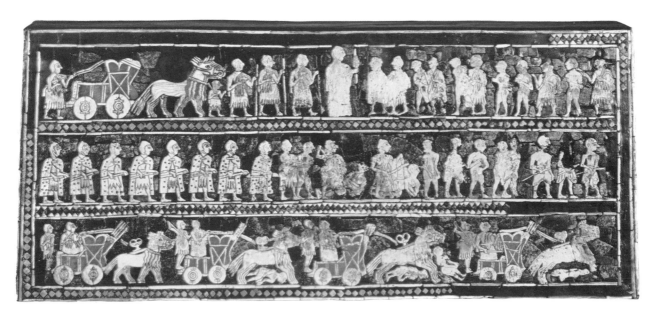

23 SCENES OF WAR. UR, IRAQ

Life-size Sumerian sculpture is represented by the
25 statue of a slightly later ruler, about 2100 BC, almost
certainly Gudea of the state of Lagash. This statue
would have been set up in a temple, to encourage the
god to look after the ruler's interests. Most Mesopotamian statues are far smaller than this (Case 5), as the
blocks of stone had to be brought from outside the
Tigris–Euphrates plain, and the problems of moving
them must have been considerable.

The remaining cases in this room show aspects of
Assyrian and Babylonian art and civilization. There is
always an apparent contrast between technical
sophistication and traditional modes of belief. In Case
2, for example, there are fragments of glass as old as
1500 BC, and a tablet giving detailed instructions on
the manufacture of glazes. In Case 13, on the other
hand, are statues of the demons to which every kind
of human misfortune was attributed. We have to
remember, when we look at objects of this kind, that
Mesopotamian civilization operated on assumptions
about the universe that were far removed from those
which many of us take for granted. In order to appreciate all that Mesopotamian works of art have to offer,
we must try to understand them on their own terms.

25 GUDEA, A SUMERIAN RULER. LAGASH, IRAQ

Some of the earliest prehistoric towns developed on the Anatolian plateau, in what is now Turkey, but urban civilization did not expand there as rapidly as in Mesopotamia. In the third millennium BC Anatolia was probably an important source of copper, and fine examples of metalwork have been found in tombs at Alaca Hüyük, about 2300 BC. A silver bull with high horns probably derives from this group. In the Yortan area, to the south of Troy, an undistinguished type of black burnished pottery was used (Case 1), but those who could afford it possessed metal vessels such as an elegant two-handled silver cup.

26   Assyrian merchants brought writing to Anatolia, and in the second millennium the Hittites, who spoke an Indo-European language, built an empire which extended into Syria and shared a border with the Egyptians. Case 2 includes a cuneiform tablet from their capital city at Bogazköy, but the Museum's most remarkable example of Hittite workmanship is a series of miniature figures made of lapis lazuli, steatite and gold, which represent Hittite gods and dignitaries. They were found in a grave at Carchemish on the Euphrates, a town which retained some aspects of Hittite culture long after the empire had collapsed about 1200 BC. The language of Carchemish was related to Hittite, and was written in a hieroglyphic script; there are examples of this on the sculptured slabs displayed on the landing outside this room. The style of the sculptures themselves, however, is clearly reminiscent of Assyrian art; most of them were in fact made in the ninth and eighth centuries BC, when Carchemish was an important trading centre under Assyrian protection. The other articles from Carchemish in Cases 2 and 3 indicate the cosmopolitan character of what is sometimes called 'Syro-Hittite' art. Case 3 also includes examples of perhaps the first coins ever minted; they come from the kingdom of Lydia, on the fringe of the Greek world.

   The kingdom of Urartu (about 850–600 BC) included the eastern provinces of modern Turkey, Russian Armenia, and part of Iran. It too was strongly influenced by Assyrian civilization, as can be seen in the fine collection of Urartian bronzes from Toprak Kale near Van. (Compare the pictures of Assyrian campaigns in Urartu, shown on the Balawat Gates in the downstairs gallery.) Case 4 includes several fragments of bronze furniture, which may have belonged to a throne of the national god Haldi. A winged figure with a female head probably derives from the rim of a cauldron; this shape was widely imitated in Greek and Etruscan art. An Urartian model castle, and examples of arms and armour, are exhibited in Cases 5 and 6, together with a round bronze shield elaborately decorated with processions of animals. In between are some Urartian texts written in a version of the cuneiform script.

26 HITTITE GOD. ANATOLIA

The most famous site of Iran (Persia) is undoubtedly the Achaemenid capital of Persepolis. Its palaces and public buildings stand on a massive artificial platform, backed dramatically by bare rocky hills, about thirty-five miles from modern Shiraz. Its sculptured walls have a distinctive, highly finished style, characteristic of the art of the Persian Empire which, extending from Egypt to Turkestan, borrowed freely from all the ancient cultures it superseded. Fragments of these carvings, brought to England in the last century, line the corridor between the Anatolian and Iranian Rooms. A huge column-base, also excavated at Persepolis, will be exhibited on the landing outside the Anatolian Room.

The land of Elam, with its capital of Susa, was the oldest centre of literate civilization in Iran (Case 7). It counts in many ways as an extension of Mesopotamia, and the terracotta statue of a female, which probably decorated a temple about 1500 BC, is closely related in style to Mesopotamian work.

In the third millennium BC various Iranian products, including carved steatite vessels, were imported from the plateau into Mesopotamia, and Mesopotamian shapes and motifs were copied in Iran itself during the second millennium. They can be seen, more or less recognizable, on numerous articles of silver and bronze, in Cases 1–6. The Luristan horse-harness is in a highly individual style, and was probably made between 1200 and 800 BC. Unhappily, most of this material comes from unstratified contexts, and is hard to place chronologically. Some belts from Azerbaijan, decorated with animals and geometric motifs, are regarded as Caucasian in style.

The Ziwiye Treasure (Case 9) has been attributed to many groups of people, and indicates how freely decorative motifs and stylistic idiosyncracies travel

27 ARMLET. OXUS TREASURE

from place to place. It may have been buried between 750 and 600 BC. The Achaemenid empire was finally established through the capture of Babylon by Cyrus in 539 BC; this was recorded on a cylinder (Case 11), which asserts that the Persian conquest liberated the people from their oppressors. The Museum is singularly fortunate in its collection of Achaemenid work. The Susa archer is a large-scale example in glazed brick. Among smaller works of art, one of the finest is a silver and partly gilded rhyton with a griffin's head. It was used to drink from, the liquid being poured into the mouth through a hole in the griffin's chest.

The Oxus Treasure

The Oxus Treasure (Cases 12–14) probably belonged to a temple where offerings had accumulated for several centuries; it was eventually buried, perhaps about 200 BC, and rediscovered in 1877. A group of merchants carried it to India, where it was sold to a British officer, and most of it eventually came to the British Museum as part of the Franks bequest. Many of the objects are typically Achaemenid in style and quality. Others, notably some of the finger-rings, show the influence of Greek art. One item of particular interest is the model chariot drawn by four small ponies. Others worth noting include the pair of armlets, decorated with griffins' heads and once inlaid with glass or semi-precious stones, and the large gold fish, really a bottle, with an aperture at its mouth. A simpler form of art is represented on a series of gold plaques for sewing on clothes, while an elaborate scabbard, with scenes of lion-hunts, recalls some of the Assyrian sculptures downstairs.

The coins which came on the market at the same time as the Oxus Treasure, and which may have formed part of it, comprise material from two distinct periods: both the Achaemenid empire, with its

32 SASSANIAN SILVER DISH

mixture of currency, and the kingdoms set up by Alexander the Great and his successors. The royal Achaemenid gold and silver coins (*darics* and *sigloi* respectively) are characterized by the figure of an archer traditionally recognized as the Great King. Apart from these there are the coins issued by individual imperial governors or satraps, mainly at Tarsos in southern Anatolia during the fourth century BC; one of these shows a fine seated satrap, with the supreme god Ahuramazda above.

The original hoard, if indeed it was a single hoard, also contained coins of the Greek world which circulated in the Persian empire (minted at Akanthos and Byzantion in northern Greece as well as other cities, including Athens) and eastern imitations of these. There were apparently included many of the common silver coins of Alexander the Great whose mint at Babylon also produced gold double-*darics* continuing the Achaemenid type; these too appear in the hoard. Then come the issues of Alexander's successors, Seleucus I, Antiochus I and Antiochus II, and perhaps even a few of the first independent Greek rulers of Bactria (e.g. Diodotus, c. 250 BC). Finally, another group of very rare and obscure coins, which seem to belong to north-eastern Persia and to the early Greek period, are those of a certain Andragoras and of the Iranian ruler Vahsuvar (?).

The Parthians

The conquests of Alexander the Great destroyed the Persian Empire, but from about 250 BC his Greek successors were gradually replaced by a local dynasty, the Parthians, who had their early capital at Hecatompylos in north-eastern Iran. Work produced in the Parthian period, from about 150 BC to AD 224 (Cases 15–18), is often based on Greek models, but older Iranian themes tend to intrude. The gold masks from Nineveh were originally placed in graves, over the faces of the dead. The blue-glazed coffin from Warka is decorated with figures of armed men, made by pressing a mould into the damp clay.

Parthian coins are particularly valuable for reconstructing the period's political history, our knowledge of which often depends on sporadic references in western literature. During the reign of Mithridates I (171–138 BC) Parthian control was extended over a large part of Iran and Babylonia. At first the Parthian rulers accepted the existing standards of civilization.

This is clearly reflected in the coins, on which appear portraits of the individual rulers often displayed in Greek style wearing a simple diadem around the head, but otherwise often shown in a royal tiara or helmet. The royal titles, in Greek, were placed on the reverse of the coins and the date when given was still based on the Seleucid era starting 312 BC. At a later stage the style of the coinage changes perceptibly. The portraits become harsher and less realistic, more recognizably oriental monarchs; some of the later ones such as Volagases IV (AD 147–191) have an almost 'Babylonian' appearance.

The Sassanians

The process of orientalizing Hellenistic art was completed under the kings of the Sassanian dynasty (AD 224–642), who regarded themselves as heirs of the Achaemenids and retained a religious centre at Istakhr, a city in the neighbourhood of Persepolis. Their goldsmiths and silversmiths showed great skill in the use of embossing, chasing, engraving and gilding, and other craftsmen continued ancient Near Eastern traditions of fine workmanship. One silver dish shows Shapur II hunting stags; on another Bahram V is shown hunting lions, and a partially gilded silver vase is decorated with vineyard scenes framed in stylized grape vines. Contacts with the classical world are shown by seals depicting 'Leda and the swan' and 'a wolf suckling Romulus and Remus'; both seals bear Pahlavi inscriptions.

In coinage, also, the Sassanians broke with Hellenistic traditions. Pahlavi writing finally replaced Greek. As an indication that Zoroastrianism was the official religion, a fire-altar tended by two royal or priestly figures appeared on the reverse. The coins, which are mainly of silver – gold was minted on special occasions only – carry portrait busts of the kings, who are distinguished from each other by their characteristic crowns. Ardashir I (AD 224–241), the first independent Sassanian king, has no fewer than five distinctive head-dresses, probably marking different stages in his assumption of power. In one instance, on the coinage of Bahram II (AD 276–293), a whole family is depicted – the King, the Queen, and the Crown Prince. Boran (AD 630–631) was the only woman ruler in her own right to portray herself on coins in this series.

28 ACHAEMENID. DARIC   29 VAHSUVAR. STATER   31 VOLAGASES IV. TETRADRADRACHM   33 BAHRAM II. DRACHM

30 GOLD MASK FROM PARTHIAN GRAVE. NINEVEH

The display here illustrates the history of writing from its origins down to the emergence of the alphabet. The first written records seem to have been receipts, lumps of clay in which rows of dots, representing numbers, were written beside seal-impressions; such receipts have been found from Syria to central Iran, and may date back to 3500 BC. The Museum's collection begins (Case 2) at a slightly later stage, when the dotted numbers were accompanied by simple pictures. The head of an ox, for example, was used to indicate that the number of dots referred to the number of oxen. Each symbol became increasingly stylized with time, until it was no longer recognizable as the picture of an object, and merely consisted of a geometric pattern representing a particular word or syllable.

We cannot say exactly when it was recognized that this method of keeping accounts had become a suitable means of recording far more elaborate things, such as religious incantations. The process was probably gradual, but it had been completed by about 2500 BC in the Sumerian cities of southern Mesopotamia. The script, which we know as cuneiform, was eventually used to write records of many kinds in several different languages (Case 3), and it continued in use until the first century AD. The material on which it was written remained, most commonly, damp clay; this was available everywhere, retained its shape when dry, and could always be baked if a permanent record was required.

Cases 4–9 indicate the wide range of cuneiform literature; most of these clay tablets are written in Akkadian, the language which replaced Sumerian in Mesopotamia. A fine hexagonal prism, once buried in the foundations of an Assyrian palace, describes how Sennacherib besieged Jerusalem about 701 BC. A broken tablet from Nineveh tells the Mesopotamian legend of a flood which devastated the entire world; the text has some striking resemblances to the story of Noah's ark. Another tablet is shaped like a sheep's liver, and was used to teach student priests how to foretell the future from the entrails of sacrificed animals. Yet another depicts a crude map of the world, with Babylon at the centre and Ocean all around; this is the prototype of a view of the world which prevailed widely until the time of Columbus. The Babylonians also made extremely elaborate astronomical observations, using a system of mathematical notation which was comparable with the decimal system but required more sophisticated handling. A large tablet explains how to calculate the areas of a variety of geometrical shapes.

Ashurbanipal, an Assyrian king (668–627 BC) who is portrayed in Case 9, ostentatiously carrying a basket of bricks to rebuild a temple, had a high regard for traditional literature. He collected a vast library at Nineveh, and most of what has been recovered is

34 TABLET WITH A FLOOD LEGEND. NINEVEH

36 AKKADIAN CYLINDER-SEAL IMPRESSIONS

now in the British Museum, though only a tiny proportion is on display. This is a main source of our knowledge of formal cuneiform literature. No less important for our understanding of early civilization are the administrative tablets, census lists, legal contracts, and letters exchanged between men and women of many different positions in the state (Cases 7 and 8); one letter still retains part of its clay envelope. Mesopotamia has also produced the earliest known code of laws; this was written slightly earlier than the reign of the most famous law-giver, Hammurabi of Babylon (about 1750 BC), who is represented by a stela on the wall opposite.

Cuneiform tablets, like prehistoric receipts, were often signed by means of seals. Generally cylindrical in shape, they were rolled over the surface of the clay. The carvings on these seals, though miniature in size, are among the finest products of ancient Mesopotamian art. There are many different styles, but the best of all are perhaps those produced in the Agade period, about 2370–2100 BC. One has to look at them very closely to appreciate the quality of workmanship and the concentrated vitality of the figures. The pair illustrated show two extremes of subject-matter: one, a procession of people, and the other, a struggle between a legendary hero and a lion.

The cuneiform script consisted of signs, each of which represented a whole word or syllable. Over the years, in the hands of many different writers, it grew extraordinarily complicated: a single sign came to represent several different syllables, and one syllable came to be represented by several different signs. About 1500 BC an entirely new type of writing is recorded for the first time in the Sinai peninsula. This was the alphabet, in which each sign represented one consonant and nothing more (Case 1). This system, far simpler than syllabic cuneiform, spread among the Phoenicians and other Semitic-speaking peoples of the eastern coast of the Mediterranean. The inhabitants of Ugarit, modern Ras Shamra near Lattakia, and subsequently the Achaemenid kings, used alphabets written in types of cuneiform. Both were eventually replaced by alphabets derived from the Phoenician, which could be written at greater speed on materials like paper.

This Semitic alphabet developed in several directions. Hebrew, as written on the tomb of Shebnaiah at Jerusalem, eventually became the square Hebrew script still used today. The Aramaic script, used through much of Western Asia for centuries, had several descendants including Armenian. The Arabic script is again derived from the early Semitic alphabet. The Greeks borrowed their own alphabet from the Phoenicians, and the Russians took theirs from the Greek. Most western European languages now use the Latin alphabet which derives from the same source.

35 BABYLONIAN GEOMETRICAL PROBLEMS

37 TOMB PORTRAIT. PALMYRA, SYRIA

Syrian civilization shared the prehistoric background of Mesopotamia. The finds from a temple at Tell Brak, about 2900 BC, include a frieze of carved stone and gold which has no identifiably local characteristics. In the Sumerian period, however, and in the second millennium BC, Syria seems to have borrowed more from Mesopotamian and other civilizations than it contributed itself. Two of the most important centres were Ebla, south of Aleppo, and Mari in the Euphrates valley.

The design of the statue of King Idrimi, dated about 1600 BC, from Alalakh (modern Açana in Turkey), is distantly related to the seated statues of Sumerian worshippers; but its stylized features and uncomfortable pose are almost prehistoric in spirit. Small bronze statues which represent Syrian gods often combine technical dexterity with a very crude style. Many of them must have been owned by private families, and been regarded as household gods.

The subject-matter of the sculptures from Tell Halaf is based ultimately on third-millennium models, and this led an early archaeologist to the conclusion that the sculptures were far older than they really were. In fact they were produced about 1000–800 BC, and belong at the tail-end of a tradition of provincial imitations. The carving is coarse, but the stone itself is of poor quality. It has been suggested that their surface was once smoothed with plaster, which would have greatly improved their appearance.

The Phoenicians, living on the Mediterranean coast, established an extensive network of trading stations overseas. They themselves produced works of art which borrowed freely from every culture with which they came into contact. The biggest contributor was Egypt, and this influence can be clearly seen in the sphinxes and decorative motifs on a series of bronze bowls. The bowls themselves were found in the Assyrian capital city of Nimrud, and must have been made between 900 and 700 BC. The Ivory Room contains other examples of Phoenician work which found favour with the Assyrian kings.

Cyprus was among the islands colonized from Phoenicia; an elaborate silver bowl, showing both Egyptian and Assyrian influence, comes from a grave at Amathus. A Phoenician cemetery has also been discovered as far west as Tharros in Sardinia, and a selection of jewellery and pottery is displayed. The most famous of all Phoenician settlements, however, was the city of Carthage in what is now Tunisia; the Carthaginian Empire was at one time a serious rival of Rome. There are a number of stelae inscribed in the Phoenician (Punic) script; some were erected over the graves of children who had probably been sacrificed to the local god, a practice noted by several Greek and Roman authors.

Syria in the Roman period was a frontier province, and the desert city of Palmyra, or Tadmor, retained a considerable degree of freedom. It was situated on an oasis dominating the most direct trade-route between the Syrian coast and the important Mesopotamian territories of the Parthian and Sassanian empires. Its control of the transit trade greatly enriched the city, especially in the second and third centuries AD, and the principal families built themselves imposing tombs in the suburbs. Each individual grave was provided with a stone portrait of the deceased, and their style is a strange amalgam of eastern and western influences. They are worth comparing with some of the painted portraits in the Coptic Gallery of the Egyptian Department.

Other late objects from Syria, including stone statuary from the Hauran, are variable in style, but the glassware shows great originality; indeed, the blowing of glass was probably invented in Syria. Some pottery bowls, with Aramaic incantations written across them, were originally buried for magical purposes.

58 THE IVORY ROOM

Ivory, a material which can be carved in the greatest detail, was popular in the ancient world, especially in Syria. Elephants once lived there wild, but the last were killed about the eighth century BC; even after this, however, merchants continued to obtain tusks from Africa, and possibly from India too.

Sometimes a single article, such as a toilet-box, was made from one piece of ivory, or from several small pieces fastened together. A larger object, such as a chair, might be made entirely of ivory members: one piece is apparently a furniture-leg. More often, however, there were ivory panels, plain or carved, forming a decorative veneer over a wooden framework, or stitched on to the leather backing of a horse's harness. Most of the fragments so far found probably belonged to furniture, and some even have alphabetic marks on the back, which indicated to the carpenter where to fix them.

The majority come from the palaces of Nimrud, where several stores of this furniture have been excavated. Some are blackened by fire, but others

39 ALABASTER HEAD. SOUTH ARABIA

retain the brilliant whiteness of fresh ivory. This can be misleading, as ivories were sometimes stained in different colours, and the richer pieces were covered with gold-leaf. Colour was also provided by red and blue inlays; these were normally made of glass, but we occasionally encounter carnelian and lapis lazuli too, for instance on a plaque which shows a lioness holding an African by the neck. The delicate carving of this small panel is among the finest examples of Phoenician workmanship. It must be dated between 900 and 700 BC, a period during which large quantities of ivory furniture were transported to Assyria as war booty or as tribute.

The Phoenician ivories are often inspired by Egyptian models, so much so that some of them at first sight might seem to be Egyptian work. Towns in inland Syria, including probably Damascus and Hama, had their own schools of ivory craftsmen; these inland ivories are less polished in style, but often show greater vigour and originality. Ivories were also carved in Urartu and Babylonia. Those made in Assyria itself are lightly incised, or cut in low relief like the stone sculptures; they are seldom comparable with those imported from the West.

Notable motifs on the Syrian and Phoenician ivories include the sphinx, the griffin, the grazing deer, the cow turning to lick her suckling calf, and the 'Woman at the Window', believed to be a picture of one of the Phoenician goddesses of reproduction and fertility. She also appears, in a slightly different version,

among the decorative panels on Ashurbanipal's couch in the Assyrian Basement. It would be invidious, however, to insist on the importance of any one or two of the ivories on display here. They were in fact mass-produced; but each one seems to have some individual felicity of carving. We can see that the Phoenician reputation for ingenuity, mentioned by the early Greeks, was thoroughly well deserved.

59 THE SOUTH ARABIAN LANDING

Most South Arabian antiquities have come from what are now the territories of Yemen and South Yemen, the home of the legendary Queen of Sheba. The ancient history of this area is virtually unknown, but it was famous for the production of aromatic spices and incense; its reputed wealth attracted invaders from Rome, Iran, and Ethiopia. One of the more delicate objects on display is, appropriately, a bronze incense-burner; its handle represents an oryx, or antelope with highly exaggerated horns.

The South Arabians had their own alphabetic script, which appears on several monuments, and a distinctive style of primitive sculpture, sometimes reminiscent of modern work. A great bronze altar, with projecting bulls' heads and massive rows of sphinxes, recalls the art of Western Asia before the Greeks. Two fine heads, however, in bronze and translucent stone, are obviously influenced by Greco–Roman standards of portraiture.

38 CARVED IVORY. NIMRUD, IRAQ

Museum of Mankind – Ethnography

Museum of Mankind – Ethnography

In 1970 the Ethnography Department moved from the British Museum to its new galleries in Burlington Gardens. The Department contains the anthropological collections of the British Museum, which are the finest of their kind in the world. The collections come from the indigenous peoples of Africa, Australia and the Pacific Islands, North and South America, and from certain parts of Asia and Europe; both recent and ancient cultures are represented. This material is presented in regularly changing exhibitions which illustrate the enormous variety of human societies and cultures and the art and artefacts they created. Some of these exhibitions show the ways of life of particular peoples, their art and religion, while others concentrate on specific features of their cultures. In addition a selection of the Museum's finest artistic treasures is constantly on display. Current exhibitions are described in the Museum's published programme. Although the Department's magnificent collections are now housed away from the British Museum they date from the Museum's foundation. When Sir Hans Sloane's collections were purchased by the Government in 1753 among the 'artificial curiosities' acquired were a number of ethnographic specimens which are now among the Department's most valued possessions. To these were added many collections made during the great exploratory and colonial enterprises of the eighteenth and nineteenth centuries and these, in turn, have been augmented in the present century by collections from both public and private sources and by materials obtained by scientific expeditions to all parts of the world.

For convenience this material will be dealt with here by broad geographic areas in the same way that it is organized in the Museum itself.

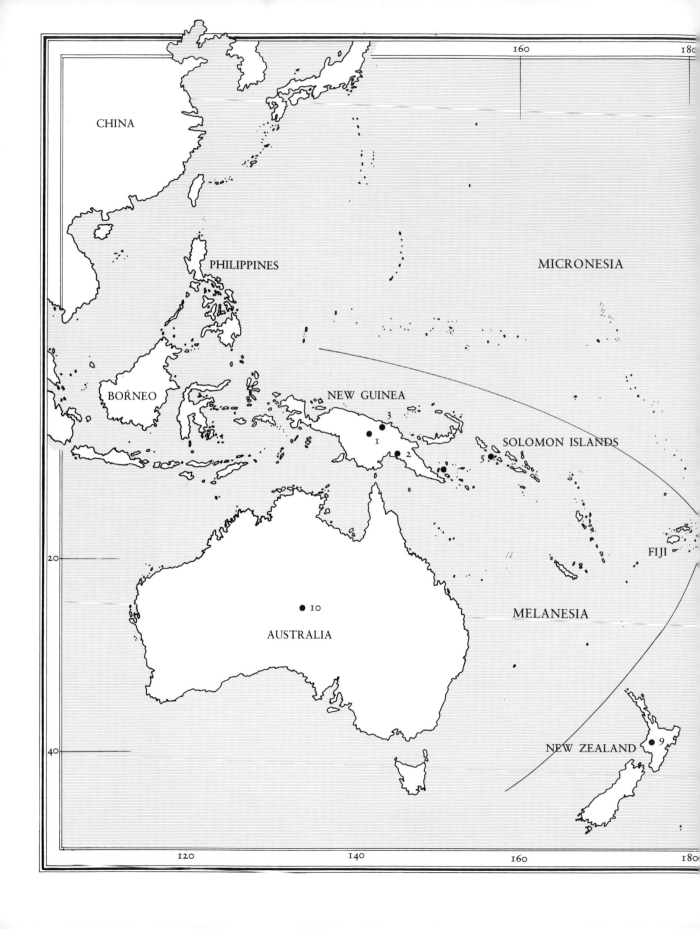

CHINA

PHILIPPINES

MICRONESIA

BORNEO

NEW GUINEA

3

1

2

SOLOMON ISLANDS

5

FIJI

20

MELANESIA

10

AUSTRALIA

NEW ZEALAND   9

40

160

180

120

140

160

180

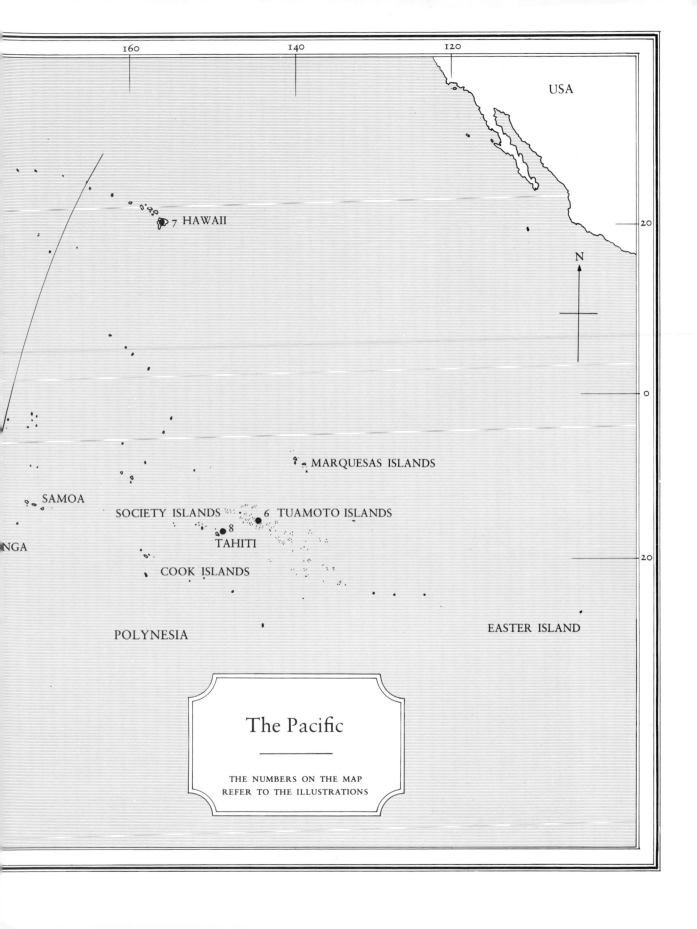

160 140 120

USA

20

N

0

7 HAWAII

MARQUESAS ISLANDS

SAMOA

SOCIETY ISLANDS   6 TUAMOTO ISLANDS

NGA   8
TAHITI

COOK ISLANDS   20

POLYNESIA   EASTER ISLAND

The Pacific

THE NUMBERS ON THE MAP
REFER TO THE ILLUSTRATIONS

1 SHIELD FROM THE NEW GUINEA HIGHLANDS

2 MASK FROM THE PAPUAN GULF, NEW GUINEA

The numerous islands scattered across the vast expanse of the Pacific Ocean show an amazing diversity of societies and a wide variety of cultural invention. The majority of the people of the area grow crops, although fishing is important around most small islands and on the coasts of the larger land masses. The area as a whole can be divided into three sections according to the culture and racial type of the inhabitants. These are Melanesia, stretching from New Guinea to Fiji; Micronesia, the scattering of islands to the north, and Polynesia, the vast area from Tonga to Easter Island and from Hawaii to New Zealand. The continent of Australia was populated by peoples who lived by hunting and gathering wild plants and had a distinctive culture of their own.

The peoples of Melanesia and New Guinea traditionally lived in small independent communities. Although some of the coastal peoples made long voyages by canoe to exchange goods and to trade, inland communication was made difficult by the tropical forest and, in the New Guinea Highlands, by the terrain. These factors seem to have encouraged the development of many distinct regional cultures and local groups which were often in a state of war with one another. Even today feuding and raiding between nearby communities continues in parts of New Guinea. In many parts of Melanesia weapons and shields were beautifully decorated. The large shield illustrated is coloured with ochre, lime and soot, and was obtained in the Telefomin area of New Guinea by the British Museum expedition of 1964–65.

Although the Melanesians, like other Pacific peoples, had no metals before the coming of Europeans they developed a remarkable variety of manufacturing techniques using tools of stone, bone and shell. Each island or district had its local style of manufactures and art. In some areas wood-carving was highly developed, in others shell-working, modelling in clay and vegetable pastes, or making feather ornaments. The illustration shows a mask from the Papuan Gulf of New Guinea, which demonstrates this resourceful use of materials. This has a cane frame, tightly covered with a layer of barkcloth, made by pounding and felting together the inner bark of a tree. The painted design is outlined with strips of cane and the cape of vegetable fibre concealed the wearer's body.

Masks were used in many parts of lowland New Guinea and the eastern islands of Melanesia. Like so many Melanesian works of art they had a religious purpose, and were worn in festivals by dancers impersonating spirits. In the Papuan Gulf such masks were secretly made by men to represent spirits of the forest who were believed to make a short annual visit to the village to dance among the people before returning once again to the trees.

Throughout most of Melanesia men spent much of their time in large well-built club houses, where, among other things, they made and stored sacred objects such as masks in preparation for esoteric rituals. The club house buildings were the Melanesians' finest architectural achievements and in some areas they were truly spectacular, pillared with the trunks of tall trees and adorned with elaborate carvings or painted designs. The wooden sculpture illustrated is a post from such a club house, made by the Iatmul of the Sepik River area of New Guinea, a region famed for the skill of its local sculptors. It probably represents a spirit, perhaps an ancestor, although the details of its significance are unknown.

Carvings such as this were shaped with an adze or axe fitted with a blade of ground and polished stone. The illustration shows an axe from the islands to the east of New Guinea. Although basically similar to those used for woodworking this object is a work of art in itself, with its thin polished greenstone blade and delicately carved haft. Like various other finely made objects, such axes were used mainly for elaborate ceremonial exchanges which created and confirmed bonds between communities throughout Melanesia. Such exchanges sometimes involved islands separated by hundreds of miles of ocean, and large parties of men travelled in canoes built mainly for this purpose.

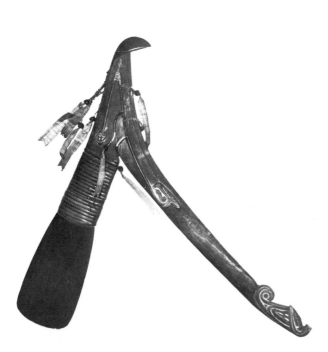

4 AXE FROM THE MASSIM AREA OF MELANESIA

3 HOUSEPOST FROM NORTHERN NEW GUINEA

5 CANOE PROW FROM THE SOLOMON ISLANDS

The outrigger canoe was common in Melanesia, although the Solomon Islanders developed long graceful canoes without outriggers, which might carry almost one hundred men on raids as well as trading expeditions. These canoes were often masterpieces of craftsmanship, built of many planks stitched together with cane and caulked with resinous vegetable paste. Painted black and inlaid with gleaming shell, the largest and finest of these bore on the prow a half figure like the one illustrated, which probably represented a water spirit protecting the vessel.

Such carvings are not only fine examples of the local style of sculpture but also demonstrate the Solomon Islanders' special skill in working shell. Each piece of inlay was individually ground from hard pearl shell and sunk into a groove in the wood, firmly embedded in resinous paste. This style of decoration is typical of the south-east Solomon Islands, and was used to good effect on their many fine wooden objects. Here and elsewhere shell was also worked into fishhooks, ornamental plaques and small flat beads which, when strung together in elaborate necklaces and other ornaments, were used for ceremonial exchange.

In contrast to Melanesia the people of Polynesia, although separated from one another by thousands of miles of ocean, all shared one basic culture and spoke variants of a single language. This culture has suffered heavily in most places from European influences, and the Museum's Polynesian material is particularly important because it includes many pieces collected by the first explorers and early missionaries.

The Polynesians have many tales of how their islands were populated by migrations over vast stretches of ocean. Such long voyages were seldom made in more recent times but most Polynesians remained expert boat builders and seamen. In the Tuamotus, a group of coral atolls where good land and large trees were scarce, the people built canoes with what little wood was available by ingeniously fitting together many small pieces of timber. These were sewn together with plaited coconut fibre, the common boat-building technique of Polynesia. The canoe illustrated is a masterpiece of precise carpentry, using mainly shell cutting tools. Such small canoes were used for fishing, important on islands of poor agricultural yield, but in places such as Tahiti and Tonga enormous canoes with double hulls were used for carrying large numbers of warriors to war and, in earlier times, for colonizing expeditions.

6 CANOE FROM THE TUAMOTU ISLANDS

The most heavily populated Polynesian islands had well developed systems of aristocratic government with hereditary chiefs who could sometimes muster armies large enough to conquer neighbouring districts or islands. Chiefs were recognized even in poorer islands such as the Tuamotus, but in places such as Tonga, Samoa, Tahiti and Hawaii their authority was particularly strong, and their persons sacred. Of the special insignia, often including red feathers, which these chiefs wore, those from Hawaii are among the most impressive. The illustration shows a Hawaiian crested helmet of basketry which is entirely covered with small feathers. In this case the feathers are bound on to cords which cover the sides and are attached to fine netting on the top to create a masterpiece of skilled craftsmanship. Elaborate and beautiful cloaks and capes covered with feathers were also worn. The Department has a major collection of this extremely rare and valuable Hawaiian work, as well as many rare or unique examples of chiefs' insignia from other parts of Polynesia.

A particularly interesting item illustrated here is a complete costume worn in rituals for mourning the dead in Tahiti. It reveals several of the crafts in which Polynesians excelled. The body is covered with drapes of barkcloth, soft and flexible, which was a common Polynesian clothing material. Polished plaques of pearl shell, widely favoured for ornaments, cover the face in perhaps the only type of mask used in Polynesia, and they also adorn the wooden breastpiece. From the latter hangs a fine veil of many small pieces of pearl shell, pierced and strung on vegetable fibre, and below this is a barkcloth apron studded with pieces of polished coconut shell. Pendants of black cockerel feathers, which were also worn by dancers, hang at the sides of the costume, and tail feathers of the frigate bird, often used in headdresses, form a halo. The wearer's back is covered with netting to which bunches of black feathers are tied. This costume was collected on one of Captain Cook's voyages. The collector mounted it on wooden easel and when it was dismantled recently for conservation it was found that a Tahitian religious figure of wood had been used to form a support for the top of the costume.

7 FEATHERED HELMET FROM HAWAII

8 MOURNER'S COSTUME FROM TAHITI

The Polynesian culture developed by the Maori of New Zealand is characterized by a sophisticated art style very different from that of the central Polynesian islands, whence the Maoris' ancestors emigrated long ago. Besides the prolific use of wood carving in architecture and the decoration of useful objects, the Maoris worked bone and stone with equal success. 9 The illustration shows a good example of the type of neck pendant, made of local greenstone, which was commonly worn by persons of rank. Its form reveals the technique of slow grinding by which it was made.

In Australia the Aborigines lived entirely by gathering wild plant food, and by hunting and fishing. Although their material possessions were few and simple, the Aborigines had an intimate knowledge of their natural environment which enabled them to live in even the most arid deserts of central Australia. In the rich coastal areas, long since settled by Europeans, they once found food in abundance. The Aborigines also devised perhaps the world's most complex way of organizing kin relationships, which was matched by the complexity of their religion. Much time and energy was spent in religious rituals, in which men enacted the exploits of long distant ancestors, animal people who shaped the world and founded human society, and whom they believed were still present in the natural world. The stone plaque illustrated, known as 10 a *Churinga*, is a symbol of certain of these beings, and is engraved with designs illustrating how the ancestors of a certain clan came from the ground. Such stone and wooden tablets were kept hidden in sacred places which women or uninitiated boys were forbidden even to approach.

The many fine paintings on bark, which some Aborigine groups produced, also show scenes from sacred tales. Paintings were also made on rocks as well as on the ground and on the bodies of participants in religious rituals. The Museum's Australian collections show how a rich cultural life can be created with even the simplest economy and technology.

9 GREENSTONE 'TIKI' FROM NEW ZEALAND

10 STONE 'CHURINGA' FROM CENTRAL AUSTRALIA

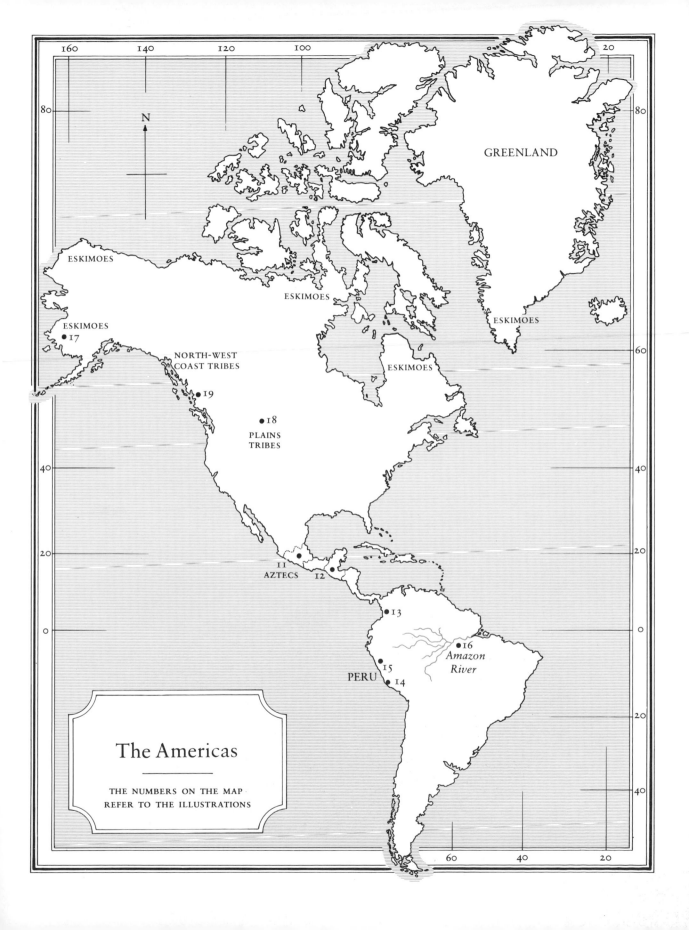

160   140   120   100   20

N

80   80

GREENLAND

ESKIMOES

ESKIMOES

ESKIMOES

ESKIMOES
● 17

NORTH-WEST
COAST TRIBES

ESKIMOES

60

● 19

● 18
PLAINS
TRIBES

40   40

20   20

11
AZTECS
● 12

● 13   0

● 16
*Amazon
River*

● 15
PERU   ● 14

20

The Americas

THE NUMBERS ON THE MAP
REFER TO THE ILLUSTRATIONS

40

60   40   20

When the Spaniards conquered the Mexican empire of the Aztecs in the early sixteenth century they destroyed the last of a long succession of civilizations which had flourished in this area for centuries. The Department's collections include extensive archaeological material from many of these earlier cultures. Notable among these are a number of fine jade carvings made by the Olmec, often regarded as the earliest of the major Middle-American civilizations, flourishing as long ago as 1000 BC.

The cultures of the time of the Spanish Conquest are represented by a number of important pieces of perishable materials which would probably have disappeared had they not been brought to Europe at that time. Perhaps the most remarkable of these are the famous Aztec period mosaics of turquoise and other materials of which the Department has one of the world's finest collections. The example illustrated is a mask in the form of two intertwined rattlesnakes 11 fashioned in different shades of turquoise. The close fitting pieces of stone, shaped without the aid of metal tools, are stuck with a resinous gum to a carved wooden base. The mask is thought to represent the god Quetzalcoatl, the 'Feathered Serpent' and his plumes are shown at the sides of the mask. The piece fits the contemporary description of a mask given by the Emperor Moctezuma to Cortes, who was thought to be Quetzalcoatl in person. The turquoise mosaics in the Museum's collections show the meticulous skill of pre-Columbian craftsmen and the elaboration which art reached in the Central American area.

In south-east Mexico, Yucatan, and the neighbouring countries of Guatemala and Belize, the ancient civilization of the Maya once flourished. The ceremonial centres of monumental stone architecture, built in the classic period of their civilization, were abandoned and engulfed by the tropical forest long before the Spaniards subdued the Maya in the sixteenth century and were only rediscovered in the eighteenth and nineteenth centuries. The Department benefited from a number of expeditions by British explorers and archaeologists, and besides examples of fine jades, pottery and other material, has a large collection of casts and originals of architectural stone 12 sculpture. The illustration shows a stone lintel from the site of Yaxchilan in Mexico, a good example of an art in which many ancient peoples of Middle America excelled. It shows a kneeling worshipper, elaborately dressed in flower patterned fabric, making an offering to a god who is emerging from the jaws of a serpent. The glyphs at the top of this scene are examples of the most highly developed system of writing to be found among the native peoples of the New World. Apart from those relating to their complex calendrical system these Maya glyphs remain largely undeciphered.

11 MOSAIC MASK FROM MEXICO

12 LINTEL FROM A MAYA BUILDING

The artistic achievements of ancient America seem the more remarkable for the fact that very little use was made of metals. The Mexicans worked gold and silver, as did the peoples of Columbia and Peru, but the use of copper and bronze, suitable for sharp tools, only developed to an appreciable extent among the later pre-conquest peoples, particularly in Peru. However, some of these people did produce masterpieces of art and craftsmanship in precious metals using a variety of quite sophisticated techniques. The gold figurine illustrated is in the Quimbaya style of Columbia and was made by the 'lost wax' technique.

13 The object was first made in wax and coated with clay. The wax was melted out, metal poured in and then the clay mould was broken away to reveal a metal cast. The figure is hollow, with an opening on top of the head, and probably served as a container for lime powder which was taken while chewing coca leaves.

13 GOLD FIGURINE FROM COLOMBIA

15 POT FROM THE MOCHICA CULTURE, PERU

14 TEXTILE FROM PARACAS, PERU

The civilizations of Peru, of which that of the conquering Incas was only the last of many, are well represented in the collections by a wide range of archaeological material. The semi-desert conditions of coastal Peru have preserved many of the precious wood, cloth and feather objects with which the dead were buried, often in lavish style. The district of Paracas is especially noted for the beautiful textiles
14 discovered in graves, an example of which is illustrated. As in other parts of South and Middle America wool and cotton cloth was woven on a simple loom of a type still used by the rural Indians, the elaborate patterns being woven into the cloth by a variety of techniques.

Peruvian graves are also noted for fine pottery which in some cases was made specially for placing in burials. The use of pottery was general among the ancient American civilizations, as well as in large areas of South and North America in more recent times. The potter's wheel was never used, but the ancient Peruvians in particular developed the use of clay moulds, in several pieces, with which they produced fine, thin walled pottery in a variety of complex forms. The
15 pot illustrated is in one of the styles of the Mochica people of the Moche valley. The face upon it has the type of features found in the present-day inhabitants of the area, and may have been a portrait, while the spout has the characteristic 'stirrup' shape.

The Museum also has extensive collections from the more recent and modern native peoples of South America, particularly the many small tribes of the tropical forest areas. Unlike the highly populated areas of Middle America and Peru, where political units ranged from small states to empires, the Indians of the forests live in widely scattered independent villages. Among their various crafts, these people produce beautiful featherwork, like the headdress
16 illustrated from central Brazil. Such treasured objects were worn while dancing in religious festivals.

16 FEATHER HEADDRESS FROM BRAZIL

A large part of the North American material in the collections is much more recent than the extensive archaeological collections from Middle and South America. It was obtained from peoples whose native cultures endured as late as the eighteenth or nineteenth centuries, until they were overwhelmed by the tide of European settlement. An exception is the large collection, made by Squier and Davis, of objects from the prehistoric cultures of Ohio. This is particularly notable for the numerous stone carvings, such as tobacco pipes, in the forms of animals and birds.

Throughout North America hunting provided an important source of food, usually supplementing that obtained from wild plants or from agriculture, which was practised in parts of the eastern and south-western United States. No people were so completely dependent on hunting and fishing as the Eskimo, whose harsh habitat on the northern coasts of the continent is very poor in plant foods. The hunting life of the Eskimo is reflected in their art, and particularly in the sculpture which, traditionally, adorned useful objects, tools and weapons. The illustration shows a wooden eyeshade which gave protection from the fierce glare of the sun reflected from the ice and snow. The Eskimo excelled in the carving of bone and ivory, which was used for a variety of purposes from harpoon fittings to snow knives and sled runners, besides carvings such as those which adorn this eyeshade. Carvings were often made as charms or amulets and worn in the clothing for protection and good fortune. This may have been the motive for portraying whales and walruses on the eyeshade which might be worn while hunting such animals.

The meticulous craftsmanship of the Eskimo is also shown in the Department's collection of their tailored skin garments, which often employ furs of different

17

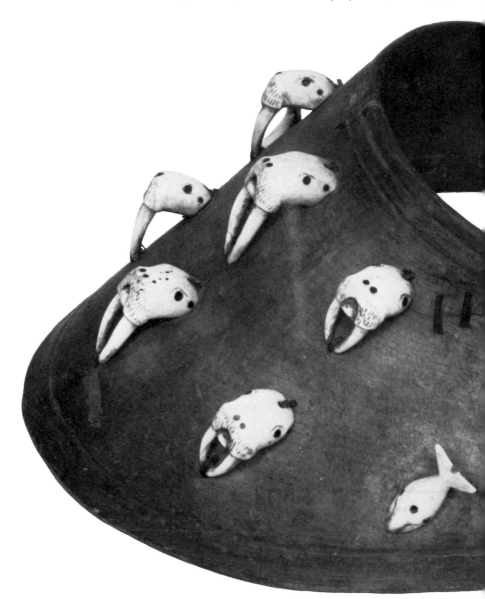

types and shades for decorative effect. While these may represent the height of development in North American craftsmanship in skins, work from other areas, particularly the Great Plains, also shows masterly handling of this material.

The Plains Indians lived mainly by hunting the bison (or 'buffalo') and other large game. From the hides of these animals they fashioned their tents, storage bags and cases and clothing, all well adapted for transporting in pursuit of the migratory herds. The hide shirt is an example of Plains decorative art at its most elaborate. Good quality skins of small game animals were generally used for such fine garments in preference to that of the buffalo, and the hide was painstakingly worked until it was uniformly soft and supple. The form of the shirt is simple. It is open at the sides, and the sleeves are left open from armpit to elbow. The edges of the shirt, which conform to the

original shape of the hide, would hang in shaggy drapes, accentuated by the strands of now largely fur-less ermine skin which are attached to the sleeves and shoulders. The embroidered chest panel and bands on sleeves and shoulders are worked in dyed porcupine quills, a material which in later times was supplanted by imported beads for this purpose. Shirts of this type were worn for ceremonial occasions to show the status of the wearer. This example, from the Blackfoot, was probably a religious object, owned and worn according to rituals which contributed to the owner's store of supernatural power. The paintings, a buffalo head and eagles, probably represent spiritual beings from which such power was obtained.

The Indians of the north-west coast of North America are famous for their sculpture in wood, which surpasses that of any other area of North America in both stylistic development and quantity. The richness

17 EYESHADE FROM THE ALASKAN ESKIMO

[267]

19 MASK FROM THE NORTH-WEST COAST OF AMERICA

of their food supply, which was based on the fish of the rivers and sea, allowed these people to pass much of the year in permanent settlements. These villages contained large well-made houses built of timber from the abundant forests. An enormous variety of useful objects, as well as ritual paraphernalia, was made of wood, carved and painted in a formal yet flexible style. Perhaps the most famous carvings from this area are the totem poles, fine examples of which are in the Department's collections. The theme of this art is broadly religious in that the animals, birds and other creatures represented were beings with supernatural powers. Often the motifs refer to characters in ancient tales, including the non-human clan ancestors of the owners whose inherited rank and status was thus proclaimed by their possessions. The small mask illustrated seems to portray a raven, an important religious character, with a combination of animal and human features indicating the human characteristics shared by animals and birds. The exact meaning or use is not recorded, but it seems to be the type of mask or plaque made for the front of a headdress which was worn ceremonially by persons of high rank.

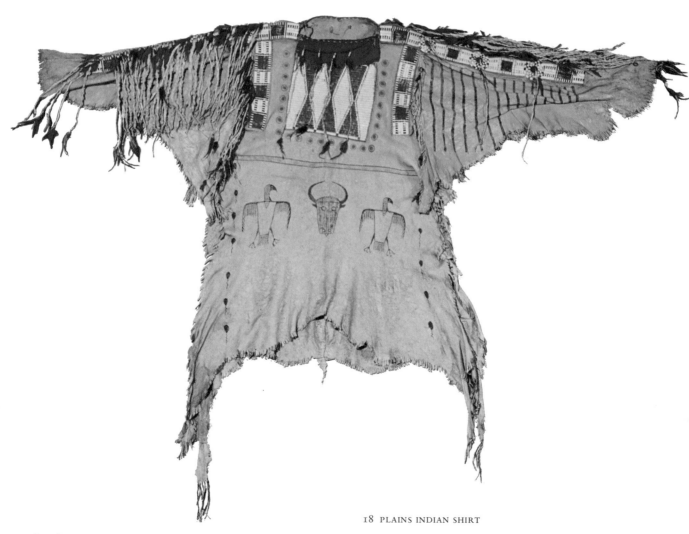

18 PLAINS INDIAN SHIRT

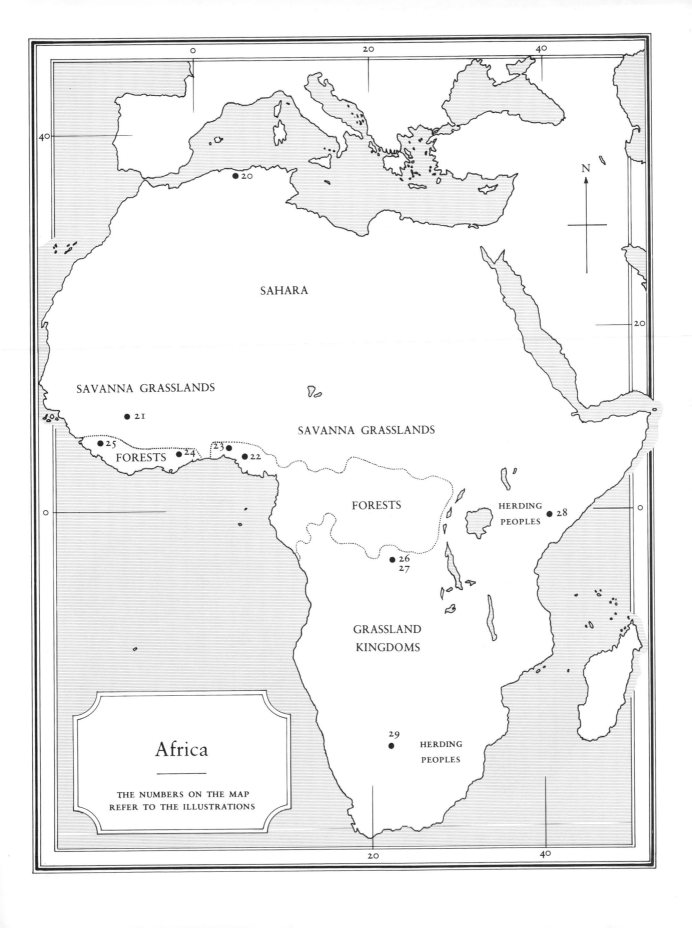

SAHARA

SAVANNA GRASSLANDS

● 21

● 25

FORESTS ● 24 ● 23 ● 22

SAVANNA GRASSLANDS

FORESTS

HERDING
PEOPLES

● 28

● 26
27

GRASSLAND
KINGDOMS

29
●

HERDING
PEOPLES

20 ●

N

Africa

———

THE NUMBERS ON THE MAP
REFER TO THE ILLUSTRATIONS

Africa can be divided into a number of broad ecological and cultural regions. The arid lands of the Sahara, less fertile now than in the past, now support only nomadic groups while the regions of heavier rainfall to the south of the Sahara and in the centre and east of the continent are mainly inhabited by settled agricultural communities. Semi-nomadic herdsmen inhabit a broad zone stretching from the southern Sudan to South Africa and pastoral societies are also found in the more open regions of West Africa. Smali bands of hunting and gathering peoples, representing the original African way of life, still survive in a few parts of South and Central Africa.

Much of the culture of North Africa, formerly influenced by the classical world, has come under Islamic domination since the seventh century AD. The Berber groups who were prominent in this area before the Arab incursions still survive in both nomadic and settled groups. Among the former the Tuareg of the Sahara, who once controlled the trade routes across the desert, have concentrated their artistic skills on jewellery and the trappings for their camels. Among the settled Berber groups the Kabyles of Algeria are famous for their pottery which seems to represent the continuation of a prehistoric Mediterranean tradi-

20 tion. The Kabyle pottery illustrated, like all African pottery, was made without the use of the wheel but it nevertheless shows a remarkable regularity of form. Like most African pottery it is painted and not glazed, and illustrates the careful embellishment of useful objects which is a characteristic feature of African culture.

South of the Sahara the earliest African states seem to have developed in the savannahs and forests of West Africa from the eighth century AD onwards. Long before Europeans began to explore the West African coast in the fifteenth century the trans-Saharan trade routes connected this area to the Mediterranean and Islamic worlds. Along these routes Islam spread to West Africa where it became widespread by the eighteenth century, and where it was the main religion of many of the powerful savannah states.

The Islamic prohibition of representing humans or living creatures is reflected in the material culture of these Muslim peoples, although the prohibition is not strictly observed everywhere. Nevertheless the great religious sculpture for which much of West Africa is famous is seldom found in Muslim areas and creativity in these regions tends to be devoted to the decoration of buildings, leather-work and clothing. The elaborately decorated man's gown illustrated is

22 COSTUME MASK FROM BENIN, NIGERIA

23 BRONZE HEAD FROM IFE, NIGERIA

21 from the Manding, a largely Muslim people who now occupy wide areas of West Africa from Senegal to Ghana. The cotton material, woven in narrow strips on a simple hand loom characteristic of West African weaving, is dyed in different shades of indigo, a favourite local dyestuff. Coloured patterns are woven into the cloth, embroidered upon it, or formed by appliqué.

In the non-Muslim kingdoms which extended into the forests of Ghana and Nigeria, certain valuable objects or materials were the prerogative of kings and chiefs, the tangible symbols of their divinely instituted authority. Craftsmen were attached to the rulers' courts, and produced distinctive art forms. Perhaps the most remarkable collection of African 'court art' in the Museum is of bronze castings and ivories from the royal palace in the city of Benin, centre of an empire in Nigeria. The early sixteenth-century ivory mask
22 illustrated was made to be worn at the belt as part of the king's regalia. The human heads on its diadem represent Portuguese visitors long familiar to the people of Benin as the first European traders in the area.

The famous bronze head illustrated is older than
23 the finest Benin bronzes, which date from the sixteenth century. This is one of several pieces in a similar naturalistic style which were discovered at the town

26 FIGURE OF A KING FROM ZAÏRE

25 SANDE MASK FROM SIERRA LEONE

of Ife, traditionally the most ancient of the Yoruba kingdoms of south-west Nigeria. It was made by the lost wax technique, commonly used in metal casting in West Africa.

In Ghana the king and major chiefs of Ashanti made extensive use of local gold and imported silver for their regalia. This forest empire, established in the eighteenth century, controlled the local gold trade as a means of obtaining firearms from Europeans on the coast. Taxes, tolls and controlled mining supplied the gold from which court craftsmen fashioned personal ornaments and ceremonial objects. On the chief's helmet illustrated there are woodcarvings overlaid with gold foil and cast-gold beads. Besides a large collection of goldwork the Department also has a quantity of the charming miniature brass sculptures of humans, living creatures and everyday objects, which the Ashanti and their neighbours used for weighing gold dust.

While the kings' courts are centres of artistic activity in West Africa, the Department's collections also reflect the place of art in the lives of ordinary people in these kingdoms as well as in those parts of Africa which were never subject to state governments before European rule. Most communities of the dense tropical forests which extend along the southern coast of West Africa to the Congo basin were generally small and largely self-supporting. Their people farmed and hunted in the vast forests, which also provided them with protection against military conquest by the more powerful savannah states. The independence and relative isolation of many of these communities may explain why many of these people, who were prolific sculptors in wood, produced work in such a large variety of local styles. Many of their carvings and masks were created for religious purposes. This is the case with the mask from Sierra Leone illustrated. It was commissioned for, and worn by, members of a women's society known as Sande, which educated girls and initiated them into adult life. Sande masks portray the local ideals of feminine beauty with smooth features, rings of neck fat and elaborate hair braiding.

21 GOWN FROM THE MANDING OF WEST AFRICA

Closed societies for men or women are common among the forest and savannah peoples, and were usually influential in the affairs of local communities. It should be understood that African masks are more than works of art or parts of costumes to local people. Some were not made to be worn, or to be seen clearly, and, in local eyes, their importance derives from the dangerous powers with which they have been imbued by various rites.

To the south of the tropical forests many of the peoples of the grasslands and open woodlands were organized into sizeable states of a rather different character to those of West Africa. In both areas the people were mainly farmers but whereas the kings of West Africa drew much of their wealth from trade, in the southern savannah states the people contributed a portion of their crops for the upkeep of the kings and their courts. The grassland people, like those of the forest, are fine sculptors and much of their work is used in the royal courts. Thus the Bakuba of Zaïre commemorated their kings in the now famous

26 'portrait' statues, of which the Department has three. Each king is distinguished in the sculpture by objects symbolic of his reign, and the figure illustrated is identified as King Shamba Bolangongo by the game board before his knees. The king, who probably reigned in the seventeenth century, is said to have introduced the game of mankala, now common throughout Africa, among his own people to cure them of gambling. His portrait also shows items of costume resembling those still worn by Bakuba kings. The carving itself, though said to be a portrait made at the time of the king's death, is probably a copy of an older piece. Like many other works of art associated with kingship in Africa these carvings serve to commemorate individual rulers and also to express the continuity of the ruling group.

The sculpture and other art of this area tends to be decorative, embellishing objects of everyday use which also serve to reflect the status of their owners. Besides many remarkable woodcarvings in the Museum's 27 collections such as decorated cups, stools, headrests

24 HELMET WITH GOLD ORNAMENTS FROM ASHANTI

20 POTTERY FROM ALGERIA

27 RAFFIA CLOTH FROM ZAÏRE

[273]

and boxes, these people also produced cloth, woven in beautiful geometric designs from unspun raffia fibres. Cloths of this sort were used as a form of currency, as well as for dress.

Large areas of East and southern Africa were, in the past, dominated by herding peoples who travelled the land in search of grazing for their cattle. Cattle are the prized possession of these people; not simply their livelihood, but the symbol of their whole way of life. These nomads do not burden themselves with many material possessions but they may wear elaborate personal ornaments and hair dress. As warriors, the men prize fine weapons, and the Masai shield illustrated shows the care lavished upon these things. It is of cowhide, strengthened at the rim with wood, and the painted designs indicate its owner's clan affiliation. Herdsmen not only defended their own herds and raided those of their neighbours, but in some cases subdued settled peoples and established themselves as ruling aristocracies. The Zulu and Matabele of southern Africa organized large armies which put up a formidable opposition to white settlers.

From South Africa the Department has a collection of material from the Bushmen, who now inhabit only a few areas of the Kalahari desert. With the Hottentots of the Cape, the Congo Pygmies and the Hadza of Tanzania, the Bushmen are the remnants of the hunting peoples who formerly occupied large areas of Africa. The Bushmen still produce rock paintings and engravings of the type found throughout the areas they once occupied and one of these, in the Department's possession, is shown in the illustration.

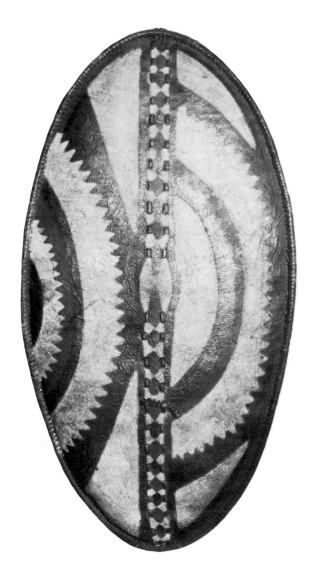

28 SHIELD FROM THE MASAI OF EAST AFRICA

29 ROCK ENGRAVING FROM SOUTHERN AFRICA

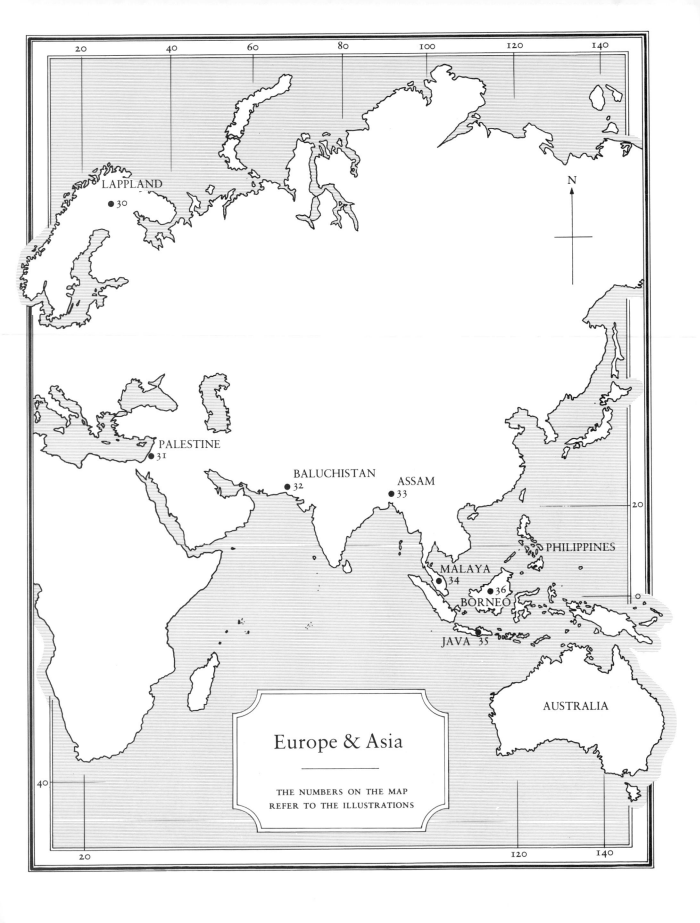

LAPPLAND
● 30

N

PALESTINE
● 31

BALUCHISTAN
● 32

ASSAM
● 33

PHILIPPINES

MALAYA
● 34

BORNEO
● 36

JAVA 35

AUSTRALIA

Europe & Asia

———

THE NUMBERS ON THE MAP
REFER TO THE ILLUSTRATIONS

30 DRUM FROM LAPPLAND

33 HELMET FROM THE NAGAS OF ASSAM

31 EMBROIDERED DRESS FROM PALESTINE

32 RUG FROM BALUCHISTAN

Many of the Department's Asian and European collections come from groups whose cultures were distinct from those of the urban civilizations which have long dominated these continents. The cultures represented in the collections include both the peasant and minority cultures which surround the urban centres, and the tribal cultures which are still wide-spread in areas such as South-east Asia. Such European cultures are represented in the collections by folk arts from Greece and the Balkans and, from northern Europe, by material from the Lapps. These people, traditionally nomadic herders of reindeer, are the sole surviving European representatives of the old Arctic reindeer hunting culture, traces of which extend to Siberia, from where the Department also has material. The drum illustrated was part of the original Sloane collection, and thus dates back at least to the first part of the eighteenth century. Made of reindeer hide 30 stretched over a hollow wooden bowl, it is of the type used by religious specialists or *shamans* before the imposition of Christianity upon the Lapps in the seventeenth and eighteenth centuries. As in Siberia in recent times the drum was played to help induce a state of trance during which the *shaman* was believed to communicate with the spirits. The paintings on the drumhead probably represent these beings.

The Department's collections from the Near East are particularly rich in textiles. The dress illustrated is 31 from Palestine, one of a number of pieces collected on research expeditions by members of the Department. Such dresses, of linen woven locally on simple hand looms, were made and embroidered by the women of rural Arab communities. Formerly each district had its own style of embroidery, a consequence of their

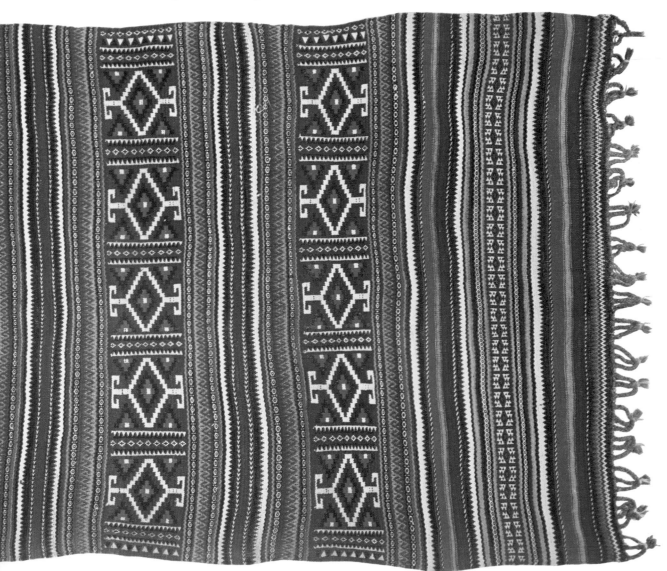

isolation and the lack of contact between the different villages. This example is from a village near Jaffa.

Textiles are also well represented by the Department's collections from the Baluchi nomads of Afghanistan and Pakistan. These tribes, who journey back and forth across the high desert of the area in search of sustenance for their herds, weave an astonishing variety of bags and rugs on simple looms. 32 The rug illustrated shows the elaboration of geometric designs which is found among this people and the fine quality of the weaving produced by their women.

In the forested hills of Assam and Burma a number of different peoples traditionally remained independent of the neighbouring state governments. The Nagas of Assam live in autonomous farming villages which, in the past, were frequently at war with one another. Much of the Museum's Naga material consists of the elaborate costume ornaments and decorated weapons through which the men proclaimed their warlike prowess and achievements such as the killings to their credit. Among these are helmets 33 of plaited cane, often decorated with coloured orchid stems and dyed goat hair. The one illustrated also has pig's tusks and a chinstrap of claws.

Some crafts in the various kingdoms of Malaya and the Indonesian Islands reached their fullest development in the work of specialists attached to the royal courts. Their work has a richness in style and materials not often found in the objects used by the ordinary people. This is the case with the Malayan dagger illustrated, which, from its quality, must have belonged to a man of wealth and high aristocratic 34 rank. This type of weapon, the *kris*, traditionally forms an essential part of a man's costume in Indonesia. It is worn with the sheath tucked inside the waist of the sarong and was used for fighting at close quarters. The patterned blade is the result of forging with alternate layers of different quality iron. *Kris* were believed to possess magical powers of protection over their owners and had to be handled with appropriate rituals.

34 DAGGER FROM MALAYA

Perhaps the most remarkable collection from the kingdoms of Indonesia was made by Sir Stamford Raffles, the Lieutenant-Governor of Java from 1811 to 1816. The shadow puppet illustrated is one of the large number that he brought to England with an orchestra of the type used to accompany the puppet plays. Such plays, in which the audience watches shadows cast by the puppets on a cloth screen, or the puppets themselves, are a popular form of entertainment in South-east Asia. Javanese puppets are more elaborate and skilfully made than any others and have a distinctive style. They are cut from stiff parchment pierced with great precision and delicately painted and gilded on both sides. Many of the puppets portray characters from the great Hindu epics on which numbers of the plays are based. The Raffles collection is exceptionally fine and the numerous puppets it contains are of outstanding beauty.

The establishment of kingdoms in Malaya and the Indonesian Islands was largely the result of conquests via the seas on which communication and commerce throughout the area depended. These kingdoms were generally restricted to accessible coastal areas and never extended effective control into the heavily forested interiors of Malaya and the larger islands. While the religion of the kingdoms has been influenced by Hinduism, Buddism and Islam at various times, these religions seldom penetrated to the forest peoples.

The people of the interior of Borneo, as in other islands such as Sumatra and the Celebes, traditionally live in small independent villages. In Borneo wood working is highly developed, not only in the architecture of the large wooden houses which shelter whole communities of relatives, but in religious sculpture and the adornment of weapons and useful objects. The carving illustrated represents a dragon and was used as a seat by a priest while enlisting the aid of the gods. The priest's spirit, released from his body during a trance, was carried to meet the gods by the dragon.

It is impossible to describe more than a small selection of the Ethnography Department's many and varied collections in a short space. In the course of time much of this material will be put on exhibition, but of necessity most will be in storage at any one time although it will be accessible to serious students. The Department also holds regular film shows and has perhaps the largest public library of anthropology in the country, which visitors are welcome to use.

35 SHADOW PUPPET FROM JAVA

36 SEAT IN DRAGON FORM FROM BORNEO

		Registration No.	Dimensions	Donor
32	The Pitt Rivers flint knife with carved ivory handle	(68512)	Lgth. 24 cm	
33	Sculptured head of the Late Period	(67969)	Ht. 17·5 cm	
34	Mummy of Artemidorus with a portrait of the deceased	(21810)	Ht. 1·67 m	Given by H. Martyn Kennard
35	Tapestry depicting two cupids in a boat	(20717)	84 × 94 cm	Given by the Rev. G. Chester

Greek & Roman antiquities

		Registration No.	Dimensions	Donor
1a	Cycladic Idol	1932 10–18 1	20·9 cm	Given by Sir Arthur Evans
1b	Cycladic Idol	Sculpture A7	11·1 cm	
1c	Cycladic Idol	Sculpture A17	49·5 cm	Given by Viscount Strangford
2	Bronze bull and acrobat. c. 1600 BC	1966 4–28 1	Lgth. 15·5 cm	
3	Minoan gold pendant	Jewellery 762	Ht. 6 cm	
4	Marble decoration from the 'Treasury of Atreus'	Sculpture A53	Ht. 41·4 cm	
5	Pitcher with 'Geometric' decoration, c. 740 BC	1878 8–12 8	Ht. 21·5 cm	
6	Clay plate from Rhodes	1860 4–4 1	Diam. 39·5 cm	
7	Cast bronze griffin's head	1870 3–15 16	Ht. 23·4 cm	
8	Wine-jar signed by Exekias	Vase B210	Ht. 41·5 cm	
9	Wine-jar signed by Exekias; detail	Vase B210	Ht. of vase 41·5 cm	
10	Cup signed by Epiktetos; detail. c. 520 BC	Vase E3	Diam. of cup 33 cm	
11	Bronze statuette of a banqueter	1954 10–18 1	Lgth. 10·4 cm	Purchased with the help of the National Art-Collections Fund
12	Marble statue of a young man	Sculpture B474	Ht. 77·3 cm	
13	Limestone frieze from Xanthos, Lycia	Sculpture B299–306	Ht. 41·9 cm	
14	Cup signed by Epiktetos; detail of interior. c. 510 BC	Vase E38	Diam. of roundel 14 cm	
15	Wine-cooler signed Douris, 490–480 BC	Vase E768	Ht. 28 cm	
16	Cup showing a girl picking apples	Vase D5	Diam. 13·6 cm	
17	From the West Frieze of the Parthenon	Slab II	Ht. 99 cm	
18	From the East Pediment of the Parthenon	Figures K, L, M	Lgth. of group 3·15 m	
19	From the East Pediment of the Parthenon	Figures D, E, F, G	Ht. of E 1·21 m Ht. of G 1·73 m	
20	Frieze from the Temple of Apollo at Bassae; detail	Sculpture 522	Ht. 64·2 cm	
21	Marble figure of a Nereid from the 'Nereid Monument'	Sculpture 909	Ht. 1·4 m	
22	Caryatid from the Erechtheion, Athens	Sculpture 407	Ht. 2·31 m	
23	Water-jar signed by the potter Meidias	Vase E224	Ht. 52 cm	
24	Banded onyx seal. Mid 5th century BC	Gem 511	Lgth. 1·6 cm	
25	Bronze head of a Berber from the Temple of Apollo at Cyrene	Bronze 208	Ht. 30·5 cm	
26	Marble statue, perhaps Mausolus, from the Mausoleum at Halicarnassus	Sculpture 1000	Ht. 3·01 m	
27	Marble column drum from the temple of Artemis at Ephesus	Sculpture 1206	Ht. 1·82 m	
28	Marble statue of Demeter; from Cnidus	Sculpture 1300	Ht. 1·47 m	
29	Bronze head of Sophocles	Bronze 847	Ht. 34·8 cm	Given by the Earl of Exeter
30	Glass bowl with gold-leaf decoration	1871 5–18 2	Diam. 19·3 cm	Given by the Executors of Felix Slade
31	The Portland Vase; Roman cameo glass	Gem 4036	Ht. 24·8 cm	Purchased with funds bequeathed by James Rose Vallentin
32	Fresco painting from a villa near Pompeii	Painting 19	Ht. 32 cm	
33	Bust of 'Clytie'; perhaps a portrait of Antonia, daughter of Mark Antony	Sculpture 1874	Ht. 57 cm	
34	Porphyry head of a Tetrarch	1974 12–13 1	Ht. 43 cm	Purchased with the help of the Shaw Fund
35	Naxos. Squatting Silenus. Tetradrachm	P.C.G. II.C. 48	27 mm	Given by Clayton Mordaunt Cracherode
36	Syracuse. 'Demarateion'. Decadrachm	P.C.C. II.C. 54	33 × 35 mm	
37	Syracuse. Decadrachm by Euainetos	1946 1–1 1413	37 mm	Given by Dr A. H. Lloyd
38	Phaistos. Herakles and the Hydra. Stater	P.C.G. IV.B. 24	21 mm	Given by Clayton Mordaunt Cracherode
39	Antimachus of Bactria. Tetradrachm	P.C.G. V.A.20	33 mm	
40	Cleopatra VII. Tetradrachm	P.C.G. VII.A. 20	27 mm	Bredgar Treasure Trove
41	Claudius. Imper Recept. Aureus Imperial Portraits	1957 10–10 Claudius 5	20 mm	Treasure Trove
42	Julius Caesar. Aureus	B.M.C. Gaul 75	18 mm	Given by Clayton Mordaunt Cracherode
	Augustus. Aureus	B.M.C. 481	19 mm	Given by Edward Wigan
	Nero. Aureus	B.M.C. 77	18 mm	Given by Clayton Mordaunt Cracherode
43	Hadrian. Aureus	B.M.C. 671 A	19 mm	Given by Sir Allan George Clark
44	Marcus Aurelius. Aureus	B.M.C. 486	19 mm	Given by Edward Wigan

Medieval & Later antiquities

		Registration No.	Dimensions	Donor
1	The Lycurgus Cup; a glass cage-cup depicting the death of Lycurgus, trapped in the vine; Italy or Alexandria. c. AD 400	1958 12–2 1	Ht. 20 cm	Purchased with the aid of the National Art-Collections Fund, 1958
2	The Marriage Casket of Projecta from the Esquiline Treasure; Roman. Late 4th century AD	66 12–29 1	Ht. 28 cm Lgth. 55 cm Wdth. 43 cm	
3	Ivory plaque carved with a figure of the Archangel Michael; Byzantine. c. AD 519–527	OA 4312	Ht. 41 cm Wdth. 14·5 cm	
4	The helmet from the Sutton Hoo ship-burial, reconstructed. The iron is covered in decorated tinned bronze sheets and the features enriched with silver wire, gilt-bronze and garnet; Swedish. Before c. AD 625	1939 10–10; Inventory 93	Ht. 31·8 cm	Given by Mrs E. M. Pretty, 1939

	Registration No.	Dimensions	Donor
5 Glass drinking horn found near Bingerbrück, W. Germany; Frankish. Early 5th century	73 5–2 212	Lgth. 34 cm	Given by the Executors of Felix Slade. 1873
6 Brooches of the Migration Period with Germanic 'Animal Style' Ornament			
Left – Gilt-bronze square-headed brooch from Chessel Down, Isle of Wight. 6th century.	67 7–29 5	Lgth. 14 cm	
Centre – Gilt-bronze and garnet disc-on-bow brooch from Gotland, Sweden. 7th century	1921 11–1 222	Lgth. 6·1 cm	
Right – Silver-gilt radiate brooch from Gotland, Sweden. 5th century	1921 11–1 217	Lgth. 12·2 cm	
7 Gold filigree pendant with garnet cloisonné settings in the form of bird heads; from Faversham, Kent. 7th century	1145 70	Diam. 3·5 cm	Bequeathed by W. Gibbs. 1870
8 Ivory Byzantine Borradaile triptych, said to have come from a convent at Rheims. 10th century	1923 12–5 1	Ht. 27·3 cm	Bequeathed by C. Borradaile, 1923
9 Rock crystal disc engraved with scenes from the story of Susannah, known as the Lothar Crystal; Carolingian. 9th century. Set in a later mount	55 12–1 5	Diam. 11·4 cm	
10 Knight from the hoard of ivory chessmen found on the Isle of Lewis, 1831; Scandinavian. 12th century	31 11–1	Ht. 10 cm	
11 Enamel plaque bearing a representation of Samson carrying away the gates of Gaza; from the valley of the Meuse. c. 1180	88 11–10 2	Ht. 11·1 cm	Given by Sir Augustus Wollaston Franks, 1888
12 Gilt-bronze crozier head in the manner of the goldsmith Hugo d'Oignies; north-eastern France. c. 1225–30	98 5–21 1	Ht. 38 cm	
13 Silver seal-die of Isabella of Hainault. Late 12th century	1970 9–4 1	Ht. 9·6 cm	
14 Medieval stringed musical instrument known as a gittern; English. c. 1285–1300	1963 10–5 1	Lgth. 70 cm	Purchased with the aid of the Pilgrim Trust and the National Art-Collections Fund, 1963
15 The Royal Gold Cup of the Kings of France and England. Enamelled with scenes from the Life of St Agnes; French. 1380–81	92 5–1 1	Ht. 23·6 cm	Purchased by private subscription and a special Treasury grant, 1892
16 Shield of parade, for use at a tournament; Flemish. 15th century	63 5–1 1	Ht. 83 cm	Given by the Rev. John Wilson D.D., 1863
17 Green-glazed pottery face jug. Found in the City of London. Late 13th or early 14th century	55 10–29 11	Ht. 11·2 cm	
18 Panel of mosaic floor tiles. From Rievaulx Abbey, Yorkshire. 13th century	1947 5–5	Ht. 131·2 cm	Purchased with the aid of the National Art-Collections Fund, 1947
19 Tile pavement from the house of a merchant, William Canynges, Bristol. Late 15th century	1947 5–5	Lgth. 577·5 cm	Purchased with the aid of the National Art-Collections Fund, 1947
20 Carillon Clock. Made in 1589 by Isaac Habrecht, of Strasborg (1544–1620). The earliest surviving weight-driven musical clock on a 'domestic' scale	88 12–1 100	Ht. 152·5 cm Wdth. 39·4 cm	Bequeathed by O. Octavius S. Morgan, 1888
21 The Emperor Rudolf 'Nef' or Ship-clock; an automaton attributed to Hans Schlottheim, Prague. c. 1580–1600	66 10–30 1	Ht. 99 cm Lgth. 76·2 cm	Given by C. Octavius S. Morgan, 1888
22 French gold enamelled watch with a movement signed: 'D. Bouquet, Londini' 1650	88 12–1 219	Diam. 4·2 cm	Bequeathed by C. Octavius S. Morgan, 1888
23 Equation timepiece with mercurial pendulum by George Graham, London. c. 1730	Ilbert Collection CAI 2132	Ht. 234 cm	Given by Mr Gilbert Edgar, C.B.E., 1958
24 'Rolling-ball' timepiece by French, of the Royal Exchange, London, c. 1810, copying a design patented by Sir William Congreve, F.R.S., in 1808	Ilbert Collection CAI 2137	Ht. 61 cm Wdth. 43 cm	Given by Mr Gilbert Edgar, C.B.E., 1958
25 The Lyte Jewel. A gold enamelled locket containing a portrait of King James I (1603–25) painted by Nicholas Hilliard. Presented by the King in 1610 to Mr Thomas Lyte, a gentleman of Somerset; English. 1610	Waddesdon Catalogue No: 167	Lgth. 7·9 cm	Bequeathed by Baron Ferdinand de Rothschild, M.P., 1898
26 Nautilus-shell cup with silver-gilt mounts. Hall-marks Antwerp. 1555	Waddesdon Catalogue No: 115	Ht. 22·8 cm	Bequeathed by Baron Ferdinand de Rothschild, M.P., 1898
27 Shield of hammered iron; damascened with gold and plated with silver. Dated 1554 and signed by Giorgio Ghisi of Mantua (1520–82), who worked in Rome and Mantua; Italian. 1554	Waddesdon Catalogue No: 5	Diam. 54·6 cm	Bequeathed by Baron Ferdinand de Rothschild, M.P., 1898
28 Rosary bead of boxwood, carved with sacred subjects and inscriptions; Flemish. Early 16th century	Waddesdon Catalogue No: 236	Lgth. 13·2 cm	Bequeathed by Baron Ferdinand de Rothschild, M.P., 1898
29 The Holy Thorn Reliquary, made of gold and enamelled about 1400–10, for Jean, Duc de Berri, Uncle of Charles VI, King of France. The Holy Thorn from the Crown of Thorns is set in a cabochon sapphire behind a rock-crystal 'window'	Waddesdon Catalogue No: 67	Ht. 29·5 cm	Bequeathed by Baron Ferdinand de Rothschild, M.P., 1898
30 Rochester Tazza. Silver-gilt tazza and cover from Rochester Cathedral; London hall-marks, for the years 1528, 1531 and 1532	1971 5–2 1–2	Ht. 22·6 cm Diam. 23 cm	
31 Painted Enamel Triptych. The Entombment flanked by the Deposition and Resurrection. Probably by Nardon Pénicaud (active 1493–1541); Limoges, France. c. 1510	1913 12–20 6	Left panel: 22 × 10·55 cm Centre Panel: 21·9 × 25·8 cm Right Panel: 21·9 × 10·6 cm	Bequeathed by Rev. A. H. S. Barwell
32 Silver-gilt ewer and basin by Pierre Harache. London hall-marks, 1697. Engraved with the arms of 1st Duke of	1969 7–5 28A & B	Ewer: Ht. 30·5 cm Basin: Diam. 65·6 cm	Bequeathed by Peter Wilding. 1969

		Registration No.	Dimensions	Donor
	Devonshire (1640–1707)			
33	Prince Rupert (1619–62) wearing the 'collar' and 'mantle' of the Garter. Made of salt-glazed stoneware with touches of gilding at the Fulham Pottery, London, by John Dwight. c. 1670–5	71 6–13 1	Ht. 61 cm	
34	Medal of John Paleologus, by Pisanello	B.M.C. 19	10·3 cm	Given by King George III
35	Porcelain group: The Lady and a Girl Pedlar. Modelled by Kändler and Reinicke, made at Meissen. c. 1745	1952 11–1 1	Ht. 17·2 cm	
36	Glass goblet with enamelled decoration; Venice. Late 15th century	Slade Catalogue No: 361	Ht. 22·3 cm / Diam. 10·5 cm	Bequeathed by F. Slade, 1868
37	Cloisonné enamel locket-pendant, with Japanese-style images. By Alexis Falize (1811–98, retired 1876). French, c. 1869	Hull Grundy Collection HG 470	Ht. 5·4 cm	Given by Professor and Mrs Hull Grundy, 1978

Museum of Mankind

		Registration No.	Dimensions	Donor
1	Shield from the New Guinea Highlands	1964 Oc 3.81	Ht. 151 cm	
2	Mask from the Papuan Gulf, New Guinea	+2486	Ht. 165 cm	Given by Sir Augustus Wollaston Franks
3	House post from northern New Guinea	1964 Oc 6.1	Ht. 254 cm	
4	Axe from the Massim area of Melanesia	+ 4587	Lgth. 63 cm (Along the handle)	Given by Professor Charles Stewart
5	Canoe prow from the Solomon Islands	1927 10–22 1	Ht. 33 cm (Of figure)	Given by the Trustees of the Lady Lever Art Gallery
6	Canoe from the Tuamotu Islands	N.N.	Lgth. 388 cm	
7	Feathered helmet from Hawai	N.N.	Ht. 35 cm	
8	Mourner's costume from Tahiti	TAH 78	Ht. 220 cm	Given by Captain James Cook
9	Greenstone 'tiki' from New Zealand	S825	Ht. 13 cm	
10	Stone 'churinga' from central Australia	1935 4–12 1	Lgth. 41 cm	
11	Mosaic mask from Mexico	N.N.	Ht. 17 cm	
12	Stone lintel from a Maya building		Ht. 128 cm	Given by A. P. Maudslay
13	Gold figurine from Colombia	1940 Amll. 2	Ht. 13 cm	Given by the National Art-Collections Fund
14	Textile from Paracas, Peru	1933 12–16 3	Wdth. 24 cm	Given by H. Van den Bergh, through the National Art-Collections Fund
15	Pot from the Mochica culture, Peru	1947 Am 16.12	Ht. 31 cm	
16	Feather headdress from Brazil	1931 7–18 5	Ht. 50 cm	
17	Eyeshade from the Alaskan Eskimo	1931 7–21 4	Lgth. 27 cm	
18	Plains Indian shirt	N.N.	Ht. 160 cm (Overall)	
19	Mask from the north-west coast of America	6437	Ht. 27 cm	Given by J. L. Brenchley
20	Pottery from Algeria	(left to right) N.N.; 1922 10–19 1 1907 10–16 1	Ht. 28 cm (Centre)	Given by J. H. Reynolds
21	Gown from the Manding of West Africa	2798	Ht. 93 cm (Shoulder to hem)	Given by Mrs Eustace Smith
22	Costume-mask from Benin, Nigeria	1910 5–13 1	Ht. 24 cm	
23	Bronze head from Ife, Nigeria	1939 Af 34.1	Ht. 36 cm	Given by the National Art-Collections Fund
24	Gold ornamented helmet from Ashanti, Ghana	1900 4–2 1	Ht. 25 cm	
25	Sande mask from Sierra Leone	1910 7–22 10	Ht. 35 cm	
26	Figure of a king from Zaïre	1909 12–10 1	Ht. 54 cm	Given by E. Torday
27	Raffia cloth from Zaïre	Q73 Af506 507 & 514	(Scale on picture)	
28	Shield from the Masai of East Africa	1904 11–120	Ht. 124 cm	
29	Rock engraving from southern Africa	1886 11–23 1	Wdth. 43 cm	Given by the Kimberley Local Committee (Colonial and Indian Exhibition) through F. Schute (Royal Colonial Inst.)
30	Drum from Lappland	Sloane 1103	Ht. 39 cm	
31	Woman's embroidered dress from Palestine	1968 As 4.31	Ht. 139 cm	
32	Rug from Baluchistan	1970 As 21.3	Wdth. 172 cm	
33	Helmet from the Nagas of Assam	1954 As 7.75	Ht. 24 cm	Given by the Trustees of the Wellcome Museum of Medical Science
34	Dagger from Malaya	1928–125	Lgth. 49 cm (Blade & hilt)	
35	Shadow puppet from Java	59 12–28 547	Ht. 85 cm (Excluding prop)	
36	Seat in dragon form from Borneo	1905–785	Lgth. 182 cm	

Oriental antiquities

		Registration No.	Dimensions	Donor
1	Reliquary. Gold set with rubies. Afghanistan: from Bimaran. 2nd–3rd century AD	1900 2–9 1	Ht. 6·7 cm	
2	The Buddha Bronze. Central India: from Dhanesar Khera, near Allahabad. Gupta period: 5th century AD	1969 7–25 1	Ht. 32·4 cm	Brooke Sewell Bequest
3	Ganesa. Sandstone. Western India. 8th century AD	1964 12–21 1	Ht. 81·3 cm	Brooke Sewell Fund
4	Lovers. Sandstone. Central India. Candella: late 10th century AD	1964 4–13 1	Ht. 58·5 cm	Brooke Sewell Fund
5	A Bodhisattva with attendants. Ivory enclosed in wooden	1968 5–21 1	Ht. 14·6 cm	

	Registration No.	Dimensions	Donor
panel of a shrine. India: Kashmir. 1st half of 8th century AD		ivory: 9·5 cm	
6 Manasa, the snake goddess. Bronze inlaid with silver. Eastern India. c. AD 750	1969 1–15 1	Ht. 45·7 cm	Brooke Sewell Fund
7 Durga killing the buffalo demon. Sandstone. India: Orissa. 8th century AD	1872 7–1 89	Ht. 43·2 cm	Bridge Collection
8 Sarasvati, Goddess of Wisdom. Bronze. India: Deccan. Western Ganga: 10th century AD	1957 10–21 1	Ht. 33·3 cm	Given by P. T. Brooke Sewell
9 Garuda. Granite. South India. Pallava: c. AD 700	1968 10–16 1	Ht. 127·1 cm	Brooke Sewell Fund
10 Siva Vishapaharana. Bronze. South India. Cola: c. AD 960	1970 9–21 1	Ht. 59 cm	Brooke Sewell Fund and Bequest
11 The Bodhisattva Tara. Gilt-bronze. Sri Lanka: found near Trincomalee. 12th century AD	1830 6–12 4	Ht. 144·9 cm	Given by Sir Robert Brownrigg
12 The Buddha. Bronze. Burma. Pagan period: 12th century AD	1971 7–27 1	Ht. 33 cm	Brooke Sewell Fund
13 The Dikpalaka Nairrita. Volcanic stone. Java. 9th–10th century AD	1861 10–10 1	Ht. 88·3 cm	Given by Charles Millet
14 Demetrius. Tetradrachm. Bactria	B.M.C.2	33 mm	Given by the India Office
15 Archebius. Tetradrachm. Bactria	1959 11–1 1	30 × 33 mm	
16 Vima Kadphises. Gold Coin	B.M.C. 2	25 mm	
17 Samudra Gupta. Playing lyre. Gold coin	B.M.C. 53	22 mm	
18 Samudra Gupta. Horse before altar. Gold coin	B.M.C. 59	21 mm	
19 Ewer. Brass, engraved and inlaid with copper, silver and gold. North Mesopotamia: made at Mosul by Shuja'ibn Man'a of Mosul. Dated AD 1232–3	1866 12–29 61	Ht. 30·4 cm	
20 Pilgrim flask. Glass, gilded and enamelled. Syria. AD 1250–60	1869 1–20 3	Ht. 23 cm Wdth. 21·3 cm	Given by the Executors of Felix Slade
21 Astrolabe. Brass, engraved and inlaid with copper and silver. Egypt: made in Cairo by 'Abd al-Karim of Cairo. Dated AD 1235–6	1855 7–9 1	Ht. 39·4 cm	
22 Dish. Pottery, painted in two shades of blue, aubergine and green. Turkey: Iznik. AD 1540–50	1878 12–30 530	Diam. 39·4 cm	Henderson Bequest
23 'Abd al-Malik. Figure type. Dinar	1954 10–11 2	18 × 20 mm	Given by Professor P. Grierson
24 'Abd al-Malik. Inscription. Dinar	B.M.C. 188	20 mm	
25 Saladin. Bronze coin	B.M.C. 276	26 × 28 mm	
26 Jahangir. Gold Mohur	B.M.C. 314	22 mm	Bequeathed by R. Payne Knight
27 ⎰ Middle spade coin from An 1	B.M.C. 8	63 × 41 mm	
⎨ Early knife of Ch'in	B.M.C. 56	187 × 28 mm	
⎱ Copper cash of T'ang dynasty	1884 5–11 755	24 mm	
28 Ritual vessel: tsun. Bronze. China. Shang dynasty: 12th–11th century BC			
29 Wine vessel: hu. One of a pair. Bronze. China. Eastern Chou period: 5th century BC	1972 2–29 1a	Ht. 48·3 cm	Given by Mrs U. E. K. Cull and her family in memory of A. E. K. Cull, Knight of St John of Jerusalem
30 Model of a watchtower. Earthenware. China. Han dynasty: 1st–2nd century AD	1929 7–16 1	Ht. 86·5 cm	Given by Mrs Chester Beatty
31 Camel. Glazed earthenware. China: from the tomb of Liu T'ing-hsün (died AD 728). T'ang dynasty (AD 618–906)	1936 10–12 228	Ht. 84 cm	
32 Phoenix-headed ewer. Stoneware. China. T'ang dynasty: 10th century AD	1936 10–12 206	Ht. 34·5 cm	
33 Pillow. Tz'u-chou type. Stoneware. China. Sung dynasty (AD 960–1279)	1936 10–12 169	Lgth. 32 cm	
34 Ewer and Basin. Porcelain, with ying-ch'ing glaze. China. Sung dynasty (AD 960–1279)	1936 10–12 153	Ht. of ewer: 20·3 cm. Diam. of basin: 18·9 cm	
35 Jar. Porcelain, decorated in underglaze cobalt blue with ch'i-lin, phoenixes and peonies. China. Yüan dynasty. c. AD 1350	1960 7–28 1	Ht. 48 cm	Brooke Sewell Bequest
36 Vase. Porcelain, decorated with parrots on a flowering branch of pomegranate. China. Ming dynasty: period of Hsuan-te (AD 1426–35)	1972 6–21 1	Ht. 33·2 cm	Given by His Excellency Walter H. Annenberg
37 Box with design of parrots and lotus scrolls. Cloisonné enamels. China. Ming dynasty: late 15th century AD	1940 12–14 314	Diam. 25 cm	Given by Mrs B. Z. Seligman
38 Dish. Porcelain. China. Ch'ing dynasty. K'ang hsi period (1662–1723)	F511	Diam. 34·3 cm	Given by Sir Augustus Wollaston Franks
39 Sutra Box. Lacquer, inlaid with mother-of-pearl and silver wire. Korea. Koryo dynasty: 13th century AD	1966 12–21 1	Lgth. 47·2 cm	Brooke Sewell Bequest
40 Haniwa in the form of a woman. Red pottery. Japan. Great Tombs period: 5th–6th century AD	F2210	Ht. 55 cm	Given by Sir Augustus Wollaston Franks
41 Seated figure of the Bodhisattva Miroku (Maitreya). Gilt-bronze. Japan. Early Buddhist period: 2nd half of 7th century AD	1963 2–14 1	Ht. 31 cm	National Art-Collections Fund, Mrs W. Sedgwick, Sir Alan and Lady Barlow, Mrs B. Z. Seligman, J. P. Dubose and the R. J. Sainsbury Discretionary Settlement
42 Gigaku mask of a young man. Wood, gesso and traces of paint. Japan. Nara period: 8th century AD	1954 10–21 1	Ht. 28·5 cm	National Art-Collections Fund and Sir Chester Beatty
43 Document box decorated with insects. Lacquer inlaid with mother-of-pearl. Japan. Heian period: 12th century AD	1965 10–12 1	Lgth. 44 cm	Brooke Sewell Bequest
44 Figure of a young man. From Burghley House. Porcelain decorated with Kakiemon style enamels. Japan. Edo period: late 17th century AD	F1214+	Ht. 30·3 cm	Given by Sir Augustus Wollaston Franks

Prehistoric & Romano-British antiquities

		Registration No.	Dimensions	Donor
1	Stone hand axe from Olduvai Gorge, Tanzania. Lower Palaeolithic (Acheulian). *c.* 500,000–100,000 BC	1934 12–14 71	Lgth. 15·5 cm	Given by Dr L. S. B. Leakey
2	Flint blade from Volgu, Saône-et-Loire, France. Upper Palaeolithic (Solutrean). *c.* 18,000 BC	Sturge 582 A	Lgth. 28·4 cm	Bequeathed by Dr Allen Sturge
3	Reindeer sculpture in mammoth tusk from Bruniquel, Tarn-et-Garonne, France. Upper Palaeolithic (Magdalenian). *c.* 17,000–11,000 BC		Lgth. 20·3 cm	Purchased by the Trustees of the Christy Fund
4	Mammoth sculpture in reindeer antler from Bruniquel, Tarn-et-Garonne, France. Upper Palaeolithic (Magdalenian). *c.* 17,000–11,000 BC		Lgth. 12 cm	Purchased by the Trustees of the Christy Fund
5	Antler frontlet head-dress from Star Carr, N. Yorkshire. Mesolithic (Maglemosean). *c.* 7500 BC	1953 2–8 1	Lgth. 17·5 cm	Given by Professor J. G. D. Clark
6	Seated figurine in clay from Vinča, Yugoslavia. Neolithic (Vinča-Pločnik). *c.* 3500 BC	1939 7–4 1	Ht. 17 cm	
7	Figurine in calcite from Ain Sakhri, Jordan. Mesolithic (Early Natufian). *c.* 10,000 BC	1958 10–7 1	Lgth. 10·2 cm	
8	Chalk figurine from Grime's Graves, Norfolk. Neolithic. *c.* 2200 BC	1959 7–12 1	Ht. 10·7 cm	Bequeathed by A. L. Armstrong
9	Beaker from Barnack, Cambridgeshire. Early Bronze Age. *c.* 1800 BC	P1975 9–11 4	Ht. 24 cm	Given by the Trustees of the Burghley Estate Trust
10	Gold cup from Rillaton, Cornwall. Early Bronze Age. *c.* 1700–1400 BC		Ht. 8 cm	Placed on permanent loan by HM King Edward VIII
11	Gold lunula from Mangerton, Co. Kerry, Ireland. Early Bronze Age. *c.* 1800–1500 BC	1871 4–1 1	Diam. 15·5 cm	
12	Jet necklace from Melfort, Strathclyde, Scotland. Early Bronze Age. *c.* 1600 BC	1890 4–10 1	Wdth. 27·7 cm	
13	Bronze shield from Aberystwyth, Dyfed, Wales. Late Bronze Age. *c.* 800 BC	1873 2–10 2	Diam. 67 cm	Given by Sir Augustus Wollaston Franks
14	Chalk 'drums' from Folkton, North Yorkshire. Early Bronze Age. *c.* 1800 BC	1893 12–28 15, 16, 17	Diam. 14·2, 12·1, 10·4 cm	Given by the Rev. W. Greenwell
15	Dish from the Degerfeld, Tailfingen, Württemberg, Germany. Early Iron Age (Hallstatt-Alb Salem). *c.* 700–550 BC	1908 8–1 239	Diam. 40 cm	Given by Sir John Brunner and Sir Henry Howorth
16	Urn from Prunay, Marne, France. Iron Age (La Tène). *c.* 300 BC	ML 2734	Ht. 30·9 cm	
17a, 17b	Bronze flagon from Basse-Yutz, Moselle, France. Iron Age (La Tène). *c.* 400 BC	1929 5–11 1	Ht. 39 cm	
18a	Electrum torc from Snettisham, Norfolk. Iron Age (La Tène). *c.* 50 BC	1951 4–2 2	Diam. 19·6 cm	Treasure Trove
18a, 18b	Second electrum torc and gold bracelet from Snettisham, Norfolk. Iron Age (La Tène). *c.* 50 BC	1951 4–2 3 / 1951 4–2 4	Diam. 10·1 cm / Diam. 8·2 cm	Treasure Trove / Treasure Trove
19	Bronze torc from Courtisols, Marne, France. Iron Age (La Tène). *c.* 300 BC	ML 1711	Diam. 15·7 cm	
20	Bronze mirror from Desborough, Northamptonshire. Iron Age (La Tène). *c.* AD 1–50	1924 1–9 1	Lgth. 34·9 cm	Given by the National Art-Collections Fund
21	Bronze shield from the River Witham, Lincolnshire. Iron Age (La Tène). *c.* 200–100 BC	1872 12–13 1	Lgth. 110·4 cm	Given by Sir Augustus Wollaston Franks
22	Bronze helmet from the River Thames at Waterloo Bridge, London. Iron Age (La Tène). *c.* 50 BC		Wdth. 42 cm	Deposited by the Thames Conservancy
23, 24	Iron firedog from a grave at Welwyn, Hertfordshire. Iron Age (La Tène). *c.* 50–10 BC	1911 12–8 2	Ht. 96·5 cm	Given by Mrs A. J. Neall
25	Glass gaming pieces from a grave at Welwyn Garden City, Hertfordshire. Iron Age (La Tène). *c.* 25 BC	1967 2–2 42–65	Diam. 2·5–2·8 cm	Given by the Welwyn Garden City Development Corporation
26	Great dish (silver) from the Mildenhall Treasure, found at Mildenhall, Suffolk. Roman. *c.* AD 350	1946 10–7 1	Diam. 60·5 cm	Treasure Trove
27	Section of the wall-plaster from Lullingstone Roman villa, Kent. Romano-British. *c.* AD 350	1967 4–7 1	Wdth. of section 140 cm	Given by Kent County Council
28	Section of mosaic pavement from Hinton St Mary Roman villa, Dorset. Romano-British. *c.* AD 350	1965 4–9 1	Diam. of central roundel 95 cm	
29	Bowl (samian ware – Southern Gaulish) from Great St Helen's, London. Gallo-Roman. AD 80–90	1931 12–11 1	Diam. 24·4 cm	
30	Glass flagon from Bayford, Kent. Roman. AD 180–220	1883 12–13 295	Ht. 22·2 cm	
31	Bronze helmet from Ribchester, Lancashire. Roman. *c.* AD 80	Towneley Collection (1814)	Ht. 25·7 cm	
32	Bronze statue of the Emperor Nero from Barking Hall, Suffolk. Roman. 1st century AD	1813 2–131	Ht. 62 cm	Given by the Earl of Ashburnham
33	Bronze ornament from Icklingham, Suffolk. Romano-British. *c.* 2nd century AD	1935 4–16 1	Diam. 5·5 cm	

Prints & Drawings

		Registration No.	Dimensions	Donor
1	Sandro Botticelli 1444–1510. 'Abundance' or 'Autumn' Drawing in pen and brown ink and wash, heightened with white, on pink prepared paper, *c.* 1480	1895-9-15-447	31·7 × 44·7 cm	
2	Andrea Mantegna 1431–1506: Mars, Venus (?) and Diana. Drawing in pen and brown ink with brown, blue and pink	1861-8-10-2	36·4 × 31·7 cm	

		Registration No.	Dimensions	Donor
	wash. *c.* 1490–1500			
3	Raphael 1483–1520. Study for the Borghese *Entombment*. Drawing in pen and ink, 1506–7	1855–2–14–1	23 × 31·9 cm	Chambers Hall Gift, 1855
4	Michelangelo 1475–1564. The Virgin and Child. Drawing in black chalk, *c.* 1535	Pp. 1 58	31·7 × 19·1 cm	Payne Knight Bequest, 1824
5	Pietro da Cortona 1596–1669. Jason and the Golden Fleece: Allegory of the Arms of the Borghese Family. Drawing in black chalk and pen and brown wash, heightened with white, *c.* 1630	1941–11–8–16	39·8 × 52·8 cm	Given by the National Art-Collections Fund
6	Giovanni Battista Tiepolo 1696–1770. Entrance to a Farm-Yard. Drawing in pen and brown ink and wash	1936–10–10–17	17·1 × 28·3 cm	
7	Antonio Canale, called Canaletto 1697–1768. Roofs and Chimneys in Venice; view from the Artist's House. Drawing in pen and brown wash	1910–2–12–22	30·3 × 44 cm	George Salting Bequest, 1910
8	Albrecht Dürer 1471–1528. A House in a Lake ('Weierhaus'). Drawing in watercolour and body colour, *c.* 1495/6	5218–165	21·3 × 22·5 cm	Sir Hans Sloane Bequest, 1753
9	Albrecht Dürer 1471–1528. A Windisch Peasant Woman. Drawing in pen and brown ink and brown wash, dated 1505	1920–3–24–1	41·6 × 28·1 cm	
10	Rogier van der Weyden 1397/1400–1464. Portrait of a Young Woman. Drawing in metalpoint on cream-coloured prepared paper	1874–8–8–2266	16·6 × 11·6 cm	
11	Lucas van Leyden 1494–1533. Study for a *Virgin and Child*. Drawing in black chalk, *c.* 1525	1892–8–4–15	21 × 17·1 cm	
12	Pieter Bruegel the Elder *c.* 1530–69. Landscape. Drawing in pen and brown ink	1963–10–12–1	24·4 × 35·2 cm	
13	Peter Paul Rubens 1577–1640. Dancing Peasants. Drawing in pen and brown ink, *c.* 1636	1920–10–12–1	27·3 × 25·1 cm	
14	Peter Paul Rubens 1577–1640. The Artist's first wife, Isabella Brant. Drawing in black, red and white chalk, *c.* 1625	1893–7–31–21	38·1 × 29·2 cm	
15	Anthonie van Dyck 1599–1641. Landscape. Drawing in pen and brown ink, 1634	Oo. 9–49	18·5 × 28 cm	Payne Knight Bequest, 1824
16	Jacob Jordaens 1593–1678. The Falconer: design for a Tapestry. Drawing in brown wash and bodycolour	1865–7–8–627	35·2 × 45·4 cm	
17	Rembrandt 1606–69. The Good Samaritan. Drawing in pen and brown wash, *c.* 1642	1860–6–16–122	18·4 × 28·7 cm	
18	Claude Lorrain 1600–82. Landscape with Pine Trees. Drawing in pen and brown ink and brown and grey wash	Oo. 7–230	32·2 × 21·6 cm	Payne Knight Bequest, 1824
19	Antoine Watteau 1684–1721. Studies of a Young Woman's Head. Drawing in black, red and white chalk	1895–9–15–941	33·1 × 23·8 cm	
20	Antoine Watteau 1684–1721. Design for a Fan Leaf. Drawing in watercolour and bodycolour on grey paper	1965–6–12–1	21·6 × 42·5 cm	
21	Francisco Goya 1746–1828. The Duke of Wellington. Drawing in red chalk, 1812	1862–7–12–185	23·5 × 17·8 cm	
22	William Hogarth 1697–1764. 'The Idle' Prentice at play in the Churchyard During Divine Service': study for pl. 3 of 'Industry and Idleness', 1747. Drawing in pen and brown ink and grey wash over pencil	1896–7–10–6	21·5 × 29·3 cm	
23	Thomas Gainsborough 1727–88. A Lady standing. Drawing in black and white chalk on grey paper	1910–2–12–250	49·4 × 31·3 cm	George Salting Bequest, 1910
24	William Blake 1757–1827. Beatrice on the Car with Dante and Matilda: Illustration to *Purgatorio* XXIX. Drawing in pencil and watercolour, *c.* 1825	1918–4–13–5	36·5 × 52 cm	
25	Alexander Cozens *c.* 1700–86. Mountainous landscape. Brush drawing in brown	1928–4–17–4	23 × 30·3 cm	
26	J. M. W. Turner 1775–1851. The Church of SS Giovanni e Paolo from the Palatine, Rome. Drawing in watercolour and bodycolour, 1819	T.B. CLXXXIX-39	23 × 36·7 cm	Turner Bequest
27	Thomas Girtin 1775–1802. Westminister from Lambeth: study for the *Panorama of London*. Watercolour, *c.* 1800	1855–2–14–23	29·2 × 52 cm	Chambers Hall Gift, 1855
28	John Sell Cotman 1782–1844. Greta Bridge. Watercolour, 1805	1902–5–14–17	22·7 × 32·9 cm	
29	Samuel Palmer 1805–81. Landscape with the Edge of a Cliff: from the 1824 *Sketchbook*. Drawing in pen and brown ink, 1824	1964–11–4–1 (9)	11·6 × 18·8 cm	
30	Dante Gabriel Rossetti 1828–82. Hamlet and Ophelia. Drawing in pen and brown wash, *c.* 1855	1974–4–6–11	25·8 × 10 cm	
31	Henry Moore b. 1898. Miners at the Coal-face: from the Castleford Sketchbook. Drawing in black crayon and grey wash, with touches of red and yellow crayon, 1941/2	1975–1–18–4	23·5 × 17·5 cm	Given by the Artist
32	Hercules Seghers 1589/90–1633/4. Valley with Towns, Churches and other Buildings. Etching and Drypoint printed in green and overpainted in green bodycolour. The houses and parts of the rocks and road coloured red	Sheepshanks 5531	20·3 × 33 cm	
33	Rembrandt 1606–69. 'The Three Trees'. Etching 1643	F.4–164	21·1 × 28 cm	
34	Giovanni Battista Piranesi 1720–78. A Fantastic Prison. Plate from the *Carceri d'invenzione*. Etching (second state 1761)	1910–12–14–21	53·5 × 40 cm	
35	Francisco Goya 1746–1828. *Tras el vicio viene el fornicio*	1863–11–14–791	24·5 × 35 cm	

		Registration No.	Dimensions	Donor
	('After Vice, comes Fornication'). Etching, plate 4 of 'Los Proverbios', *c.* 1820			
36	J. A. McNeill Whistler 1834–1903. 'Black Lion Wharf'. Etching	1973–9–15–15	15·2 × 22·5 cm	

Western Asiatic antiquities

1	Ashurnasirpal II, king of Assyria	118871	Ht. 113 cm	
2	Black Obelisk of Shalmaneser III	118885	Ht. 202 cm	
3	Assyrians at the source of the Tigris (detail)	124656	Ht. 26 cm	
4	Eagle-headed genie protecting a king	124585	Ht. 220 cm	
5	Battle around a siege-engine (detail)	124554	Ht. 91 cm	
6	Colossal human-headed winged bull	118808	Lgth. 486 cm	
7	Paving-stone carved as a carpet (detail)	124962	Full Lgth. 379 cm	
8	Lion and lioness in a garden	118914	Ht. 95 cm	
9	Lion shot by the Assyrian king (detail)	124864	Full Ht. 155 cm	
10	Wild asses fleeing from hounds (detail)	124877	Full Ht. 157 cm	
11	The rout of the Elamites (detail)	124801	Full Ht. 137 cm	
12	Assyrian garden with an aqueduct (detail)	124939	Full Ht. 207 cm	
13	African prisoners of war (detail)	124928	Full Ht. 113 cm	
14	Ashurbanipal feasting in a garden	124920	Ht. 56 cm	
15	Fertility goddess from ancient Palestine	130761	Ht. 8·9 cm	
16	Ossuary found at Jerusalem	126395	Ht. 38 cm	Given by Mr Gray Hill
17	Bar Kochba Revolt. Shekel	B.M.C. 5	25 × 27 mm	
18	Prehistoric bowl from Bakun, Iran	128622	Diam. 27·6 cm	
19	Neolithic skull from Jericho	127414	Ht. 20·3 cm	
20	Carved trough from Uruk (detail)	120000	Full Lgth. 96·5 cm	
21	Goat and tree from the Ur cemetery	122200	Ht. 45·7 cm	
22	Lyre-player from the Ur cemetery (detail)	121201	Full Lgth. 48·3 cm	
23	Scenes of war from the Ur cemetery	121201	Lgth. 48·3 cm	
24	Wild ass from the Ur cemetery	121348	Ht. 13·5 cm	
25	Gudea, a Sumerian ruler, from Lagash	122910	Ht. 73·6 cm	Bought with the aid of a contribution from the National Art-Collections Fund
26	Hittite god from Anatolia	126389	Ht. 3·7 cm	
27	Griffin armlet from the Oxus Treasure	124017	Diam. 12·7 cm	Franks Bequest
28	Achaemenian Daric. Archer. Oxus Treasure	B.M.C. Persia 170	20 × 17 mm	
29	Vahsuvar. Stater. Oxus Treasure	Vahsuvar 2	19 × 17 mm	
30	Gold mask from Parthian grave, AD 100–150, from Nineveh	123894	Ht. 16·5 cm	
31	Volagases IV. Tetradrachm. Parthian	G.1058	28 mm	
32	Sassanian silver dish	124091	Diam. 18 cm	
33	Bahram II. Dirhem. Sassanian	de Bode. 1845 No: 2	26 mm	Given by Baron de Bode
34	Tablet with a flood legend in the cuneiform script from Nineveh	K3375	Ht. 15·5 cm	
35	Babylonian geometrical problems	15285	Ht. 22·5 cm	
36	Akkadian cylinder-seal impressions	89137	Ht. 3·4 cm	
		89147	Ht. 3·7 cm	
37	Tomb portrait from Palmyra, Syria	125024	Ht. 53·3 cm	
38	Ivory from Nimrud	127412	Ht. 10·2 cm	
39	Alabaster head from South Arabia	116674	Ht. 18·2 cm	Given by Lt.-Cdr. C. Crauford

Information & Museum Services

The British Museum
Great Russell Street
London WC1B 3DG
Tel. 01-636-1555

Opening Hours
Monday to Saturday 10–5. Sundays 2.30–6. Closed
Christmas Eve, Christmas Day, Boxing Day, New Year's
Day, Good Friday and the first Monday in May.

Refreshments
The licensed Coffee Shop offers a choice of full meals,
tea, coffee and sandwiches. Open Monday to Saturday
10.30–4.15 and Sundays 3–5.15.

The Museum of Mankind
The Ethnography Department of the British Museum is
at the Museum of Mankind, 6 Burlington Gardens,
London W1X 2EX.

EDUCATION
The offices of the Museum Education Service are at 43
Russell Square. The staff of the Education Office are
available by appointment to advise teachers about visits
to the Museum, and to give illustrated talks to school
and college students on topics related to the Museum's
collections.

FILMS
Films are shown in the Lecture Theatre every day except
Saturdays, Sundays and Mondays, and also at the
Museum of Mankind, Burlington Gardens; there is no
entrance charge.

A programme of lectures, gallery talks and films,
covering a two-monthly period, is available free of
charge from the information desks.

GALLERY PHOTOGRAPHY
Photography of Museum exhibits (not material on loan)
using a hand-held camera is permitted in the galleries.
Flash bulbs or electronic flash may also be used.
Permission must be obtained from the Photographic
Service for photography in the galleries requiring a
tripod, and for all filming.

INFORMATION
There are information desks at both entrances of the
Museum and at the Museum of Mankind. The staff will
be pleased to answer visitors' questions about the
Museum's collections and special exhibitions.

LECTURES
Lectures and gallery talks are given every day except
Sundays and Mondays.

PHOTOGRAPHIC SERVICE
Members of the public may order prints and

transparencies of most of the objects in the Museum.
Ektachromes, but not slides, may be hired. Information
and price lists are available from the Photographic
Service.

PUBLICATIONS
Books, replicas and other publications are sold at the
shop in the Front Hall. Postcards, slides and posters are
available at the bookstall to the west of the Main
Entrance. There is also a shop at the Museum of
Mankind.

SOUND COMMENTARIES
Individual recorded commentaries to some of the
Museum's collections can be hired. Inquire at the
information desks.

SPECIAL EXHIBITIONS
The British Museum mounts a series of special changing
exhibitions which focus more detailed attention on
certain aspects of the permanent collections and/or show
related material from other major collections. An
exhibition programme is available on request.

STUDENTS' ROOMS
Admission to the Departmental Students' Rooms is by
prior arrangement only. Staff are however available
without appointment to give opinions on objects relating
to the Museum's collections from Monday to Friday
2–4.30. (Prints and Drawings 2.15–4, Oriental
2.15–4.30.) No valuations can be given.

WHEELCHAIRS
Wheelchairs are available by prior arrangement at both
the Main Entrance in Great Russell Street and the North
Entrance in Montague Place. Lifts at both entrances give
access to the upper galleries. Toilet facilities for disabled
visitors are located in the Egyptian Sculpture Gallery and
the New Wing Special Exhibitions Gallery, both on the
ground floor.

Join The British Museum Society
What the Society has to offer: * A chance to
support Britain's greatest cultural institution.
* Private views of the museum's special exhibitions.
* An informative and lavishly-illustrated magazine,
issued three times a year. * Regular lectures by
experts on the museum's treasures. * Visits 'behind
the scenes' at the museum. * Expeditions at home
and abroad. * Comfortable members' room.
Further details from the secretary, The British
Museum Society, c/o The British Museum, London
WC1B 3DG.
Tel. 01–636 1555 ext. 605.